Understanding Collaborative Consumption

ELGAR UNDERSTANDING SERIES

This series elucidates fundamental knowledge and foundational research on significant topics and themes across the social sciences. It provides a basis for understanding the key elements of the subject, with expert insight offering a clear and concise exposition.

Illuminating the pertinent issues, each book is authored or edited by a leading scholar in the field, providing clarity and definition, and presenting a comprehensive and authoritative account of the topic. Collectively and individually, these books will advance knowledge and understanding of contemporary issues and challenges.

For a full list of Edward Elgar published titles, including the titles in this series, visit our website at www.e-elgar.com.

Understanding Collaborative Consumption

Edited by

Pia A. Albinsson

Beroth Professor of Marketing, Marketing & Supply Chain Management, Walker College of Business, Appalachian State University, USA

B. Yasanthi Perera

Assistant Professor, Department of Organizational Behaviour, Human Resources, Entrepreneurship, and Ethics, Goodman School of Business, Brock University, Canada

Stephanie J. Lawson

Associate Professor of Marketing, Marketing & Supply Chain Management, Walker College of Business, Appalachian State University, USA

ELGAR UNDERSTANDING SERIES

Cheltenham, UK • Northampton, MA, USA

Published by
Edward Elgar Publishing Limited
The Lypiatts
15 Lansdown Road
Cheltenham
Glos GL50 2JA
UK

Edward Elgar Publishing, Inc.
William Pratt House
9 Dewey Court
Northampton
Massachusetts 01060
USA

A catalogue record for this book
is available from the British Library

Library of Congress Control Number: 2024930584

This book is available electronically in the **Elgar**online
Business subject collection
http://dx.doi.org/10.4337/9781035307531

ISBN 978 1 0353 0752 4 (cased)
ISBN 978 1 0353 0753 1 (eBook)

Printed and bound by CPI Group (UK) Ltd, Croydon, CR0 4YY

To My Loving Family and Community – Pia A. Albinsson
For my dear parents and my siblings and their families, with much love. Thank you – B. Yasanthi Perera
To my family – Jonathan and the Brooksies. You are my love, magic, and greatest adventure – Stephanie J. Lawson

Contents

Contributors

Pia A. Albinsson (Ph.D., New Mexico State University) is endowed Beroth Professor of Marketing in the Walker College of Business at Appalachian State University, where she has been teaching since 2009. Her research, which mainly focuses on collaborative consumption, sustainability, consumer well-being, and advertising effectiveness, has been published in *Journal of Public Policy & Marketing*, *Journal of the Association for Consumer Research*, *Journal of Macromarketing*, *Journal of Consumer Behaviour*, *Journal of Consumer Marketing*, *European Journal of Marketing*, and *Journal of Consumer Affairs* among others. She has previously co-authored a book on Uber, and co-edited a book on *The Rise of the Sharing Economy* with B. Yasanthi Perera.

Dan R. Bradbury (Ph.D., Florida State University) is a researcher with a keen focus on CSR-related subjects, notably financial decentralization, sustainability, and AI utilization. His work delves into cutting-edge methodological techniques, with particular proficiency in systematic reviews and large language modeling.

Jan-Hendrik Bucher is a Ph.D., student at the Institute for Marketing and Customer Insight at the University of St. Gallen, Switzerland. In his qualitative research at the intersection of marketing, sociology, and psychology he explores novel market and consumption phenomena. Jan-Hendrik Bucher graduated with a master's degree in Brand Management and Marketing Communication from the University of Southern Denmark.

Lagnajita Chatterjee is an Assistant Professor of Marketing at Worcester State University, where she has been teaching since 2020. Her research includes investigating consumer emotions, digital marketing, financial well-being, and digital healthcare. Her work has been published in the *Journal of the Academy of Marketing Sciences*, the *Journal of Business Research*, and the *Journal of Consumer Affairs*.

Eileen Davenport is an Associate Faculty member of Royal Roads University where she primarily works as an academic research supervisor and mentor. She has a BA from University of Exeter and an MA and MPhil from Nottingham Trent University. Eileen has published foundational articles on

Fair Trade studies and her work has combined applied policy research and academic research on skills, training and labour, industrial restructuring, and NGO capacity building.

Alexander Davidson is an Assistant Professor of Marketing at the Mike Ilitch School of Business, Wayne State University, Detroit, Michigan. He earned his Ph.D. from Concordia University in Montreal, Quebec. His research explores the sharing economy and consumer behavior in peer-to-peer platforms with an emphasis on political and public policy issues. He has published in the *Journal of Consumer Psychology, Journal of Public Policy & Marketing, Journal of Business Ethics*, and the *Journal of Business Research*, among others.

Irene Di Bernardo, Ph.D., is a Research Fellow at University of Naples Federico II. Her research interests converge on the study of how service technologies (i.e., service and social robots) improve human well-being and transform the human experience. She has participated in national and international conferences.

Amy Greiner Fehl is an Assistant Professor of Marketing at Georgia Gwinnett College. Her research appears in *Psychology & Marketing*, *Journal of Personal Selling & Sales Management*, and *Journal of Service Research*, among others. She explores transformative healthcare policy, collective restoration after marketplace violence, and connection through meaning-making in sales and services marketing. She employs mixed methods for many of her projects to explore diverse perspectives, uncover unexpected relationships, and move closer to a richer understanding of the phenomena of interest.

Meegan Feori-Payne, Ph.D., is an Assistant Professor of Marketing at California State University San Marcos. Her research areas are product development, innovation, sustainability, and social media. Her work has been published in the *Journal of Global Fashion Marketing, International Journal of Fashion Design, Technology and Education*, and *Family and Consumer Sciences Research Journal.*

Mark R. Gleim is an Associate Professor of Marketing in the Harbert College of Business at Auburn University. He earned his Ph.D. from Florida State University. His research interests include access-based consumption, collaborative consumption, services marketing, the metaverse, sustainability, and marketing strategy. His research has appeared in the *Journal of the Academy of Marketing Science, Journal of Retailing, Journal of Service Research, Journal of Business Research, European Journal of Marketing*, and *Marketing Letters*, among other outlets.

Johanna Gollnhofer, Ph.D., is Associate Professor for Marketing and leads the Institute for Marketing and Customer Insight (IMC-HSG) at the University of St. Gallen, Switzerland. She is also the academic director of the Master in Marketing Management (MiMM-HSG). Her research is published, among others, in the *Journal of Consumer Research, Organization Studies* and *Strategy & Management.*

Antje R. H. Graul, Ph.D., is Assistant Professor of Marketing at Utah State University. Her research examines consumer decision making and consumer adoption of sustainable products and services, such as collaborative consumption objects or electric vehicles. She published in the *Journal of Consumer Psychology, Journal of Business Research,* and *Journal of the Academy of Marketing Science.* She is the USU Campus Director of the NSF funded Research Center for "Advancing Sustainability through Powered Infrastructure for Roadway Electrification" (ASPIRE).

Merlyn A. Griffiths, Ph.D., is an Associate Professor of Marketing and Department Head of the Marketing, Entrepreneurship, Hospitality and Tourism Department at the University of North Carolina-Greensboro in the Bryan School of Business and Economics. Her research interests include consumer consumption behaviors, branding and services marketing and her award-winning research is published in leading academic journals. She is the co-author of the textbook *Mastering the Art: An Entrepreneurial Guide to a Profit-Driven Marketing Plan* with Dr. Channelle James.

Yang (Jenny) Guo, Ph.D., is an Assistant Professor of Marketing at the State University of New York (SUNY)-Binghamton. Her recent work explores the sharing economy's potential in maximizing financially constrained consumers' happiness (published in *Frontiers in Psychology*) and in reducing perceived social inequality in the context of access-based luxury goods consumption (published in *Market Letters*). She is currently teaching Consumer Behavior and Social Media Marketing. During her free time, she likes doing yoga.

Hugo Guyader, Ph.D., is Assistant Professor of Marketing at Linköping University, Sweden. His research is focused on sustainable consumer behaviors and business models that challenge traditional modes of consumption, particularly in the contemporary contexts of the "sharing economy" and the circular economy. Based on a mixed-method approach to data collection with surveys, experiments, participant observations, interviews and (n)ethnography, he has published in marketing, sustainability, and service journals. He also co-authored a coursebook *Marketing & Sustainability* that he uses in his teaching.

Channelle D. James, Ph.D., teaches social and sustainable entrepreneurship in the Bryan School of Business and Economics at the University of North Carolina at Greensboro in the Department of Marketing, Entrepreneurship,

Hospitality, and Tourism. Dr. James also serves as the Dean's Fellow for School Climate. She publishes based on her research in sustainable/social entrepreneurship, diversity, and community support of entrepreneurship for vulnerable communities.

Bernadette Kamleitner is full Professor of Marketing with focus on Consumer Research at WU Vienna University of Economics and Business, Austria. Her internationally recognized research is positioned at the cross-section of psychology and marketing. Her particular research interests comprise the psychological underpinnings and consequences of experiences of ownership, financial decision making and consumer responses to contemporary societal developments such as a need for more sustainable behaviors and an increase in digitalization.

Chantell LaPan, Ph.D., is an Assistant Professor in the Department of Marketing, Entrepreneurship, Hospitality, and Tourism at UNC Greensboro. Her research focuses on rural tourism development, with a particular interest in agritourism, microentrepreneurship, and issues of social justice.

Stephanie J. Lawson, Ph.D., is an Associate Professor of Marketing at Appalachian State University. She earned her B.A. in Communication, MBA, and Ph.D. from Florida State University. Her research interests include collaborative consumption and marketing issues related to indigenous culture. Her research has appeared in the *Journal of Business Research, Journal of the Academy of Marketing Science*, and *Marketing Letters* among others.

Hanna Leipämaa-Leskinen, University of Vaasa, School of Marketing and Communication, Vaasa, Finland is Associate Professor of Marketing. Her research interests are in consumer culture theory, practice theory, consumer resistance and food consumption. She has published in journals such as *European Journal of Marketing, Qualitative Market Research* and *Journal of Consumer Culture.*

Will Low is Professor of Sustainable Business Practice in the School of Business at Royal Roads University. He trained as an economist at UBC (BA and MA) and LSE (Ph.D.). Will is internationally recognized for research which helped to define the field of fair trade studies, and he also works on labor rights and alternative food networks.

Hannu Makkonen, University of Vaasa, School of Marketing and Communication, Vaasa, Finland, is Professor of Marketing. His research interests are innovation management, innovation ecosystems, and value creation logics in industrial networks and relationships. His recent work has been published in *Industrial Marketing Management, Technovation, Journal of Business Research, Marketing Theory, Technological Forecasting and Social*

Change, Journal of Service Management, Journal of Business & Industrial Marketing, and *Technology Analysis & Strategic Management.*

Marlys Mason is the Associate Dean, Spears Chair in Business Administration, and Professor of Marketing in the Spears School of Business at Oklahoma State University. Her research centers around consumer health and well-being, vulnerability, coping and resiliency, health information, and public policy. Her work has appeared in the *Journal of Consumer Research, Journal of Public Policy & Marketing, Journal of Business Research, Journal of Consumer Affairs, Journal of Marketing Management, Journal of Macromarketing,* and more.

Debi P. Mishra, Ph.D., is an Associate Professor of Marketing at the State University of New York (SUNY)-Binghamton. His research and teaching interests are in marketing strategy and inter-firm relationships. Dr. Mishra has published over 30 refereed articles in books and journals such as the *Journal of Marketing Research,* the *Journal of Business Research, Journal of Retailing and Consumer Services,* and the *Journal of Consumer Marketing.* Currently, he serves as an Associate Editor of the *Journal of Consumer Marketing.*

Adrienne F. Muldrow, Ph.D., is an Assistant Professor in the School of Communication at East Carolina University. Her research seeks to understand the psychological underpinnings of communication effects that impact various dimensions of an individual's well-being, mainly in health, business, and cyber environments. Her research has been published in journals such as the *Journal of Consumer Marketing, Journal of Marketing Communications,* and the *International Journal of Advertising.*

Xiaodong Nie, Ph.D., is an Assistant Professor at the University of Washington Bothell. Her research interests are in consumer cultural psychology, with a specific emphasis on how cultural identity affects consumer decision making, such as engaging in collaborative consumption. Her work has been published in premier marketing journals, such as *Journal of Marketing Research.* She regularly presents at top marketing conferences, such as ACR and SCP. During her free time, she likes to build Legos.

Elina Närvänen, Tampere University, Faculty of Management and Business, Tampere, Finland is Professor of Services and Retailing. She leads a research group that focuses on sustainability and the circular economy. Her research interests are also in collective consumption, practice theory, and qualitative research methods. She has recently published in the *Journal of Consumer Research, European Journal of Marketing,* and *Industrial Marketing Management.*

Lucie K. Ozanne is a Professor of Marketing in the Business School at the University of Canterbury, Christchurch, New Zealand. Lucie is a consumer researcher who works in the Transformative Consumer Research (TCR) area. Her recent research focuses on community, organizational and family resilience, sustainability, and alternative and environmentally motivated consumption behavior, including the sharing economy.

B. Yasanthi Perera is an Assistant Professor in the Department of Organizational Behaviour, Human Resources, Entrepreneurship, and Ethics at Brock University. Yasanthi's research interests include collaborative consumption, immigrant and social entrepreneurship, and consumer activism. Her work has been published in multiple journals including *Journal of the Association for Consumer Research, Journal of Small Business and Enterprise Development*, and *Journal of Marketing Theory and Practice*. She has also co-authored a book (*Uber*) and co-edited another (*The Rise of the Sharing Economy*) with Pia A. Albinsson.

Rebeca Perren, Ph.D., is an Associate Professor of Marketing at California State University San Marcos. Her research explores the intersection of social and market domains in consumption, particularly as facilitated by technology. Her work has been published in the *Journal of Marketing, Journal of Business Research, Journal of Consumer Marketing*, and the *Journal of Promotion Management*. She co-edited a special issue of the *Journal of Marketing Education* on diversity in marketing education and the *Handbook on Intra-Cultural Marketing*.

Angelo Ranieri, Ph.D., is a Research Fellow at the University of Naples Federico II. His research topics converge on the study of service innovation thanks to the use of new technologies, such as service robots, conversational agents, and the blockchain. He participated in national and international conferences.

Susanne Ruckelshausen, M.Sc., is a Teaching and Research Associate and is currently pursuing her Ph.D. at WU Vienna University of Economics and Business, Austria. With academic qualifications in psychology at both the bachelor's and master's levels, she teaches Marketing and Consumer Psychology courses at the Institute for Marketing and Consumer Research. Her research focuses on sustainable and moral consumer behavior.

Birgit Teufer, MA, is a scientist and lecturer at the Institute of Business and Psychology at the Distance-Learning University of Applied Sciences (FERNFH). Before her current role, she was associated with IMC Krems, Austria, and carried out her PhD research at the University of Klagenfurt, delving into the dynamics of collaborative consumption in consumer networks and accompanying social innovations. Her further research interests are in (green) marketing and consumer behavior research, consumer perceptions and sustainable development. She has (co-)published various articles in top journals such as *Journal of Consumer Affairs*, *BMJ Open*, *The Lancet Psychiatry*, or *Scientific Reports*.

Aristeidis Theotokis, Ph.D., is Professor of Marketing at University of Leeds, UK. Prof. Theotokis conducts research in the areas of consumer psychology, retailing, and shopper marketing. He examines theories and phenomena in the areas of behavioral decision making, behavioral economics, and social and cognitive psychology. His research has been published in world-leading academic journals, such as *Journal of Marketing Research*, *Journal of Retailing*, *Journal of Business Ethics*, *Journal of Interactive Marketing* and *Journal of Advertising* among others.

Marco Tregua, Ph.D., is an Associate Professor in Management at University Federico II of Naples. He has been lecturer at University L'Orientale of Naples and at Universidad de Jaén. He participated in national and international conferences, and he published papers on value creation, management, and ethics in international journals. His main areas of interest are service studies, international management, and smart innovation.

Niklas Woermann, Ph.D., is Associate Professor for Marketing and head of studies at SDU Business School, University of Southern Denmark, Denmark. His research focuses on how technology shapes consumer experience, services, and interactions. Multidisciplinary in his education, research and outlook, Niklas has published in the *Journal of Consumer Research*, the *American Behavioural Scientist*, and with key publishers in sociology.

Foreword

Cait Lamberton

In *The Third Pillar: How Markets and the State Leave the Community Behind*, Raghuram Rajan (2019) discusses three major institutions that shape our lives: the state, the market, and the community. He argues that, after the community-building – if traumatic – experiences of the Great Depression and the Second World War, the market asserted itself with a vengeance. Because standard economic exchange seemed the surest path to prosperity, it was able to co-opt community as a preferred path to well-being. In turn, community was progressively weakened. The state retreated, presumably to allow the market to build a bedrock on which society could rest.

However, economic and global crises in the first decades of the new millennium showed the potential precarity inherent in an overly dominant market. Now, Rajan suggests, we are thrown back to community. But given the undernourished state of many communities, they cannot pick up the market's dropped rocks alone. So Rajan presents us with a problem: What form of community might be robust enough to make up for the deficiencies of the state, to repair what is broken in society, and to challenge the sometimes over-developed power of the market?

The words "collaborative consumption" appear nowhere in Rajan's book. However, the book you currently hold makes a strong argument that collaborative consumption may offer at least a partial answer. It is possible that collaborative consumption, as a market–community hybrid, can outperform the market, state, or community when acting alone. Throughout the chapters of this book, these three pillars can be seen to interact with one another. This collaborative consumption thus presents us with test cases of the multiple relationships that may exist: We can see that the market, community, and state may correct one another's deficiencies, lend each other tools, subvert the good of one with the perils of another, or shape the roles that people can take in each. As we read, we therefore begin to develop a novel – and necessary – view of the true potential of collaborative consumption.

In Guyader's Chapter 2, we see the way that the market and community intersect at a broader level. On one hand, this is a paradox: we need to be mindful of the tensions that can emerge when people whose goals align more closely with that of community share a system with people whose goals align more closely with that of the market. But by recognizing the tensions that arise across processes related to belonging, performing, learning, and organizing we can anticipate and accommodate the needs of all involved.

If well-structured, collaborative consumption may also make up for the market's deficiencies. In Chapter 12, for example, Low and Davenport highlight the fact that employees need more than space in which to carry out marketplace functions. We can imagine that, as the community related to corporate structures and workplaces has weakened, people have suffered a true loss of community. The type of collaborative experience that can be fostered by co-working spaces may be able to mitigate this damage. A deep understanding of the conditions under which such spaces can pick up the threads necessary to build community will be critical in determining whether the market's deficiencies can be corrected.

It is also possible that, through collaborative consumption, the marketplace supports certain aspects of communities that exist at both small and large scale. For example, in Chapter 9, Ruckelshausen and Kamleitner describe how collaborative consumption places the tools of the market at the disposal of people who share a community. This may serve in some cases to tighten bonds further, as shown in their description of hand-me-down experiences. In other cases, exchanges can make the most of brand-related communities, as described in Feori-Payne, Perren, and Lawson's chapter on resale apparel programs (Chapter 10).

We also see cases where communities return the favor, contributing to the market through collaborative consumption. The marketplace in turn shapes the communities formed to provide value. In Chapter 11, Gleim and Davidson discuss the roles, classifications, and earnings of gig workers, providing a nuanced case study of the way that community and marketplace become interwoven.

Collaborative consumption approaches can also extend community in ways that market approaches alone would fail to achieve. For example, in Chapter 3, Bucher, Gollnhofer, and Woermann vividly depict an interrelatedness of community and marketplace that encompasses geography and heterogeneity. Whereas a straight market approach would likely segment speedrunners in terms of their ability, accomplishments, or, perhaps, "customer lifetime value," a collaborative prosumption community structures itself in ways that can reach all interested members.

In Chapter 4, Graul and Theotokis demonstrate how marketplace factors can shape participation in collaborative communities. Specifically, their work highlights the varying degree to which consumers have internalized marketplace ideologies. This, in turn, affects consumers' roles in collaborative communities. For some consumers, market-related goals and preferences – that is, desires driven by materialism – bring them to collaborative communities primarily in the interest of extracting value. For others, the weaker allure of the material market allows them to take their place as donors to a collaborative community. Similarly, Guo, Nie, and Mishra's Chapter 16 shows the influence of three marketplace megatrends (sustainability, minimalism, and digitalization) on peoples' likelihood of joining a collaborative consumption system. Because consumers are heterogeneous in their immersion in these market trends, so will be their access to collaborative consumption and the potential community it may offer.

Though there is still much to learn, we also see hints that the market–community hybrid may be able to thrive without creating burdens for Rajan's third pillar – the state. Rather, collaborative communities can develop self-regulating practices that apply both to the social value in the group and to its economic exchanges. This organic, systematic self-regulation is described by Leipämaa-Leskinen, Närvänen, and Makkonen in Chapter 5. It remains to be seen whether the state will be needed to ensure that collaborative systems that engage with the market as their central focus – such as those involved in cryptocurrency and other decentralized finance – can maintain aspects of both in a healthy, if distributed, community while also facilitating fair and trustworthy value exchange. To this end, Chatterjee, Albinsson, Bradbury, and Muldrow's Chapter 15 lays out a set of insightful and pressing research questions.

But we should not discount the leverage that can be created if we connect collaborative communities to broader institutions, such as those that the state can facilitate. We see in Teufer's Chapter 7 that community alone cannot save the world. Rather, her investigation makes clear that multiple institutions – likely including both the market and the state – will be necessary to promote holistic improvement in our planet's health. Similarly, Chapter 13's authors (Ranieri, Tregua, and Di Bernardo) argue compellingly that collaborative consumption's responsiveness to environmental needs in the food industry will be determined by its ability to reach across the supply chain, likely involving multiple market, community, and state-related entities.

This book also teaches us that there is much at stake in this market–community hybrid. Tragedies in the marketplace have become terribly common. In quite beautiful ways, collaborative consumption can help us heal; Fehl and Mason analyze collective trauma and grieving in Chapter 8, highlighting the way in which this can unfold. Trauma is inescapable. If we lose the ability to collaboratively memorialize, share identities, and create rituals related to healing, these traumas may leave scars that not only mar communities, but also distort the market and strain the state over the long term.

The stakes are also high because collaborative consumption itself, if co-opted by the marketplace and the state, may undermine both community and personal well-being. This possibility is comprehensively described in

Chapter 14, by Griffiths, LaPan, and James. These authors offer strong recommendations that may be implemented to achieve a better set of outcomes.

Taken together, then, collaborative consumption presents a laboratory we can use to understand the interrelatedness of the market, state, and community. This laboratory allows us to see the power that collaborative consumption may have to simultaneously heal tears in community and support a more humane and productive marketplace. The chapters show us the remarkable way this may come about: collaborative consumption can span massive geographical ranges and subvert damaging types of nationalist or enclave-based populism. As such, it can present the type of "open access market to include and connect a diverse set of local communities" that Rajan (2019, p. 285) suggests offers a path toward a successful and thriving society. Further, facilitated with the type of technology that allows people to identify themselves, understand one another, form relationships, and build trust, collaborative consumption can do something that the market alone struggles to accomplish: allow exchange at scale without destroying identity.

Thus, this book offers a hopeful response to Rajan's dilemma. Few would argue that the market has failed to be the panacea it was once hoped to be, and few would contest the suggestion that, as the market ascended, community weakened. By blending aspects of both community and market, and often without the need for or in cooperation with the state, collaborative consumption may offer us a path that revitalizes all three.

As readers of this book, we should also consider ourselves participants in one of the repair cafés described by Ozanne in Chapter 6. In a very real sense, everyone who has written for, browsed, or purchased this volume belongs to a community that must be dedicated to repair. Some of us will have the task of identifying the things in collaborative consumption that are broken, bringing them to the attention of scholars, practitioners, and policymakers. But some of us will also – or at the same time – be ready to advise, design, and carry out the repairs needed by our markets, communities, and regulating bodies. Hopefully, the understanding of collaborative consumption shared in this book will offer us both guidance and optimism as we undertake the work together.

Cait Lamberton
Alberto I. Duran President's Distinguished Professor
Professor of Marketing
The Wharton School, USA

REFERENCES

Rajan, R. (2019). *The third pillar: how markets and the state leave the community behind*. Penguin.

PART I

Framework for understanding CC

1. *Understanding Collaborative Consumption*: an overview

B. Yasanthi Perera, Pia A. Albinsson, and Stephanie J. Lawson

We are excited to introduce this book, *Understanding Collaborative Consumption*, which represents a collaborative effort among nearly 40 scholars from around the world. As editors of and contributors to this work, our hope is that it will provide readers with a deeper understanding of Collaborative Consumption (CC). Excluding this chapter, this book, meant for both students and scholars, presents 15 chapters through a five-part guiding framework grounded in distinct aspects of CC (Figure 1.1). We begin with an overview of how the Sharing Economy (SE) and CC came to be part of consumers' daily lives through community efforts and new entrepreneurial business innovations.

Partly fueled by various movements and trends (e.g., convenience, efficiency, sustainability, voluntary simplicity) stemming from societal-level concerns (e.g., climate change, resource depletion), the modern-day SE continues to expand in scope and breadth. Defined as "a scalable socioeconomic system that employs technology-enabled platforms to provide users with temporary access to tangible and intangible resources that may be crowdsourced" (Eckhardt et al., 2019, p. 7), some of the exchanges within the SE entail CC.

At present, peer-to-peer (or rather stranger-to-stranger), based CC is commonplace in diverse contexts, from service sharing systems to crowdfunding. Relative to conventional consumption that is largely based on the outright transfer of ownership, CC is defined as "the set of resource circulation systems which enable consumers to both obtain and provide, temporarily or permanently, valuable resources or services through direct interaction with other consumers or through a mediator" (Ertz et al., 2016, p. 1). Thus, given the varied modes of engagement and consumption, the CC-based SE encompasses a range of organizational forms, including those facilitating swapping, renting, and exchanging (Habibi et al., 2017), directly or through intermediaries. However, from inception to date, large platform companies such as Airbnb, Uber, and Zipcar dominate the CC and SE landscape in terms of popular press coverage and scholarly attention (Perera & Albinsson, 2020; Sundararajan, 2013; Zervas et al., 2021).

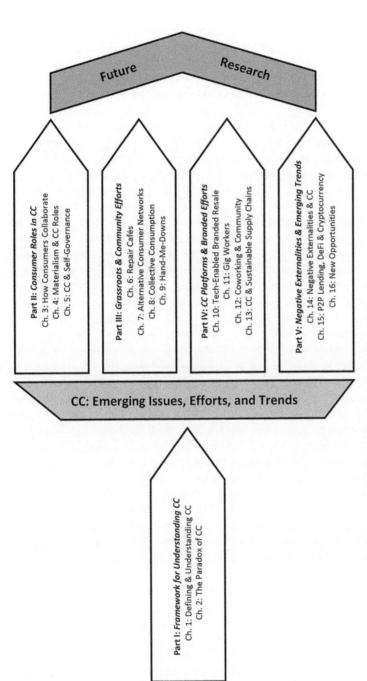

Future

Research

Part II: *Consumer Roles in CC*
Ch. 3: How Consumers Collaborate
Ch. 4: Materialism & CC Roles
Ch. 5: CC & Self-Governance

Part III: *Grassroots & Community Efforts*
Ch. 6: Repair Cafés
Ch. 7: Alternative Consumer Networks
Ch. 8: Collective Consumption
Ch. 9: Hand-Me-Downs

Part IV: *CC Platforms & Branded Efforts*
Ch. 10: Tech-Enabled Branded Resale
Ch. 11: Gig Workers
Ch. 12: Coworking & Community
Ch. 13: CC & Sustainable Supply Chains

Part V: *Negative Externalities & Emerging Trends*
Ch. 14: Negative Externalities & CC
Ch. 15: P2P Lending, DeFi & Cryptocurrency
Ch. 16: New Opportunities

CC: Emerging Issues, Efforts, and Trends

Part I: *Framework for Understanding CC*
Ch. 1: Defining & Understanding CC
Ch. 2: The Paradox of CC

Figure 1.1   Framework for understanding collaborative consumption

Through facilitating and normalizing service interactions between strangers, Uber, Airbnb, and others like them have undoubtedly transformed consumers' and providers' experiences and disrupted industries. By operating through peer providers who oftentimes use their personal possessions (i.e., a vehicle, a home) to deliver a service (i.e., a ride, a stay) to users for a cost, these platforms offer flexibility and convenience. Companies earn revenues for organizing the user–provider experience (e.g., training providers/gig workers, establishing operating standards and guidelines, matching providers and users, enabling monetary exchange, and providing oversight through reputational/ trust metrics). While the potential exists for interaction and the cultivation of social bonds, in purest terms Uber and Airbnb and other larger technology platforms are capitalist institutional logic-based entities that facilitate reciprocity-based marketplace exchanges. As such, the term "sharing" is somewhat of a misnomer for such interactions (e.g., Belk, 2014a; Habibi et al., 2017). In evaluating the distinction between the commonly understood notion of sharing and the type of sharing that occurs within the SE, Belk (2014b, p.7) posits the term pseudo-sharing as the "commodity exchange and potential exploitation of consumer co-creators" under the semblance of sharing. Essentially, pseudo-sharing pertains to self-interested/egoistic motivations, the expectation of reciprocity, an absence of community, and the involvement of money (Belk, 2014b). These are all hallmarks of the type of sharing facilitated by primarily profit-oriented platform intermediaries. In building upon this distinction, Habibi et al. (2017) present a sharing–exchange continuum extending from pure sharing to pure exchange. Pure sharing entails the creation of social bonds and social capital to some extent, and feelings of joint ownership of the objects being shared, with no monetary exchange or expectations of reciprocity. At the other extreme, pure exchange entails reciprocity and money exchange with no sense of joint ownership nor emphasis on social bonds. Besides sharing-based and exchange-based organizations, the continuum includes dual-mode-based entities (e.g., Airbnb, Uber) situated at the mid-point, which present a mix of the two extreme forms (Habibi et al., 2017). While this depiction presents a means for differentiating between SE entities, another more basic way of differentiating is to examine the level of commercialization or the goals underlying CC (Lamberton, 2016). To do so, one must determine whether the entity in question is more oriented toward revenue/profit generation based on a conventional model with an SE/CC twist (e.g., an Uber peer-to-peer provider offers rides for a fee like a taxicab employee), or whether there are some alternative social-value-related aims at play (e.g., relational goals; Lamberton, 2016). Given various concerns regarding the mainstream platform-based SE including negative externalities (e.g., Griffiths et al., 2019) and worker exploitation (Ahsan, 2020), a fuller examination of the SE is warranted to harness its potential. To this end, both the SE and CC emphasize the potential for facilitating social interaction and fostering connections (e.g., Botsman & Rogers, 2010; Albinsson & Perera, 2012; Veen, 2019), among other benefits. This is critical given that, in recent times, medical professionals, governmental bodies, academics, and others have sounded the alarm on the prevailing loneliness epidemic (e.g., Murthy, 2023; Griffiths et al., 2022). In fact, in May 2023, US Surgeon General Vivek Murthy noted the widespread occurrence of "social disconnectedness" and called for a "movement to mend the social fabric of our nation." This would require, in his words, the collective efforts of "individuals and families, schools and workplaces, health care and public health systems, technology companies, governments, faith organizations, and communities" (Murthy, 2023). To address the pandemic and build healthier communities, Murthy called for developing and strengthening relationships and "supporting community efforts to rebuild social connection[s]" (Murthy, 2023). Thus, examining community efforts within the SE/CC space that extend beyond surface-level service interactions is a valuable avenue of exploration because, in the process of delivering their specific services or products, they may also address loneliness and isolation (Albinsson et al., 2021).

There are numerous studies examining CC or CC-type behaviors in relation to community. For instance, time banks are informal volunteer-based community exchange systems through which individuals can provide and obtain assistance in terms of goods, services, advice, and so on (e.g., Williams, 2004). In the process of providing a structured means of offering and asking for help, time banks can highlight hidden talents within the community, promote intergenerational exchanges, and support the vulnerable (Ozanne & Ozanne, 2011a). In doing so, they can potentially dismantle barriers between people, and develop a sense of community akin to an "extended family" (Ozanne & Ozanne, 2011a, p. 7). A study of CC-based European time banks, which promote "meaning in consumption processes" through offering an alternative to commercial exchanges, indicate that they seek to address social inequalities through community building (Laamanen et al., 2015, p. 466). Moreover, among other things, such efforts exhibit community care and promote well-being by forming neighborhood connections (Laamanen et al., 2015). All in all, such efforts "unite individuals and communities in the creation of the commons, confronting the hegemonic models of economic activity, and instigating social change" (Laamanen et al., 2015, p. 466). Depending on the definition, libraries of various goods could also be considered as promoting CC. To this end, toy lending libraries function as a community hub that develop community capacity. Studies of toy lending libraries (Ozanne & Ozanne, 2011b) indicate that they are venues for affirming deeply held values including those related to community, generosity, and environmentalism (Ozanne & Ozanne, 2009). They also contribute to the social fabric of communities by providing a venue for people to interact, exchange ideas, volunteer their expertise, and learn new skills (Ozanne & Ozanne, 2011b). Moreover, such offerings are a means of educating children on the notions of delayed gratification, good stewardship of collectively owned goods, and of being responsible citizens (Ozanne & Ozanne, 2011b), all of which are important for fostering healthy communities. Beyond toys, recent works on clothing libraries in Sweden, Denmark, and Finland (e.g., Albinsson & Perera, 2018; Pedersen & Netter, 2015; Rosenberg et al., 2023; Zamani et al., 2017) also highlight their potential for facilitating more sustainable ways of consuming clothes while developing social connections and community. Finally, a study of CC in relation to non-monetary-based private and public sharing events, including Really, Really Free Markets, found that a sense of community is both a driver and an outcome of such non-reciprocity/non-exchange-based events (Albinsson & Perera, 2012). This sampling of research indicates that community development opportunities exist in the realm of sharing and CC. As such, this edited volume highlights research that allows for a more nuanced understanding of CC beyond those offered by the tech-based platform economy. Next, we introduce contributions from scholars around the globe, with each chapter presenting a unique focus that helps the reader to understand different aspects of CC.

A FRAMEWORK FOR UNDERSTANDING COLLABORATIVE CONSUMPTION

Part I – Framework for Understanding CC

Part I includes two chapters providing an introduction and overview of CC, along with its paradoxes. While the reader can skip around to those sections or chapters that are of most interest to them, the book is divided into five parts. In the present chapter, we propose a framework for understanding CC as illustrated in Figure 1.1. Chapter 2 follows with Guyader's exploration of CC through paradox theory, which entails a discussion of the four tensions (belonging, performing, learning, and organizing) that exist between sharing and market logics of exchange.

Part II – Consumer Roles in CC

Part II includes three chapters on the various roles consumers play in CC. Chapter 3, by Bucher, Gollnhofer, and Woermann, discusses how consumers in informal online communities collaborate by engaging in prosumption practices at four distinct levels. These prosumer CC communities provide insight into how decentralized volunteer groups collaborate on complex undertakings such as open-source and platform movements. In Chapter 4, Graul and Theotokis explore how materialism plays a role in either encouraging or discouraging consumers' interest in assuming the role of users and providers in many CC contexts. They note that encouraging materialistic consumers to engage in CC could provide benefits related to sustainability, and to financial and social concerns. Finally, in Chapter 5, Leipämaa-Leskinen, Närvänen, and Makkonen explore a local food sharing platform in Finland that promotes decentralized community collaboration to self-regulate exchanges between consumers and producers.

Part III – Grassroots and Community Efforts

Part III includes four chapters on grassroots and community efforts, illustrating how many CC initiatives begin on a small scale with limited technology prior to scaling up to larger digital platforms. For example, in Chapter 6, Ozanne utilizes the notion of "ethic of care" to discuss how volunteers and other participants at repair café communities in New Zealand engage to share expertise, learn, and extend the life of products. Teufer's Chapter 7 examines the oft-touted potential of CC to facilitate sustainable consumption. This is accomplished by examining alternative consumer networks in the context of community-supported agriculture initiatives in Austria. In Chapter 8, Fehl and Mason investigate CC as a collective communal healing experience. Their work highlights the importance of acquiring physical space to process experiences, reaffirm identity, and engage in community recovery rituals following collective traumatic events. Finally, Chapter 9, by Ruckelshausen and Kamleitner, differentiates hand-me-downs from the second-hand marketplace and introduces a framework for understanding the former through the lens of psychological ownership. Hand-me-downs, which have been largely ignored in the literature, have the potential to contribute to a more efficient use of resources and the circular economy.

Part IV – CC Platforms and Branded Efforts

Part IV, which includes four chapters, takes a different perspective by examining platformed and branded efforts. Early research on commercial sharing systems has suggested that marketers should examine specific costs and utility factors in addition to usage patterns when considering extending into sharing systems (Lamberton & Rose, 2012). In Chapter 10, Feori-Payne, Perren, and Lawson take the reader on a journey showing how more established brands integrate various components of sharing systems into their business models. Chapter 11 by Gleim and Davidson examines the role of gig workers as providers of CC services. While CC platforms often rely on gig workers to perform their work, these individuals are classified as freelance workers and not employees, and they consequently lack the protections offered by employment legislation (Gleim et al., 2019). Chapter 11 also explores the role gig workers play in the CC Triad along with platforms (e.g., Uber and Airbnb) and consumers (Benoit et al., 2017). In Chapter 12, Low and Davenport investigate the impact of dog-friendly policies on cohesion and the sense of community in co-working spaces in Lisbon and London. Essentially, the authors propose that, in co-working spaces, the element of playfulness is enhanced through interactions unrelated to work and facilitated by the presence of dogs. Next, in Chapter 13, Ranieri, Tregua, and Di Bernardo examine how collaborations in the food industry facilitate sustainability throughout the supply chain.

Part V – Negative Externalities and Emerging Trends

The last section, Part V, includes three chapters that examine unintended consequences and newer developments and emerging trends in CC. For example, Chapter 14 by Griffiths, LaPan, and James explores the unintended negative externalities of CC with real social and financial costs. Specifically, they discuss the impacts of digital surveillance and human trafficking on consumers and providers, and the measures that companies and government entities have taken, and could yet take, to address these issues. Next, Chatterjee, Albinsson, Bradbury, and Muldrow (Chapter 15) examine collaborative currency systems in relation to decentralized financial platforms (DeFi) and cryptocurrency community development. Specifically, they discuss how both internal and external communities form around crypto currencies and propose a future research agenda for these emerging topics. Lastly, Chapter 16, by Guo, Nie, and Mishra, presents a theoretical framework linking consumer motives and societal trends, including sustainability, minimalism, and digitization, and proposes opportunities for future research.

DISCUSSION AND CONCLUSION

While existing research is primarily focused on large technology-based platforms (e.g., Uber, Airbnb), likely due to availability of data and high interest in the industry disruptors, SE and CC are much more than these ventures. At its core, the platformization and profit-driven initiatives in the SE are an outgrowth of community and grassroots efforts aimed at sharing knowledge in addition to goods and services. As such, this introductory chapter offers a brief overview of what the SE is and, more importantly, what CC entails in a more nuanced and broader way than existing research suggests.

Underlying the growth of the SE, the CC Triad of providers, platforms, and consumers is experiencing societal-level forces related to the loneliness epidemic and increased distrust in centralized institutions, among others. While it is not without flaws (e.g., gig worker exploitation), CC can address such concerns by bringing community and grassroots practices to the mainstream.

CC is experiencing constant evolution as companies iterate platforms, processes, and policies. While brands hope to build relationships with their consumers, CC has the ability to blend the community aspects of sharing with the transactional aspects of market exchange supporting both relational and commercial goals. The examples of consumer/provider self-regulated communities, prosumers working together online to solve complex problems, and brands facilitating resale between consumers, to name a few, offer insight into the rapidly changing commercial environment. To that end, CC has the potential to address societal issues related to consumer well-being, building community, and supporting a sustainable environment which ultimately could be CC's greatest value. The book that you hold in your hands, *Understanding Collaborative Consumption*, moves beyond what we already know, beyond the large platforms, to investigate this phenomenon in understudied community spaces including those pertaining to hand-me-downs and co-working. However, while we aimed to seek contributions from multiple disciplines, industries, and national contexts, there is a need for more perspectives from developing and emerging markets. Nonetheless, we hope that this collection of works sparks curiosity, and opens further avenues for research related to emerging issues, efforts, and trends in CC.

REFERENCES

Ahsan, M. (2020). Entrepreneurship and ethics in the sharing economy: A critical perspective. *Journal of Business Ethics*, *161*(1), 19–33.

Albinsson, P. A., & Perera, B. Y. (2012). Alternative marketplaces in the 21st century: Building community through sharing events. *Journal of Consumer Behaviour*, *11*(4), 303–315.

Albinsson, P. A., & Perera, B. Y. (2018). Access-based consumption: From ownership to non-ownership of clothing. In P. A. Albinsson & B. Y. Perera (Eds.), *The rise of the sharing economy: Exploring the challenges and opportunities of collaborative consumption* (pp. 183–212). Praeger.

Albinsson, P. A., Perera, B. Y., & Griffiths, M. A. (2021). Overcoming scarcity through efficient consumption: Innovative sharing initiatives. In T. Sigler & J. Corcoran (Eds.), *A modern guide to the urban sharing economy* (pp. 55–70). Edward Elgar Publishing. https://doi.org/10.4337/9781789909562.00011

Belk, R. (2014a). You are what you can access: Sharing and collaborative consumption online. *Journal of Business Research*, *67*(8), 1595–1600.

Belk, R. (2014b). Sharing versus pseudo-sharing in Web 2.0. *The Anthropologist*, *18*(1), 7–23.

Benoit, S., Baker, T. L., Bolton, R. N., Gruber, T., & Kandampully, J. (2017). A triadic framework for collaborative consumption (CC): Motives, activities and resources and capabilities of actors. *Journal of Business Research*, *79*, 219–227.

Botsman, R., & Rogers, R. (2010). *What's mine is yours: The rise of collaborative consumption*. HarperBusiness.

Eckhardt, G. M., Houston, M. B., Jiang, B., Lamberton, C., Rindfleisch, A., & Zervas, G. (2019). Marketing in the sharing economy. *Journal of Marketing, 83*(5), 5–27.

Ertz, M., Durif, F., & Arcand, M. (2016). Collaborative consumption: Conceptual snapshot at a buzzword. *Journal of Entrepreneurship Education, 19*(2), 1–23.

Gleim, M. R., Johnson, C. M., & Lawson, S. J. (2019). Sharers and sellers: A multi-group examination of gig economy workers' perceptions. *Journal of Business Research, 98*, 142–152.

Griffiths, M. A., Perera, B. Y., & Albinsson, P. A. (2019). Contrived surplus and negative externalities in the sharing economy. *Journal of Marketing Theory and Practice, 27*(4), 445–463.

Griffiths, M. A., Perera, B. Y., & Albinsson, P. A. (2022). Lives of the lonely: How collaborative consumption services can alleviate social isolation. *Frontiers in Psychology, 13*, 826533.

Habibi, M. R., Davidson, A., & Laroche, M. (2017). What managers should know about the sharing economy. *Business Horizons, 60*(1), 113–121.

Laamanen, M., Wahlen, S., & Campana, M. (2015). Mobilising collaborative consumption lifestyles: A comparative frame analysis of time banking. *International Journal of Consumer Studies, 39*(5), 459–467.

Lamberton, C. (2016). Collaborative consumption: A goal-based framework. *Current Opinion in Psychology, 10*, 55–59.

Lamberton, C. P., & Rose, R. L. (2012). When is ours better than mine? A framework for understanding and altering participation in commercial sharing systems. *Journal of Marketing, 76*(4), 109–125.

Murthy, V. H. (2023). *Our epidemic of loneliness and isolation: The U.S. Surgeon General's Advisory on the Healing Effects of Social Connection and Community*. US Department of Health and Human Services. https://www.hhs.gov/sites/default/files/surgeon-general-social-connection-advisory.pdf

Ozanne, L. K., & Ozanne, J. L. (2009, July 7–9). *Parental mediation of the market's influence on their children: Toy libraries as safe havens* [Paper presentation]. Academy of Marketing Annual Conference, Leeds, UK.

Ozanne, L. K., & Ozanne, J. L. (2011a). Building the strength of local community through time bank exchanges. In A. Bradshaw, C. Hackley, & P. Maclaran (Eds.), *European advances in consumer research* (Vol. 9, p. 7). Association for Consumer Research.

Ozanne, L. K., & Ozanne, J. L. (2011b). A child's right to play: The social construction of civic virtues in toy libraries. *Journal of Public Policy & Marketing, 30*(2), 264–278.

Pedersen, E. R. G., & Netter, S. (2015). Collaborative consumption: Business model opportunities and barriers for fashion libraries. *Journal of Fashion Marketing and Management, 19*(3), 258–273.

Perera, B. Y., & Albinsson, P. A. (2020). *Uber*. ABC-CLIO.

Rosenberg, L. M., Weijo, H. A., & Kerkelä, I. (2023). Consumer desires and the fluctuating balance between liquid and solid consumption: The case of Finnish clothing libraries. *Journal of Consumer Research, 50*(4), 826–847. https://doi.org/10.1093/jcr/ucad021

Sundararajan, A. (2013). From Zipcar to the sharing economy. *Harvard Business Review, 1*(1), 1–2.

Veen, E. J. (2019). Fostering community values through meal sharing with strangers. *Sustainability, 11*, 2121. https://doi.org/10.3390/su11072121

Williams, C. C. (2004). Informal volunteering: Some lessons from the United Kingdom. *Journal of Policy Analysis and Management, 23*(3), 613–616.

Zamani, B., Sandin, G., & Peters, G. M. (2017). Life cycle assessment of clothing libraries: Can collaborative consumption reduce the environmental impact of fast fashion? *Journal of Cleaner Production, 162*, 1368–1375.

Zervas, G., Proserpio, D., & Byers, J. W. (2021). A first look at online reputation on Airbnb, where every stay is above average. *Marketing Letters, 32*, 1–16.

2. The paradox of collaborative consumption

Hugo Guyader

INTRODUCTION

Collaborative consumption (CC) platforms facilitate rental services between private individuals. Since there is no change of ownership, CC practices are fundamentally different from recirculation systems and second-hand platforms (e.g., eBay). Most CC platforms are developed by for-profit organizations that integrate a business model based on fees and commissions on each transaction (e.g., Airbnb, BlaBlaCar). Yet CC is different from on-demand services offered by gig economy companies (e.g., Deliveroo, TaskRabbit) that provide services (i.e., not tangible goods, per se) that freelancers offer to earn money (Acquier et al., 2017; Frenken & Schor, 2017; Frenken, 2017). From traditional ownership-based consumption and business-to-customer interactions, to an access-based consumption and peer-to-peer (P2P) interactions, the advent of CC in the last 15 years is a unique phenomenon provoking turbulent adjustments to business activities and consumer behavior. Despite ever-growing academic interest, the conceptual definition and understanding of the CC phenomenon has remained "somewhat messy" (Albinsson & Perera, 2018, p. 6).

CC is anchored by two opposing logics: sharing and market exchange. These coexisting contradictory logics result in a paradox (Belk et al., 2019a). On the one hand, sharing is based on pro-social orientation and norms of solidarity, mutuality, generalized reciprocity, and communal belonging. On the other hand, market exchanges are based on for-profit orientation and norms of profit maximization, self-interest, and utilitarian motives (Acquier et al., 2017; Belk, 2014; Belk et al., 2019b; Eckhardt et al., 2019; Guyader, 2019; Habibi et al., 2016; Schor et al., 2016). Leading marketing scholars summarize the paradox as "the moral economy of small-scale communal sharing versus the far-flung reaches of the market economy" (Belk et al., 2019b, p. 424).

Many scholars have thus pointed out that the umbrella term "sharing economy" is an oxymoron (e.g., Eckhardt & Bardhi, 2015; Belk, 2014; Eckhardt et al., 2019; Fournier et al., 2013; Scholz, 2016; Slee, 2015).

A confusing nomenclature is problematic because, "in some of the theory and research surrounding 'the sharing economy,' sharing is so blurred with traditional marketplace exchanges as to be indistinguishable. Or more accurately, the concepts often remain distinct, but a 'sharewashing' effort is made to blur them to the extent that marketplace exchange is touted as sharing" (Price & Belk, 2016, p. 193). Previous research on the tensions between the multiple logics at play in the sharing economy highlights dominant conflicts primarily between pro-social and economic forces, but also encompasses contradictions with sustainability claims (e.g., Beverland et al., 2021; Geissinger et al., 2019; Grinevich et al., 2019; Mont et al., 2019; Saravade et al., 2020; Schor et al., 2016; Schneckenberg et al., 2023; Voytenko Palgan et al., 2017).

This chapter aims to further conceptualize CC as a paradox with both sharing and market logics at play. It will also identify, describe, and categorize the persistent contradictions and tensions between interdependent elements of the phenomenon using a paradox theory framework.

PARADOX THEORY

Paradoxes have been defined as persistent contradictions and tensions between interdependent elements (Schad et al., 2016). As society has become ever more complex, organizations have lived and thrived through dynamic yet persistent tensions (e.g., between individual and team performance, globalization and localization, short and long terms), and scholars have effectively investigated phenomena through the lens of paradox theory, mostly in management (e.g., Lewis, 2000; Schad et al., 2016; Smith & Lewis, 2011) and marketing (e.g., Gölgeci et al., 2019, 2022; Ozanne et al., 2016).

Four categories of paradoxical tensions have been conceptualized: belonging, performing, learning, and organizing. Paradoxes of belonging are based on the tensions between self-expression (individual identity) and group affiliation (collective identity); paradoxes of performing are based on contradictory interests between multiple stakeholders (e.g., cooperation/competition); paradoxes of learning are created from tensions between the old (stability) and the new (change); and paradoxes of organizing result from the conflicting demands of organizational processes and structures, such as control/autonomy or alignment/flexibility (Lewis, 2000; Schad et al., 2016; Smith & Lewis, 2011; Ozanne et al., 2016). The remainder of this chapter discusses these four categories of tensions between the sharing and market logics of the CC paradox.

TENSIONS OF BELONGING

Social psychologists have shown that people form communal sharing relationships based on generalized reciprocity (Clark & Mills, 1979; Fiske, 1992).

That is, "communal sharing relationships are based on a conception of some bounded group of people as equivalent and undifferentiated" (Fiske, 1992, p. 690). This involves kindness, altruism, love, cooperation, collectivism, and shared identity. Communal relationships are the basis for constituting a social group: exchanges within a community involve social relationships where actors participate in consumption and production with no direct reciprocity (Clark & Mills, 1979; Fiske, 1992). Such "true sharing" is driven by altruistic motives, a sense of commonality, and a need for social interactions, which is embedded in trust and bonding (Belk, 2010, 2014). That is, sharing involves the kind of communal relationships that families, friends, spouses, and romantic partners tend to have (Clark & Mills, 1979). Moreover, in communal sharing relationships, people treat all members as equals (Fiske, 1992).

By contrast, Clark and Mills (1979) would use the term "exchange relationship" to depict the expectation of reciprocation that business partners, acquaintances, and strangers have with each other as occurs in a market context. Here it is important to note the difference between the diverse types of reciprocation or reciprocity (Houston & Gassenheimer, 1987; Sahlins, 1972): (1) generalized or indirect reciprocity (i.e., gifting, sharing, helping, and acts of generosity with no expectation of receiving anything in return as takes place in the sharing logic); (2) direct reciprocity (i.e., trading, and transactions where the equivalent value of the thing received is expected in return); (3) negative reciprocity (i.e., haggling, theft, and other attempts to get something for nothing). Thus, the tensions of belonging emerge between the sharing logic (i.e., its communal relationship norms between participants who relate to each other as friends, and expectations of generalized reciprocity) and the market logic (i.e., its exchange relationship norms between participants who relate to each other as impersonal strangers and expectations of direct reciprocity so exchanges are balanced).

For example, BlaBlaCar argues that its "trusted community" members rate their level of trust in each other (88 percent) almost as much as friends (92 percent) or family (94 percent) (Mazzella & Sundararajan, 2016). This is interesting because it relates to communal relationships involving kindness, cooperation, and shared identity taking place between friends and family members (Clark & Mills, 1979; Fiske, 1992). Schor (2014, p. 7) also argues that CC is a kind of "stranger sharing" because it involves personal relationships. As such, CC concerns practices between friends of friends where the circle of people who can be trusted is further extended to form a large family. In other words, online platforms are designed to remove impersonal characteristics (Belk, 2010; Scaraboto, 2015) and emphasize the sharing logic of CC consumption.

The proponents of *true sharing* argue that the sharing economy phenomenon has its origins in communitarian, non-monetary, and non-reciprocal acts and processes (Belk, 2010; Ozanne & Ballantine, 2010). In opposition to the commercial nature of the contemporary phenomenon based on rental exchanges between private people, participants in genuine sharing initiatives (e.g., borrowing, swapping, donating practices) were motivated by anti-capitalistic and anti-consumerist ideologies (Albinsson & Perera, 2012; Martin & Upham, 2016; Ozanne & Ballantine, 2010).

The opposite of *true sharing* is the trading of possessions through market exchanges (Belk, 2010). Exchanges between buyers and sellers of goods and services are market-mediated transactions involving money, a transfer of ownership, and the goal of maximizing utility (self-interest) for all independent and impersonal parties (Bagozzi, 1975; Belk, 2010; Eckhardt & Bardhi, 2016; Houston & Gassenheimer, 1987; Hunt, 1976; Scaraboto, 2015). Sharing is not a new behavior per se; it entered the marketing realm as an alternative mode of consumption to buying. That is, sharing is about shared ownership or joint possessions characterized by a lack of exchange, and thus without direct reciprocity, self-interest, and individual ownership. Unlike commodity exchange, sharing is likely to involve caring and love, to be interpersonal and dependent, and create communal bonds (Belk, 2010).

In conclusion, people can enact different styles of participation in CC, with different degrees of sharing and market logics, which create tensions of belonging: some participants are more inclined to belong to a group of like-minded individuals, others are more in it for themselves.

TENSIONS OF PERFORMING

Performing is another tension that manifests in the dichotomy of platform roles between consumers and peer-providers. Consumers are unique individuals whose motivations can vary from an economical way to obtain goods and services, to an expectation of social benefits from P2P exchanges. But as they come to belong to a group of consumers, their personal characteristics might be reduced and generalized as only economic (instead of both/and). These socio-economic motives and their respective importance are associated with diverse consumer segments (e.g., millennials or green consumers) who might not reflect such an individual diversity of participation motives and values. Peer-providers of CC can also use their participation to compensate for their ownership costs (i.e., a utilitarian motive in line with market logic), or as an altruistic way to offer their underutilized resources for others to use (i.e., sharing logic). Once again, due to their role as peer-providers for a market-mediated mode of consumption, their individual motives are often solely reduced to the economic aspect, with no regard for the social benefits of CC.

The dichotomy of roles for CC means that platform users have different objectives, preferences, and behaviors depending on which side they stand. For example, consumers may want more choice, quality, and cheap offers, while peer-providers may want the most compensation for their underutilized possessions. Platform managers must balance each side of the platform (i.e., reach a critical mass of users) to provide a satisfactory service to both.

One critique of capitalism is that it has reduced diverse modes of exchange (e.g., bartering) to "mercantile exchange, which is objectively and subjectively oriented towards the maximization of profit, (i.e., economically) *self-interested*. It has implicitly defined other forms of exchange as noneconomic and therefore *disinterested*" (Bourdieu, 1986, p. 46, original emphasis). There are other forms of exchange with more immaterial and symbolic benefits. In other words, there are exchanges outside of the market, based not only on economic capital but also on cultural and social capital (Bourdieu, 1986). For instance, the contemporary practices of access-based carsharing, ridesharing, and P2P car rental have their origins in older practices that took place outside the market and within grassroots movements or non-profit cooperatives (i.e., without commercial orientation and sometimes even employing non-monetary practices). For instance, firms adapted the practice of car borrowing among friends and family and began to facilitate P2P car rental by developing online platforms for owners (peer-providers) to rent their car directly to other people (consumers). P2P car rental and carpooling platforms make it more efficient, convenient, and attractive to share cars by leveraging technological developments from e-commerce and social media networks (e.g., reputation system based on peer reviews, booking capabilities, online payment functionalities), to monetize private resources through platform business models. For example, BlaBlaCar considerably improved their notice board website which lacked interactive functions to make it more efficient for organizing rides. Drivers and passengers could interact in more ways with greater ease, rather than being limited by the former static and archaic notice boards and online forums. In 2011, BlaBlaCar deployed a platform business model based on a commission and a fixed fee on each seat reserved by passengers. They also developed a more performant website with search functions similar to other transportation services, including the date, the itinerary (i.e., point of origin and destination, time flexibility, possible detours, and luggage size, etc.), the number of seats requested, and the price of the rides. Recent research further shows that issues of competition and cooperation (i.e., "coopetition") between online platforms create conflicts and enhance tensions, but also increase ethical dilemmas (i.e., unethical practices over human capital or data usage, for example) and ultimately decrease firm performance (Chatterjee et al., 2023).

Car borrowing also occurred between acquaintances such as colleagues or friends of friends. However, it was difficult to arrange outside these relationships due to a lack of demand/awareness of a potential match between owner and driver arising from the limited size of an individual's social network or a lack of trust. Borrowing became a rental. P2P car rental platforms have developed business models that leverage technological capabilities (e.g., matchmaking algorithms, localization services, peer reviews) to improve utility maximization (i.e., reduce the underutilization of personal cars) and which satisfy self-interested utilitarian needs for monetization. In addition to the agreed-upon terms (e.g., price) stipulated in a contract (for accommodation or car rentals) between people taking on market roles, these elements of market logic (Bagozzi, 1975; Belk, 2010; Eckhardt & Bardhi, 2016; Houston and Gassenheimer, 1987; Hunt, 1976; Scaraboto, 2015) are likely to reinforce the exploitative processes referred to by critics of capitalism (e.g., Bourdieu, 1986). Despite the goal of increasing economic performance, CC platforms often maintain a strong emphasis on the social aspects of P2P exchanges. This is so that participants will associate their peers with friends rather than strangers and identify with their (online) community, all of which embraces the sharing logic.

The tensions of performing in the CC paradox also mean that participants who aim to reduce overconsumption and become attached to the sharing logic and communitarian ethos can clash with those who participate for economic rather than social reasons. These latter include the free riders who benefit from generalized reciprocity but do not contribute to it. They are also incompatible with organizations (e.g., foodsharing.de, freecycle.org, landshare.co.uk, and timerepublik.com) that promote shared ownership or non-monetary practices designated as anti-capitalist or anti-consumption (e.g., Gollnhofer et al., 2016; Martin & Upham, 2016; McArthur, 2015; Schor et al., 2016). Previous research has shown that Airbnb and Uber are closer to the market logic than CouchSurfing and KangaRide (a carpooling platform like BlaBlaCar) are to the sharing logic, although all these organizations facilitate exchanges between private people (Bucher et al., 2016; Davidson et al., 2018; Habibi et al., 2016). In conclusion, people can enact different styles of participation in CC, with different degrees of sharing and market logics, which create tensions of belonging: some participants are more inclined to belong to a group of like-minded individuals, while others are in it for themselves.

TENSIONS OF LEARNING

Exchange theory has been at the heart of the conceptualization of marketing as a discipline distinct from economics, especially by considering exchanges (and later, relationships) between customers buying products and suppliers producing offerings in a balanced market (e.g., Bagozzi, 1975; Houston & Gassenheimer, 1987; Hunt, 1976). That is, the essence of marketing is the transaction, a "form of exchange of values between two parties" (Hunt, 1976, p. 25). Bagozzi (1975) argued that exchanges involve both a utilitarian and a symbolic value, and "it is very difficult to separate the two" (p. 36). Houston & Gassenheimer (1987) reviewed this development of marketing theory based on the concept of exchange and confirmed that the value of exchange resides not only in the "something of value" aspect (i.e., the good, service, or offering itself) but also in the act of exchange. Furthermore, all participating parties in the exchange have the shared goal of enhancing their own "potency" (Houston & Gassenheimer, 1987). In other words, market exchanges are driven by self-interest. For instance, the sellers want to get the highest price for their goods, while the buyers want to obtain a maximum amount of goods for their money. As such, the market logic is characterized as impersonal and independent, as buyers/sellers can change identity and it does not matter who buys or sells something, so long as everybody maximizes their gains from the exchange (Belk, 2010; Scaraboto, 2015).

CC may have been born out of the digital revolution, but its beginnings in grassroots social innovation and the non-profit sector relying on volunteers' work and communities, contrast with a commercial orientation (Martin & Upham, 2016). Research on carpooling practices show that grassroots engagement and perceived "sharing authenticity" are more important factors of participation than the website looking trendy like other "sharing economy platforms" (Guyader et al., 2023). The tensions between stability and change can be seen in grassroots movements that adapted to the growing popularity of new consumption practices facilitated by digitalization while maintaining an authentic sharing ethos. Whereas the sharing logic from older non-monetary practices is maintained, contemporary practices of CC are facilitated by online platforms and smartphone apps that pertain to the market logic. Sharing economy businesses want to be associated with the positive connotations of the word community (i.e., social belonging, collective well-being, solidarity, support networks), which describes an existing set of (warm) relationships, where members (a collective body of people) express a sense of common identity and characteristics (Williams, 1976). Indeed, consumers place emphasis on the authenticity of a sharing experience and platform. Hospitality research on P2P accommodation shows that the authenticity of a platform's narrative impacts guests' expectations (Bucher et al., 2018), and that one of the drivers of loyalty is the perceived authenticity of the experience (Lalicic & Weismayer, 2018).

Popular on-demand services such as Uber leverage these icons of communal relationships in their brand communication of *the new sharing*, associating the practice of hailing a taxi via an app to carpooling. Hawlitschek et al. (2018) define sharewashing as "a platform operator's efforts of misleading consumers by purposely portraying an image of social and ecological principles while the platform's business model is actually centered around delivering utilitarian value" (p. 2639). In other words, a business committing sharewashing is not loyal to the genuine sharing ethos. The perceived sharing authenticity of diverse online platforms and the definitional issues of CC are the subjects of many debates (Guyader et al., 2023).

The tensions between radical innovation and incremental (or continuous) change in CC are essential to the diverse regulations adopted by different governments, and the difference between their short-term or long-term perspectives influences firms and consumers. For instance, some countries have limited the maximum compensation per kilometer that one can obtain from carpooling (to differentiate the practice of CC from traditional taxi services). Others have banned Uber or Airbnb from operating in certain cities, while others collaborate with these firms (on income tax issues). The question of whether to preserve the past or favor the future, or both, leads to tension between slowing down the digital revolution that online platforms engage with, without missing out on opportunities, and promoting the evolutionary adaptation of existing infrastructures to recent technological developments.

Moreover, learning tensions for CC participants translate into a need to overcome barriers to access, such as learning to use new technologies (e.g., geo-localization and online payment). For example, carpooling participants used to post their trips and phone numbers in local stores or post offices. Online platforms have now changed the process (e.g., participants need to create a profile and provide specific details), which mostly centralizes the coordination of drivers and passengers (e.g., BlaBlaCar's reservation system and the lack of contact information). In short, the tensions between the traditions of the old practice of hitchhiking or ad hoc carpooling and the modern practice of ridesharing are concerned with how to organize the shared use of a car for efficient mobility.

TENSIONS OF ORGANIZING

The tensions of organizing arise when there are conflicting demands between organizational processes and structures, particularly during periods of change (Lewis, 2000; Schad et al., 2016; Smith & Lewis, 2011). From the sharing logic perspective, the vision is that everything could be shared without any individual possessions, such as shared goods being used to the maximum extent without underutilization. From the market logic perspective, the potential economic benefits that can be realized through renting out promote the acquisition and accumulation of goods so they can be further monetized, though underutilized. Thus, entrepreneurs adapting to *the new sharing* can acquire cars or apartments, for example, to rent them out via online platforms. These professional providers (e.g., Airbnb "super hosts") entail new challenges for platform operators. They include questions such as how long should the maximum/minimum rental duration be set for consumers, whether prices are inflated when demand is higher, whether a membership price should be charged, how often goods need to be maintained and whether it is done in-house or outsourced, and the extent of the complimentary insurance coverage.

Finally, firms define the rules and guidelines for using the platform (e.g., capping monetary compensation), which institutionalizes the practice to a certain extent and determines the autonomy with which CC participants can perform a practice. Firms negotiate the adaptation of non-monetary practices from those used by circles of friends and family (borrowing a friend's car) or those developed by grassroots movements, by controlling online platforms and educating new participants, while they engage experienced participants to modify their practice and share their knowledge with newcomers. Thus, CC startups need to remain agile due to the influence of turbulent consumer demands and unstable financial markets on their geographical expansion and growth. For example, French BlaBlaCar acquired competitors in some countries, while in others it launched its own carpooling platform with a local office and a dedicated customer service team.

Different styles of CC illustrate the tensions between the various ways people participate in the same practice (e.g., Guyader, 2018, in the carpooling context). The "communal style" is embedded in the sharing logic: CC participants have a pro-social orientation, they value the community to which they feel they belong (i.e., the grassroots movement), and they resent the capitalist ideology embedded in the technological improvements of the platforms leading to a professionalization of the practice. There is a sort of "us versus them" (McArthur, 2015) situation, where "us" are the experienced users (communal style) who were sharing rides before BlaBlaCar improved the overall organization of carpooling, and "them" are the newcomers ("consumerist" and "opportunistic" styles) who adopted CC as the most fashionable and convenient alternative for an access lifestyle (Rifkin, 2000). The consumerist and opportunistic styles emphasize the commercial orientation that paying for CC entails. Platform users with such style are perceived by users with a communal style to be participating in an apparently contradictory manner. It is possible to extrapolate the practice styles to organizations facilitating CC, where those with historically anti-capitalist communities formed around non-monetary practices (e.g., Couch Surfing) close to the sharing ethos, in contrast with the market logic of more recent sharing ventures that are disrupting industry incumbents (e.g., Airbnb, Uber).

In essence, the organizing tensions of the CC paradox are based on how a platform is organized (e.g., how exchanges are structured, how the online community is regulated through terms of usage) according to either the sharing logic or the market logic.

CONCLUSION

Drawing from paradox theory to better understand CC means to focus on the paradoxical tensions between the opposite logics of sharing and market exchange, as summarized in Table 2.1. Because CC showcases elements of both, the corollary is that CC should not be conceptualized as either sharing or market exchange. For example, the functionalities of e-commerce websites adapted and integrated into platform business models based on commission (the market logic) are as important as the participants' social networks, which are also leveraged to alleviate the fear of strangers and emphasize the large community of people centered on a practice of CC (the sharing logic). This is in line with paradox theory: interdependent elements cannot be separated, they define each other, and signify "two sides of the same coin" (Lewis, 2000, p. 761). The four paradoxical tensions of CC cannot be resolved because they originate from the two opposite coexisting logics at play. These persistent tensions balance over time.

Table 2.1   The interrelated tensions of the collaborative consumption paradox

	Sharing Logic	Market Logic
Tensions of Belonging	• communal relationships between participants • peers as friends • expectations of generalized reciprocity	• exchange relationships between participants • peers as impersonal strangers • expectations of direct reciprocity so exchanges are balanced
Tensions of Performing	• pro-social participation goals (e.g., meeting new people, engaging in social interactions, belonging to a community) • organizations adopt a grassroots model to develop local communities	• utilitarian goal for participation (e.g., reduce ownership costs, find a cheaper consumption alternative) • organizations strive for economic utility, efficiency, and convenience

	Sharing Logic	Market Logic
Tensions of Learning	• lack of adaptation to technology, platform business models, and new consumer demands • communities of practice (e.g., car-pooling) are stuck in the past	• lack of roots in the original sharing ethos • organizations focused on providing on-demand services at the least operational costs (e.g., without much consideration for the actual service providers working conditions)
Tensions of Organizing	• everything could be shared, without any individual possessions • shared goods are used by the community without underutilization	• acquisition of goods is encouraged to be further monetized • potential economic benefits from rental

REFERENCES

Acquier, A., Daudigeos, T., & Pinkse, J. (2017). Promises and paradoxes of the sharing economy: An organizing framework. *Technological Forecasting and Social Change*, *125*, 1–10.

Albinsson, P. A., & Perera, B. Y. (2012). Alternative marketplaces in the 21st century: Building community through sharing events. *Journal of Consumer Behavior*, *11*, 303–315.

Albinsson, P. A., & Perera, B. Y. (2018). *The rise of the sharing economy: Exploring the challenges and opportunities of collaborative consumption.* ABC-CLIO.

Bagozzi, R. P. (1975). Marketing as exchange. *Journal of Marketing*, *39*, 32–39.

Belk, R. W. (2010). Sharing. *Journal of Consumer Research*, *36*, 715–734.

Belk, R. W. (2014). You are what you can access: Sharing and collaborative consumption online. *Journal of Business Research*, *67*, 1595–1600.

Belk, R. W., Eckhardt, G. M., & Bardhi, F. (2019a). The paradox of the sharing economy. In R. W. Belk, G. M. Eckhardt, & F. Bardhi (Eds.), *Handbook of the sharing economy* (pp. 1–8). Edward Elgar Publishing.

Belk, R. W., Eckhardt, G. M., & Bardhi, F. (2019b). *Handbook of the sharing economy.* Edward Elgar Publishing.

Beverland, M., Cankurtaran, P., & Loussaïef, L. (2021). A critical framework for examining sustainability claims of the sharing economy: Exploring the tensions within platform brand discourses. *Journal of Macromarketing*, *42*(2), 214–230.

Bourdieu, P. (1986). The forms of capital. In J. E. Richardson (Ed.), *Handbook of theory of research for the sociology of education* (pp. 46–48). Greenword Press.

Bucher, E., Fieseler, C., Fleck, M., & Lutz, C. (2018). Authenticity and the sharing economy. *Academy of Management Discoveries*, *4*(3), 294–313.

Bucher, E., Fieseler, C., & Lutz, C. (2016). What's mine is yours (for a nominal fee): Exploring the spectrum of utilitarian to altruistic motives for Internet-mediated sharing. *Computers in Human Behavior*, *62*(9), 316–326.

Chatterjee, S., Chaudhuri, R., Mikalef, P., & Sarpong, D. (2023). Coopetition in the platform economy from ethical and firm performance perspectives. *Journal of Business Research*, *157*, 113576.

Clark, M. S., & Mills, J. R. (1979). Interpersonal attraction in exchange and communal relationships. *Journal of Personality and Social Psychology*, *37*(1), 12–24.

Davidson, A., Habibi, M. R., & Laroche, M. (2018). Materialism and the sharing economy: A cross-cultural study of American and Indian consumers. *Journal of Business Research, 82*, 364–372.

Eckhardt, G. M., & Bardhi, F. (2015, January 28). The sharing economy isn't about sharing at all. *Harvard Business Review*. https://hbr.org/2015/01/the-sharing -economy-isnt-about-sharing-at-all

Eckhardt, G. M., & Bardhi, F. (2016). The relationship between access practices and economic systems. *Journal of the Association for Consumer Research, 1*(2), 210–225.

Eckhardt, G. M., Houston, M. B., Jiang, B., Lamberton, C., Rindfleisch, A., & Zervas, G. (2019). Marketing in the sharing economy. *Journal of Marketing, 83*, 5–27.

Fiske, A. P. (1992). The four elementary forms of sociality: Framework for a unified theory of social relations. *Psychological Review, 99*(4), 689–723.

Fournier, S., Eckhardt, G. M., & Bardhi, F. (2013, July). Learning to play in the new "share economy." *Harvard Business Review*. https://hbr.org/2013/07/learning-to -play-in-the-new-share-economy

Frenken, K. (2017). Political economies and environmental futures for the sharing economy. *Philosophical Transactions of the Royal Society A: Mathematical, Physical and Engineering Sciences, 375*, 20160367.

Frenken, K., & Schor, J. (2017). Putting the sharing economy into perspective. *Environmental Innovation and Societal Transitions, 23*, 3–10.

Geissinger, A., Laurell, C., Oberg, C., & Sandström, C. (2019). Tracking the institutional logics of the sharing economy. In R. W. Belk, G. M. Eckhardt, & F. Bardhi (Eds.), *Handbook of the sharing economy* (pp. 177–192). Edward Elgar Publishing.

Gölgeci, I., Karakas, F., & Tatoglu, E. (2019). Understanding demand and supply paradoxes and their role in business-to-business firms. *Industrial Marketing Management, 76*, 169–180.

Gölgeci, I., Lacka, E., Kuivalainen, O., & Story, V. (2022). Intra and inter-organizational paradoxes in product-service systems: Current insights and future research directions. *Industrial Marketing Management, 107*, 25–31.

Gollnhofer, J. F., Hellwig, K., & Morhart, F. (2016). Fair is good but what is fair? Negotiations of distributive justice in an emerging non-monetary sharing model. *Journal of the Association for Consumer Research, 1*(2), 226–245.

Grinevich, V., Huber, F., Karataş-Özkan, M., & Yavuz, Ç. (2019). Green entrepreneurship in the sharing economy: Utilising multiplicity of institutional logics. *Small Business Economics, 52*(4), 859–876.

Guyader, H. (2018). No one rides for free! Three styles of collaborative consumption. *Journal of Services Marketing, 32*(6), 692–714.

Guyader, H. (2019). *The heart & wallet paradox of collaborative consumption*. Linköping University Electronic Press.

Guyader, H., Olsson, L. E., & Friman, M. (2023). Sharing economy platforms as mainstream: Balancing pro-social and economic tensions. *Total Quality Management & Business Excellence, 34*(10), 1257–1276.

Habibi, M. R., Kim, A., & Laroche, M. (2016). From sharing to exchange: An extended framework of dual modes of collaborative nonownership consumption. *Journal of the Association for Consumer Research, 1*(2), 277–294.

Hawlitschek, F., Stofberg, N., Teubner, T., Tu, P., & Weinhardt, C. (2018). How corporate sharewashing practices undermine consumer trust. *Sustainability, 10*(8), 2638–2656.

Houston, F. S., & Gassenheimer, J. B. (1987). Marketing and exchange. *Journal of Marketing, 51*, 3–18.

Hunt, S. D. (1976). The nature and scope of marketing. *Journal of Marketing, 40*(3), 17–28.

Lalicic, L., & Weismayer, C. (2018). A model of tourists' loyalty: The case of Airbnb. *Journal of Hospitality and Tourism Technology, 9*(1), 80–93.

Lewis, M. W. (2000). Exploring paradox: Toward a more comprehensive guide. *Academy of Management Review, 25*(4), 760–776.

Martin, C. J., & Upham, P. (2016). Grassroots social innovation and the mobilisation of values in collaborative consumption: A conceptual model. *Journal of Cleaner Production, 134*(Part A), 204–213.

Mazzella, F., & Sundararajan, A. (2016). Entering the trust age. *BlaBlaCar & New York University Stern School of Business*. https://blog.blablacar.com/wp-content/uploads/2016/05/entering-the-trust-age.pdf

McArthur, E. (2015). Many-to-many exchange without money: Why people share their resources. *Consumption Markets & Culture, 18*, 239–256

Mont, O., Voytenko Palgan, Y., & Zvolska, L. (2019). How institutional work by sharing economy organizations and city governments shapes sustainability. In R. W. Belk, G. M. Eckhardt, & F. Bardhi (Eds.), *Handbook of the sharing economy* (pp. 266–276). Edward Elgar Publishing.

Ozanne, L. K., & Ballantine, P. W. (2010). Sharing as a form of anti-consumption? An examination of toy library users. *Journal of Consumer Behaviour, 9*(6), 485–498.

Ozanne, L. K., Phipps, M., Weaver, T., Carrington, M., Luchs, M., Catlin, J., Gupta, S., Santos, N., Scott, K., & Williams, J. (2016). Managing the tensions at the intersection of the triple bottom line: A paradox theory approach to sustainability management. *Journal of Public Policy & Marketing, 35*(2), 249–261.

Price, L. L., & Belk, R. W. (2016). Consumer ownership and sharing: Introduction to the issue. *Journal of the Association for Consumer Research, 1*(2), 193–197.

Rifkin, J. (2000). *The age of access: The new culture of hypercapitalism, where all of life is a paid-for experience*. J.P. Tarcher/Putnam.

Sahlins, M. D. (1972). *Stone age economics*. Aldine Atherton.

Saravade, S., Felix, R., & Fırat, A. F. (2020). From solidity to liquidity: Macro-level consumption patterns in the sharing economy. *Journal of Macromarketing, 41*(2), 284–296.

Scaraboto, D. (2015). Selling, sharing, and everything in between: The hybrid economies of collaborative networks. *Journal of Consumer Research, 42*, 152–176.

Schad, J., Lewis, M. W., Raisch, S., & Smith, W. K. (2016). Paradox research in management science: Looking back to move forward. *Academy of Management Annals, 10*(1), 5–64.

Schneckenberg, D., Roth, S., & Velamuri, V. K. (2023). Deparadoxification and value focus in sharing ventures: Concealing paradoxes in strategic decision-making. *Journal of Business Research, 162*, 113883.

Scholz, T. (2016). *Platform cooperativism: Challenging the corporate sharing economy*. Rosa Luxemburg Stiftung. https://rosalux.nyc/wp-content/uploads/2020/11/RLS-NYC_platformcoop.pdf

Schor, J. B. (2014). *Debating the sharing economy*. Great Transition Initiative. https://greattransition.org/publication/debating-the-sharing-economy

Schor, J. B., Fitzmaurice, C., & Carfagna, L. B. (2016). Paradoxes of openness and distinction in the sharing economy. *Poetics, 54*, 66–81.

Slee, T. (2015). *What's yours is mine: Against the sharing economy*. OR Books.

Smith, W. K., & Lewis, M. W. (2011). Toward a theory of paradox: A dynamic equilibrium model of organizing. *Academy of Management Review, 36*(2), 381–403.
Voytenko Palgan, Y., Zvolska, L., & Mont, O. (2017). Sustainability framings of accommodation sharing. *Environmental Innovation and Societal Transitions, 23,* 70–83.
Williams, R. (1976). *Keyword: A vocabulary of culture and society.* Oxford University Press.

PART II

Consumer roles in CC

3. How do prosumers collaborate in online communities? The four-level structure of collaborative prosumption practices

Jan-Hendrik Bucher, Johanna Gollnhofer, and Niklas Woermann

INTRODUCTION

How are collaborative practices orchestrated in online communities? Prior studies on collaboration in communities have demonstrated that collaboration among prosumers involves many difficulties. For instance, prosumers have different intentions (Gollnhofer & Schouten, 2017), levels of involvement (Scaraboto, 2015), and skills (Knudsen & Antorini, 2021). Although Chalmers Thomas et al. (2012) explore heterogeneity in consumption communities, how prosumers manage specific projects when prosuming collaboratively, despite those tensions, remains understudied. In this chapter, we uncover and conceptualize a multi-level community structure through which prosumers orchestrate prosumption practices despite tensions. By introducing distinct but selectively interconnected levels of prosumption practices, this research reveals the importance of community for orchestrating collaborative prosumption.

Our empirical study investigates speedrunning communities through qualitative research methods, using in-depth interviews and netnography. Speedrunning communities are highly mediatized online communities that are strongly based on the collaboration between globally dispersed community members. Speedrunners aim to play through video games as quickly as possible. Instead of following the games' storylines and rules, speedrunners collaboratively develop and refine solutions to beat "speed records." We find that prosumption practices in speedrunning communities do not stand on equal terms. Instead, they serve different functions, are driven by different intentions, and are directed toward different audiences. We refer to this division of prosumption practices as *functional differentiation*. By grouping together prosumption practices with similar functions and directed toward the same audience, we identify four levels with clearly distinct sets of practices, actors, and media platforms. The *member level* encompasses prosumption practices that stand alone and are not directed toward other prosumers or consumers. The *team level* comprises prosumption practices directed toward a particular group of familiar community members who work collaboratively on the same project. The *crowd level* consists of prosumption practices directed toward all community members around the globe who are interested in the same project. Finally, the *public level* addresses prosumption practices directed toward lay consumers outside the community.

Our study demonstrates that collaborative prosumption in communities requires the managed interplay of prosumption practices at all levels. We find that consumers work across different levels through upstream and downstream processes, which we define as flows of information that connect different levels of prosumption practices. By uncovering and conceptualizing a multi-level community structure, we contribute to understanding how prosumers (a) distribute prosumption practices that require different resources, tools, and skills; (b) coordinate and quality-check prosumption results; (c) communicate results internally to community members and externally to the public; and (d) use media platforms to facilitate collaborative prosumption.

First, we review the literature on collaborative prosumption communities, focusing on the multi-level arrangements of prosumption practices. Following the literature review, we describe the study design and context of speedrunning prosumption communities. Thereafter, we present and analyze our findings. Finally, we discuss our findings and provide theoretical implications.

LITERATURE REVIEW

Collaborative prosumption differs from individual prosumption. It occurs when individual prosumers work together on shared projects. Previous research studied ample instances of collaborative prosumption. Yet, researchers primarily focused on prosumers' individual perspectives (e.g., Knudsen & Antorini, 2021; Laamanen & Skålén, 2015). Studies taking a community perspective focus on hierarchical differences between community members such as core versus peripheral members (Leigh et al., 2006) or high versus low access to resources (Chalmers Thomas et al., 2012). These studies indicate that in collaborative prosumption communities, different prosumers conduct different prosumption practices. However, they do not explain *how* community members orchestrate different prosumption practices to facilitate collaboration. In the following, we review studies on collaborative prosumption, focusing on (1) whether different prosumption practices can be observed, and (2) how prosumers orchestrate different prosumption practices to facilitate collaborative prosumption.

Scaraboto (2015) studies collaborative prosumption in the geo-caching community. The study describes different prosumption practices that are essential to facilitate the hobby of geo-caching. For instance, certain members collaboratively set up and operate websites or social media platforms, produce free trail maps, or author guides that help newcomers start on the hobby. Others contribute to the community by verifying publications of new caches on community-specific media platforms, by organizing local and regional meetings or events, or by moderating discussion forums. This infrastructure and the services offered by community members facilitate others' enjoyment of geo-caching and participation in free geo-caching events. This research highlights that different prosumption practices are orchestrated to facilitate the hobby of geo-caching. However, we do not know how this orchestration is coordinated between members.

Gollnhofer and Schouten (2017) elucidate how activist prosumers collect discarded food at cooperating retailers to distribute it among other volunteering community members, as well as to the public via food banks and charities. Similar to Scaraboto (2015), Gollnhofer and Schouten describe different prosumption practices that are orchestrated to enable food sharing. While not focusing on it, they provide evidence that prosumption practices are divided among community members based on their involvement. Members at "the forefront of foodsharing" invented and guide the alternative foodsharing market. They exert political influence on the market arrangement, build and operate platforms through which foodsharers organize themselves, make agreements with retailers, and train new volunteer foodsharers. Other members execute the activist practices of gathering and distributing discarded food to food banks and charities, as well as to other community members. While this research nicely outlines the individual roles, various responsibilities, and different prosumption practices of community members, it does not focus on how different prosumption practices are orchestrated to facilitate collaborative prosumption.

Studying the cosplay prosumption community, Seregina and Weijo (2016) show how cosplayers craft and present their costumes. This research provides evidence that prosumption practices can be divided based on intra-community status. More senior members run panel discussions, judge costumes, or produce and share tutorials via community-specific media platforms such as Cosplay. com. At conventions, these members are referred to as "celebrity guests" or "invited cosplayers." Other highly engaged members manage the community by organizing events and contests or by ensuring that cosplay is featured in convention event programs. This infrastructure and the services offered by community members support cosplayers in their prosumption practices and allow them to showcase their costumes to the community. Similar to the above-reviewed instances of collaborative prosumption, cosplayers are only able to conduct their hobby through the neat interplay of different practices. While this research nicely outlines a division of prosumption practices based on the intra-community status, it does not focus on how different prosumption practices are orchestrated and thus facilitate collaborative prosumption.

Knudsen and Antorini (2021) studied collaborative prosumption in the LEGO ideas community. This research shows how community members collaborate to support particular projects initiated by individual members. Focusing on work-sharing processes, Knudsen and Antorini identified six prosumption practices in collaborative project work. Individual members develop initial designs and build models. Some community members help with digital rendering of projects, and others promote the idea outside the platform. This research highlights that essential practices to collaborative prosumption are divided based on community members' skills and involvement. Further, it shows that prosumption practices are directed toward different audiences inside and outside the project team. Although this research highlights how important the division of labor is to collaborative prosumption projects, it does not examine how different prosumption practices are orchestrated.

Our literature review shows that in collaborative prosumption communities, prosumers engage in different prosumption practices that serve distinct functions for different audiences. We call this division of prosumption practices *functional differentiation*. For instance, we identify prosumption practices directed toward the community, such as geo-cachers who verify publications of new caches or cosplayers who judge costumes of fellow community members. Further, there are prosumption practices directed toward particular teams, such as members of the LEGO ideas community who contribute to a particular project. Research also presents prosumption practices directed toward consumers outside the community, such as foodsharers who distribute discarded food to food banks and charities. Finally, there are individual prosumption practices such as those undertaken by cosplayers or geo-cachers who use the community set-up to engage in individual prosumption projects. In the reviewed studies, functionally differentiated prosumption practices result from the different roles that individuals assume in the community, their hierarchical status within the community (Seregina & Weijo, 2016), their involvement in collaborative prosumption projects (Gollnhofer & Schouten, 2017), or their skills (Knudsen & Antorini, 2021).

While the reviewed studies suggest that these functionally differentiated prosumption practices only facilitate collaborative prosumption when orchestrated, the process of how this occurs remains understudied. To address this shortcoming, we study speedrunning communities, which are highly mediatized prosumption communities that are heavily reliant on collaboration among globally dispersed community members.

CONTEXTUAL BACKGROUND: SPEEDRUNNING COMMUNITIES

Speedrunners aim to play video games as quickly as possible. Instead of following the games' storylines or rules, they develop and refine solutions to improve current speed records, often collaboratively. For instance, they identify avoidable levels, cutscenes or *glitches* (flaws in games' codes) to complete the game in the shortest time possible (Hay, 2020; Lorber, 2018). Speedrunners thereby separate the act of playing from the games' original narratives (Ford, 2018). This makes speedrunning a metagame because it transcends the prescribed intentions of any individual game.

Speedrunning has existed from the inception of video games. Since 2010, it has become a rapidly growing global phenomenon that has assumed a significant position within the gaming culture, reaching broader public attention, and even influencing the multi-billion dollar video game industry (Escobar-Lamanna, 2019; Ford, 2018; Lewis, 2020; Scully-Blaker, 2016; Warman, 2019). Worldwide, speedrunners actively engage in discussions through forums and live-streaming platforms such as Twitch, and stream and upload videos, some of which have been viewed tens of millions of times. Given its popularity today, almost every video game around has at least a small group of speedrunners formed for prosumption purposes (Escobar-Lamanna, 2019). One of the most popular websites among speedrunners is speedrun. com. It has more than 300 000 registered users, and features forums, live streams, leaderboards, guide pages, and much more. Events such as Games Done Quick and the European Speedsters Assembly reach millions online, bringing together thousands of speedrunning enthusiasts. Speedrunning communities offer a fruitful context for studying collaborative prosumption practices because (1) they are highly mediatized prosumption communities that are heavily reliant on collaboration between globally dispersed members, and (2) the process of how prosumption practices are orchestrated is very vivid.

METHOD

To answer the research question, we conducted netnographic investigations and in-depth interviews with speedrunners, and analyzed secondary data (i.e., published interviews with speedrunners), and public user-generated content.

For our netnographic inquiry, we analyzed publicly available user-generated content (e.g., posts on social networks like Facebook, Instagram, or Twitter, discussion boards like Reddit, blogs, wikis, and video and live-streaming platforms such as YouTube or Twitch), and (semi-)private content (e.g., posts in closed Facebook groups, closed Instagram profiles, closed Discord servers, or private messages). Altogether, we gathered and analyzed over 250 hours of video data and more than 1000 comments. During our netnographic inquiry, as researchers gained familiarity with the speedrunning community and its members, they became actively engaged with the context. The first author complemented the netnographic study with a physical site visit to HeroFest in Bern (Switzerland) on November 24, 2019. At this convention, speedrunners gathered, exchanged ideas, and presented their hobby to laypeople.

To overcome observational limitations (Arnould & Wallendorf, 1994), the first author conducted ten in-depth interviews (nine speedrunners and one employee of a large Japanese video game producer) with a total duration of 11:26 hours. Three of the speedrunners were casually involved in the community, while four were highly involved, hosting for instance popular YouTube or Twitch channels. Further, the first author conducted various ethnographic interviews with speedrunners and interested people during the ongoing site visit (Spradley, 1979).

In addition to in-depth interviews, we analyzed ten interviews with *the quickest gamers* which were conducted and published by David Snyder (2017). Further, we transcribed and analyzed 25 episodes of three podcasts that were recorded by and with speedrunners, and were published via YouTube or audio platforms such as Spotify (approximate total duration of 20 hours). Gathered data was processed and coded in a multistage hermeneutic process (Thompson, 1997). To reach sufficient interpretive convergence and theoretical saturation, we collected and analyzed data simultaneously rather than subsequently (Corbin & Strauss, 1990). Thus, we interpreted data iteratively, derived new questions, collected new data, and rejected and confirmed preliminary findings (Parmentier & Fischer, 2015).

FINDINGS AND ANALYSIS

Our findings show that speedrunning consists of distinct practices with different functions carried out by various people and directed toward different audiences. By identifying prosumption practices with similar functions directed toward the same audiences (i.e., not contributing to others, or contributing to a particular team, the crowd, or the public), we identify four different levels of prosumption practices: the member level, the team level, the crowd level, and the public level (Figure 3.1). In the following, we present and analyze prosumption practices on each of these levels. Subsequently, we explore how speedrunners work across them. In doing so, we identify upstream and downstream processes that are flows of information that connect different levels of prosumption practices. We also highlight the role of media platforms on and in between each of these different levels.

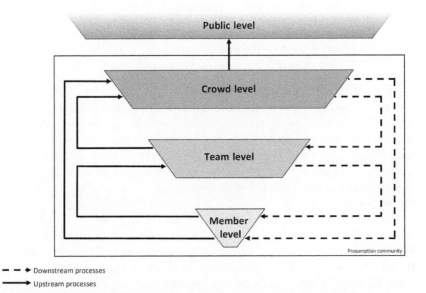

Figure 3.1   *The four-level community structure of collaborative prosumption practices*

Member Level

On the member level, speedrunners individually play through video games as quickly as possible. To do so, they first and foremost explore games to identify room for improvement. Usually, speedrunners segment games into single levels, single sections of a level, or even single button inputs, which they explore successively. Our analysis indicates that speedrunners use three practices, often used in combination, to explore video games: trial-and-error explorations, software-assisted explorations, and hypothesizing.

Most common are practices of trial-and-error. Here, individual speedrunners repeatedly play through games, trying and hoping for fast times or identifying room for improvement. Over hours, days, or weeks of repetitive activities, they identify avoidable levels, enemies, cutscenes, or glitches and thus discover opportunities to save time. One of our informants described the trial-and-error approach in speedrunning as:

> playing with the game's mechanics, trying to find something like banging your head against corners to ... explore the game, find out about how the game works and with this trial and error, ... you sort of figure out: "If I do that, then this happens," and then you dig a little more and you sort of realize the reason for that. (interview, male, 26 years old)

In some cases, their knowledge of certain video games is so far advanced that trial-and-error investigations are no longer sufficient to examine the game in more depth. To do so, some speedrunners use open-source software. "We need to take off the outer layers and understand it and find some mechanics that are hidden very, very deep down in the game" (interview, male, 20 years old). Using software allows speedrunners to examine video games' textures and loading zones, or data such as the number of frames, the position in space, or the memory cache.

Furthermore, as opposed to more unstructured trial-and-error practices, some speedrunners hypothesize possible ways to improve the playthrough by transferring previous findings to new situations in the game. In hypothesizing, they "try to come up with theoretical ideas for shortcuts or glitches" (interview, male, 20 years old). In conclusion, the member level encompasses prosumption practices that stand alone and are not directed toward others. As outlined in the literature review, this level has received the most attention in research so far (e.g., Brock & Johnson, 2021).

Team Level

On the team level, speedrunners work collaboratively on the same project. In teams of up to 20 members, they distribute individual subtasks (e.g., analyzing game code, hypothesizing new routes, or executing defined strategies). Once team members complete their subtasks, project leaders combine individual prosumption outcomes into one big picture: "It's a team effort to try to push the game to its limits" (interview, male, 20 years old). During a presentation of a finished speedrun at the Games Done Quick convention in 2019, a team leader described teamwork as an iterative process, as team members revise their fellow members' initial results several times before a project is completed: "This upcoming track features a newly found glitch that was found by [name of a team-member] and recently revised by [name of a team-member]" (presentation of a speedrun at Games Done Quick 2019). This way, unlike prosumption practices on the member level, speedrunners do not go through the entire process of speedrunning individually. Instead, they usually focus on one element such as analyzing the game's code, hypothesizing new routes, or executing defined strategies, such as crafting theories for further rooms for improvement or analyzing data: "There might be one person who is strong in one element like in doing the tricks ..., others can craft theory so well that it makes sense to try these tricks" (interview, female, 24 years old).

Team members collaborate closely and usually know each other. To share information or prosumption results with the team, speedrunners use closed Discord servers or private chats. Teamwork can last from weeks to months, and sometimes even years. During this time, speedrunners constantly revise and optimize *the run* based on new findings, strategy discussion, and countless iterations of dividing prosumption tasks and compiling prosumption outcomes. Speedrunners collaborate due to the complexity of many speedrunning projects: "usually, there's nobody in the entire group that understands everything" (interview, male, 26 years old).

In conclusion, on the team level, we summarize prosumption practices directed toward a particular group of community members that engage in collaborative teamwork. Only when put together do the individual prosumption practices form a coherent picture. Thus, practices on this level are functionally different from speedrunning prosumption practices on other levels and they have received some attention in prior research. For instance, Knudsen and Antorini (2021) studied the dynamics of teams working on the same project.

Crowd Level

On the crowd level, speedrunners carry out prosumption practices for the crowd such as legitimizing new records or compiling and archiving novel findings. Adopting the term from Kozinets et al. (2008), we define *crowds* as all speedrunners interested and involved in the same game.

When individual members or teams achieve new records, they submit a recording of the gameplay to crowd-specific platforms such as speedrun. com, speeddemosarchive.com, or tasvideos.org. To legitimize claimed records, senior crowd members (called "judges") peer-review uploaded videos. Speedrunners define judges as: "members of the site ... that have been entrusted with the responsibility of approving or rejecting movies that have been submitted" (TASVideos, 2021). They follow strict community-set guidelines (Hay, 2020). When a submission is accepted, it is made available to the community and serves as a new benchmark against which further prosumption efforts are evaluated.

Through practices of compiling and archiving, speedrunners organize prosumption outcomes such as new records, novel solutions to common problems, or hitherto unknown information to make them easily accessible to the crowd, often through crowd-specific platforms (e.g., wikis, websites, or podcasts). For other crowd members, speedrunners compile and archive prosumption results in a less structured manner on platforms such as Discord, discussion forums, or Facebook groups. In that way, they comprehend the "general knowledge of the game" (interview, male, 26 years old). Beyond submitting record playthroughs online, speedrunners present their results on crowd-specific platforms or live at conventions such as Games Done Quick.

In addition to compiling and archiving prosumption outcomes, crowd-specific platforms also provide forums for game-specific questions. Here, crowd members who do not know each other personally interact and support one another. "If I get stuck, I go to Discord and ask: 'Hey, can you help me?' ... and when people come to me in the chat and ask me: 'Hey how do you do that?' then I explain it, it's like give-and-take" (interview, male, 22 years old).

In conclusion, the crowd level comprises prosumption practices directed toward all community members worldwide who are interested in the same project. Thus, practices on this level are functionally different from prosumption practices on other levels. Crowd-level practices have received some attention in prior research. For instance, Kozinets et al. (2008) studied online creative consumer communities and studies on brand communities allude to practices on the crowd level (Muñiz & O'Guinn, 2001; Muñiz & Schau, 2005).

Public Level

On the public level, speedrunners present completed speedruns or summarize recent achievements to lay consumers outside the community. Since internal prosumption practices are mostly incomprehensible for the public, speedrunners translate prosumption practices in TV documentary-like videos that are uploaded on broadly accessible platforms such as YouTube. The videos are titled, for instance, "Mario Kart 64: The Quest for World Record Perfection," "From Challenge to Science: The History of the A Button Challenge," or "Super Mario Bros: The Human Limit." Through these videos, some of which have been viewed millions of times, speedrunners aim to entertain lay consumers and to spread the hobby. Next to presenting speedrunning to the public, speedrunners use the public attention for garnering charity donations. In this way, public-level practices can contribute to collaborative prosumption as they might lead to the recruitment of new members and resources. However, because they merely summarize and simplify previous results, these documentaries are not of interest for the speedrunners and their prosumption practices.

In conclusion, the public level comprises prosumption practices directed toward lay consumers outside the speedrunning community, which are functionally distinct from those of other levels. Most social-media-based studies embrace the notion of *the public*. For instance, Arvidsson and Caliandro (2015) explore brand publics and define the concept of "publics" as "social formations that are not based on interaction but on a continuous focus of interest and mediation" (p. 727). Yen and Dey (2019) use the term "others" to introduce the continuum between a collective "us" and an anonymous public. Yet, community practices on the public level have received scant research interest. To date, only a few collaborative prosumption community-based studies indicate that internal prosumption practices also produce value outside the community (Gollnhofer & Schouten, 2017; Woermann, 2012).

Upstream and Downstream Processes

In the following, we present how speedrunners connect the different levels of prosumption practices by discussing various upstream and downstream processes. Upstream and downstream processes are flows of information regarding prosumption practices that are directed toward higher (upstream processes) and lower levels (downstream processes) respectively.

Upstream processes

Speedrunners share novel information that might be beneficial for prosumption practices on higher levels, such as new records, identified glitches, strategy charts, and faster ways of playing through specific segments. The importance of upstream processes in speedrunning communities is reflected in the fact that members developed an implicit "code of honor" to impel upstream processes. "If I find something, I'll upload it within the next 10–15 minutes ... there's a bit of a code of honor among speedrunners stating that you actually upload the tricks you make" (interview, male, 22 years old).

Some members even share entire documents that allow fellow speedrunners to continue working on the game. This preparation and presentation of prosumption outcomes forms the basis for future prosumption practices such as optimizing or delving deeper into certain speedruns. Thus, upstream processes fuel collaborative prosumption practices.

Our findings also show that speedrunners use different media platforms on different levels. At the team level, they use platforms such as closed Discord servers or private chats that grant access only to an exclusive group. To direct information or prosumption outcomes toward the crowd level, speedrunners use open platforms such as open Twitch accounts, YouTube, crowd-specific websites, open documents (e.g., Google Docs), or open Facebook groups. Finally, to share prosumption outcomes such as completed speedruns or documentary overviews at the public level, speedrunners use popular open platforms including YouTube.

Downstream processes
When speedrunners dedicate themselves to working on a game, they usually do so by building on previous findings. By researching earlier achievements on the playthrough and analyzing their strategies and approaches, speedrunners start prosuming where their fellow community members left off. To define the starting point for their prosumption practices, they collect as much publicly available information as possible about the speedrun's current status from various sources such as wikis, podcasts, uploaded documents, Facebook groups, Twitch, YouTube, Reddit, and Discord: "I'm just watching other people that are also running the same game over and over again, ... there's so many things I can pull out ... maybe they found this little route optimization that I just hadn't thought of" (interview, male, 23 years old). As this quote shows, speedrunners use information uploaded by fellow crowd members to learn more about video games and, where possible, use it as building blocks for their own prosumption practices. When speedrunners are more deeply involved, they tend to look for more specific information that is useful for their prosumption practices. For instance, one of our informants (male, 23 years old) constantly strives to be up to date with the latest "discoveries" with the particular game he is prosuming at the moment: "I've been doing this every day actually, I go on YouTube, type in 'Spider-Reignited-Trilogy' [name of the video game] -glitch, select for the last 24 hours and I click through every single video and watch them."

With downstream processes, speedrunners aim to align their prosumption practices to the prosumption outcomes of fellow team or crowd members. In this way, as downstream processes continue or link to the consumption practices of other speedrunners, they are of great importance for collaborative prosumption in speedrunning communities.

In summary, we find that collaborative prosumption practices are functionally differentiated, driven by different intentions, and are directed toward different audiences. Grouping prosumption practices with similar functions that are directed toward the same audience, we identify four levels with distinct sets of practices, actors, and media platforms. By identifying how these different levels are connected, we demonstrate how speedrunners orchestrate functionally differentiated prosumption practices and thereby facilitate collaborative prosumption.

DISCUSSION AND CONCLUSION

Our analysis revealed the importance of community structure for collaborative prosumption. While prior research has studied practices of each level in isolation, our study finds that collaborative prosumption requires a neat interplay of practices at all levels. Complex prosumption practices like speedrunning are impossible to pursue individually at a high level but instead require consumers with different skills and passions to collaborate over long periods. The astonishing speedrunning world records are the result of years of coordinated efforts by hundreds, if not thousands of community members. However, unlike employed professionals, prosumers working in communities are volunteers so they are not managed centrally by formal power-wielding executives, and cannot be held accountable to contractual obligations. In other words, organizing collectives of prosumers is more challenging compared to managing formal, professional organizations. However, as our study indicates, collaborative prosumption is made possible by orchestration of functionally differentiated prosumption practices within a multi-level community structure supported by different media platforms. This multi-level community structure and the associated media technology is based on several key prerequisites: (a) dividing large, difficult projects into smaller, manageable tasks; (b) distributing prosumption practices requiring different resources, tools, and skills to those that possess them; (c) overseeing job progress including quality-checking results; (d) coordinating globally and temporally dispersed work; (e) aggregating, compiling, and communicating results to the crowd; (f) motivating and entertaining prosumers; and (g) communicating results to the public in order to recruit new members and resources. We suggest that prior literature does not adequately explain how globally dispersed prosumption communities can fulfill these demanding prerequisites because it has not considered community levels and the media platforms they are based on. By defining communities as a set of practices (Schau et al., 2009), assemblages (Chalmers Thomas et al., 2012), media sites (Woermann & Kirschner, 2015), or networks of desire (Kozinets et al., 2016), prior research tends to conceptualize prosumption communities as consisting of one relatively homogenous and highly interconnected level. In contrast, we find a structure of four clearly distinct levels that are characterized by distinct sets of practices, actors, and media platforms. This insight adds to our understanding of how community structures allow prosumers to collaborate on complex global projects such as open-source movements (Hemetsberger & Reinhardt, 2006, 2009; Scaraboto, 2015), fandom cultures (Kozinets, 2001; Wang, 2019), or platform economies (Kane, 2009; Kane & Ransbotham, 2012; Weltevrede & Borra, 2016).

In conclusion, we show what an analytical focus on levels of functionally differentiated practices inside prosumption communities adds to our understanding of collaborative prosumption. Our first contribution lies in our distinction between flows of information within levels and between levels (up- and downstream processes). Within levels, communication is frequent and open, but participants need a high level of knowledge and skill to be able to participate. The exchange between levels is less frequent and often more formal. Thus, information needs to be contextualized or translated in order to be informative and interesting for the audience. For instance, this is apparent in speedrunners making the community's prosumption practices and outcomes comprehensible to the public through TV documentary-like videos shared on public platforms. This insight complements prior research indicating that translation processes must occur between different community networks (Giesler, 2012) and that obligatory points of passage which exist can be used to control and manage touchpoints (Martin & Schouten, 2013). We complement this literature by showing that translation and control also occur within communities, but only between different levels.

Our second contribution concerns heterogeneity within communities. Chalmers Thomas et al. (2012) demonstrated that heterogeneous actors often collaborate in communities because they depend on each other to access complementary resources. This causes tensions across the community, which need to be managed and redressed (ibid.). In our study, we find that the multi-level structure reduces this problem greatly. Prosumers within one layer tend to be homogenous and thus freely share access to resources (i.e., knowledge or tools). In contrast, between different levels, prosumers often possess very different knowledge and skills, so that heterogeneity is pronounced and tensions can arise. For instance, we find rigorous speedrunners prosuming at the team level who dislike how some community members present themselves and speedrunning on the public level.

Third, we contribute to the practice perspective on prosumption communities (Schau et al., 2009) by showing that prosumption practices are not equally distributed across the community but are organized into different levels with limited cross-level interaction. In other words, we argue that community structure is also relevant in terms of a practice lens on community. Distinguishing between practices that (a) occur only on one level; (b) are universal to community; and (c) only occur at the interface between different levels (up- and downstream processes) can increase the depth and granularity of our understanding of communities.

REFERENCES

Arnould, E. J., & Wallendorf, M. (1994). Market-oriented ethnography: Interpretation building and marketing strategy formulation. *Journal of Marketing Research, 31*(4), 484–504. https://doi.org/10.1177/002224379403100404

Arvidsson, A., & Caliandro, A. (2015). Brand public. *Journal of Consumer Research, 42*(5), 727–748. https://doi.org/10.1093/jcr/ucv053

Brock, T., & Johnson, M. R. (2021). Video gaming as craft consumption. *Journal of Consumer Culture, 21*(1), 3–13. https://doi.org/10.1177/1469540521993904

Chalmers Thomas, T., Price, L. L., & Schau, H. J. (2012). When differences unite: Resource dependence in heterogeneous consumption communities. *Journal of Consumer Research, 39*(5), 1010–1033. https://doi.org/10.1086/666616

Corbin, J. M., & Strauss, A. (1990). Grounded theory research: Procedures, canons, and evaluative criteria. *Qualitative Sociology, 13*(1), 3–21.

Escobar-Lamanna, J. (2019). *Why speed matters: Collective action and participation in speedrunning groups* [Unpublished dissertation]. OCAD University, Toronto, Ontario, Canada.

Ford, D. (2018). *Speedrunning: Transgressive play in digital space* [Paper presentation]. Nordic DiGRA, Bergen, Norway. https://doi.org/10.13140/RG.2.2.12357 .91369

Giesler, M. (2012). How doppelgänger brand images influence the market creation process: Longitudinal insights from the rise of Botox cosmetic. *Journal of Marketing, 76*(6), 55–68.

Gollnhofer, J. F., & Schouten, J. W. (2017). Complementing the dominant social paradigm with sustainability. *Journal of Macromarketing, 37*(2), 143–152. https://doi .org/10.1177/0276146717696892

Hay, J. (2020). Fully optimized: The (post)human art of speedrunning. *Journal of Posthuman Studies, 4*(1), 5–24. https://doi.org/10.5325/jpoststud.4.1.0005

Hemetsberger, A., & Reinhardt, C. (2006). Learning and knowledge-building in open-source communities: A social-experiential approach. *Management Learning, 37*(2), 187–214. https://doi.org/10.1177/1350507606063442

Hemetsberger, A., & Reinhardt, C. (2009). Collective development in open-source communities: An activity theoretical perspective on successful online collaboration. *Organization Studies, 30*(9), 987–1008. https://doi.org/10.1177/0170840609339241

Kane, G. C. (2009, August). It's a network, not an encyclopedia: A social network perspective on Wikipedia collaboration. *Academy of Management Proceedings, 2009*(1), 1–6.

Kane, G. C., & Ransbotham, S. (2012). *Collaborative development in Wikipedia* [Paper presentation]. Collective Intelligence Conference, Cambridge, MA, USA.

Knudsen, G. H., & Antorini, Y. M. (2021). Hard work: Unanticipated collaboration in co-creation processes. *Journal of the Association for Consumer Research, 6*(4), 435–446. https://doi.org/10.1086/715545

Kozinets, R. (2001). Utopian enterprise: Articulating the meanings of Star Trek's culture of consumption. *Journal of Consumer Research, 28*(1), 67–88. https://doi .org/10.1086/321948

Kozinets, R., Hemetsberger, A., & Schau, H. J. (2008). The wisdom of consumer crowds: Collective innovation in the age of networked marketing. *Journal of Macromarketing, 28*(4), 339–354. https://doi.org/10.1177/0276146708325382

Kozinets, R., Patterson, A., & Ashman, R. (2016). Networks of desire: How technology increases our passion to consume. *Journal of Consumer Research, 43*(5), 659–682. https://doi.org/10.1093/jcr/ucw061

Laamanen, M., & Skålén, P. (2015). Collective–conflictual value co-creation: A strategic action field approach. *Marketing Theory, 15*(3), 381–400. https://doi.org/10 .1177/1470593114564905

Leigh, T. W., Peters, C., & Shelton, J. (2006). The consumer quest for authenticity: The multiplicity of meanings within the MG subculture of consumption. *Journal of the Academy of Marketing Science, 34*(4), 481–493. https://doi.org/10.1177/ 0092070306288403

Lewis, L. (2020, January 22). Super Mario in five minutes: How "speedrunning" went mainstream. *Financial Times Magazine.* https://www.ft.com/content/12c385fa-3be1 -11ea-b232-000f4477fbca

Lorber, M. (2018, July 7). *Speedruns – Gaming gegen die Zeit.* https://spielkultur.ea.de

Martin, D. M., & Schouten, J. W. (2013). Consumption-driven market emergence. *Journal of Consumer Research, 40*(5), 855–870. https://doi.org/10.1086/673196

Muñiz, A. M., Jr., & O'Guinn, T. C. (2001). Brand community. *Journal of Consumer Research, 27*(4), 412–432. https://doi.org/10.1086/319618

Muñiz, A. M., Jr., & Schau, H. J. (2005). Religiosity in the abandoned Apple Newton brand community. *Journal of Consumer Research, 31*(4), 737–747. https://doi.org/10.1086/426607

Parmentier, M.-A., & Fischer, E. (2015). Things fall apart: The dynamics of brand audience dissipation. *Journal of Consumer Research, 41*(5), 1228–1251. https://doi.org/10.1086/678907

Scaraboto, D. (2015). Selling, sharing, and everything in between: The hybrid economies of collaborative networks. *Journal of Consumer Research, 42*(1), 152–176. https://doi.org/10.1093/jcr/ucv004

Schau, H. J., Muñiz, A. M., & Arnould, E. J. (2009). How brand community practices create value. *Journal of Marketing, 73*(5), 30–51. https://doi.org/10.1509/jmkg.73.5.30

Scully-Blaker, R. (2016). *On becoming "like eSports": Twitch as a platform for the speedrunning community* [Paper presentation]. First joint conference of DiGRA and FDG, Dundee, Scotland, UK.

Seregina, A., & Weijo, H. A. (2016). Play at any cost: How cosplayers produce and sustain their ludic communal consumption experiences. *Journal of Consumer Research, 44*(1), 139–159. https://doi.org/10.1093/jcr/ucw077

Snyder, D. (2017). *Speedrunning: Interviews with the quickest gamers*. McFarland.

Spradley, J. P. (1979). *The ethnographic interview*. Wadsworth–Thomson Learning.

TASVideos. (2021). *Guidelines for judges*. Accessed October 31, 2021, from http://tasvideos.org/JudgeGuidelines.html

Thompson, C. J. (1997). Interpreting consumers: A hermeneutical framework for deriving marketing insights from the texts of consumers' consumption stories. *Journal of Marketing Research, 34*(4), 438–455.

Wang, C. L. (2019). *Handbook of research on the impact of fandom in society and consumerism*. IGI Global.

Warman, P. (2019). *Global games market report 2019*. Newzoo. https://newzoo.com/insights/trend-reports/newzoo-global-games-market-report-2019-light-version/

Weltevrede, E., & Borra, E. (2016). Platform affordances and data practices: The value of dispute on Wikipedia. *Big Data & Society, 3*(1). https://doi.org/10.1177/2053951716653418

Woermann, N. (2012). On the slope is on the screen: Prosumption, social media practices, and scopic systems in the freeskiing subculture. *American Behavioral Scientist, 56*(4), 618–640. https://doi.org/10.1177/0002764211429363

Woermann, N., & Kirschner, H. (2015). Online livestreams, community practices, and assemblages. Towards a site ontology of consumer community. *Advances in Consumer Research, 43*, 438–442. https://www.acrwebsite.org/volumes/1019801/volumes/v43/NA-43

Yen, D. A., & Dey, B. (2019). Acculturation in the social media: Myth or reality? Analysing social-media-led integration and polarisation. *Technological Forecasting and Social Change, 145*, 426–427. https://doi.org/https://doi.org/10.1016/j.techfore.2019.04.012

4. The effect of materialism on participation in collaborative consumption

Antje R. H. Graul and Aristeidis Theotokis

COLLABORATIVE CONSUMPTION AND BROADENING BOUNDARIES

While traditional economic models are premised on the assumption of buying and selling, collaborative consumption (CC) involves access rather than ownership (Lee et al., 2009). Contrary to forms of social sharing, which involve offering and using private goods to close friends or members of the family (Belk, 2010), CC is "an economic exchange, and consumers are after utilitarian, rather than social, value" (Eckhardt & Bardhi, 2015a, p. 3). Access-based CC schemes have seen a significant rise in popularity over the past decade (Bäro et al., 2022). While market reports estimated the market size of the sharing economy at US$149.9 billion in 2022, it is expected to grow to US$793.7 billion by 2028 (Absolute Reports, 2023). For instance, Airbnb, one of the most popular examples of a sharing economy venture, was listed in 2023 as the 117th most valuable company worldwide (CompaniesMarketCap.com). In February 2023, Airbnb's share price was US$129, while its all-time high was US$212.68 in February 2021 (see https://google.com/finance).

At first, CC may sound contradictory in a world where ownership of goods is of high importance. However, the user benefits from temporary ownership of the given object during the time of use. Thus, with the broadening of the boundaries of materialism, recent literature posits the emergence of a post-ownership economy (Atanasova & Eckhardt, 2021), with consumers displaying status through experiential consumption or access that fulfills materialistic goals.

Car sharing, in which consumers gain access to cars over a short period of time, is a popular example of CC. The user pays a short-term rental fee for access, and the car is returned to the provider after the agreed-upon rental period. These services allow consumers access to a car model of their choice, including distinguished luxury brands, and are currently offered by companies such as Turo in America or Drivy in Europe.

When it comes to accessing rather than owning a car, consumer-to-consumer schemes such as Turo include a provider (the car owner) and a user (the car renter). When investigating the role of individual traits such as materialism, the presence of the distinct roles of user and provider in peer-to-peer CC schemes offers interesting insights.

COLLABORATIVE CONSUMPTION: A SUSTAINABLE POST-OWNERSHIP ECONOMY

While traditional consumer behavior theories are concerned with consumers who value the purchase and possession of materialistic goods (see Lastovicka & Sirianni, 2011), CC focuses on shared access to materialistic goods (Atanasova & Eckhardt, 2021). As a result, both industry and academia have paid significant attention to the recent growth of collaborative economies and the determinants of and deterrents to consumers' participation in CC schemes.

Practitioners have presaged the beginning of a "post-ownership economy" based on short-term access (Belk, 2014, p. 1599; Atanasova & Eckhardt, 2021) that favors environmental sustainability and a reduction in consumption. Recent research has found that consumers' perceived sustainability is the leading determinant of CC usage for US and Indian consumers (Albinsson et al., 2019). However, it is important to note that other studies find that sustainable purchasing can occur irrespective of sustainability concerns (Balderjahn et al., 2018).

CC may offer both environmental and societal benefits to the consumer. Specifically, from the perspectives of the user and the provider, the reduction or replacement of original material purchases may bring financial benefits to those who participate in CC schemes. Instead of purchasing a material good, such as a car, at a high price, consumers can now utilize a car for a small monetary fee. This allows consumers with a high level of materialism to access increased material/luxury objects through CC, thereby making a societal impact. As a result, material consumers are enabled to access symbolic goods without relying on purchases or credit. In line with this argument, prior research suggests that materialism could be seen as a motivator to engage in CC as a user because the extended access to luxury or material items can heighten consumers' perceived status or prestige (Albinsson et al., 2019; Habibi et al., 2016).

While CC empowers renting consumers to gain access to a variety of products and services, it also involves the consumers who supply the objects. Such lending consumers (providers) equally experience an advantage – they gain a financial incentive for sharing their products during times they would otherwise remain unused or unoccupied (Frenken & Schor, 2017). Interestingly, CC allows for the immediate satisfaction of consumer needs and wants, thus fostering freedom of choice with regard to product categories, product brands, and service opportunities for the renter and the immediate satisfaction of financial desires for the lender.

MATERIALISM AND COLLABORATIVE CONSUMPTION

Materialism has traditionally been linked to the higher importance of possessions in consumers' lives (Belk, 1983). Based on this theoretical perspective, Belk (1983) conceptualized materialism as a personality trait that involves three distinct components. The first is possessiveness, defined as "the inclination and tendency to retain control or ownership of one's possession" (p. 514). The second is envy, which is the discomfort a person experiences due to the superiority of another individual stemming from ownership of desired possessions. The third is non-generosity, which signifies consumers' disinclination to provide or share belongings with others. These components may lead to the assumption that materialistic consumers may be reluctant to engage in sharing, which is in line with prior studies that suggest materialistic people value the acquisition of products over social relationships (Kasser & Ahuvia, 2002; Van Boven & Gilovich, 2003). A high level of materialism is further expected to be positively related to financial restrictions and being indebted (Watson, 2003). Twenge and Kasser (2013) also suggest that materialists are more competitive. However, the belief that materialists are happier when they acquire things (Watson, 2003) has not yet been sufficiently examined empirically (Richins, 2013). In particular, the concept of the sharing economy as an economic model offers distinct economic implications that dissociate the engagement in economic sharing from the social act of sharing. Media coverage and academic literature have particularly ascertained a value shift in Western countries away from materialism toward a "post-materialist self-expression" (Delhey, 2010, p. 66). Assuming that materialistic consumers increasingly value the importance of possessions in their life, materialism could represent a threat to a sustainable society.

Recent research has started to investigate further the "unexpected" (Lindblom et al., 2018) linkage between materialism and CC. This may come as a surprise because CC is seen as the beginning of a "post-ownership economy" that is based on short-term access rather than ownership of possessions (Bardhi & Eckhardt, 2015b). One could argue, based on sharing being contrary to purchasing and owning, that materialistic consumers may be reluctant to engage in the sharing economy because they prefer the actual ownership of materialistic goods as opposed to accessing them over a short period of time. For instance,

Lindblom et al. (2018) find that materialistic consumers have a more negative attitude toward sharing-based programs. However, studies also find that materialism may be positively related to consumers' actual intention to engage in CC. For example, in a survey study conducted among US consumers, Lang and Armstrong (2018) found that three personality traits, including materialism, significantly impact consumers' intention to engage in CC clothing schemes. Similarly, research by Davidson et al. (2018) revealed that Indians who have high materialism are more inclined to participate in sharing-based programs such as CouchSurfing due to the utility of the programs. By comparison, materialistic US consumers are similarly inclined to engage in CC but for different reasons, including the desire to indulge in hedonic experiences to improve their self-image. Wei et al. (2022) also find that consumers use CC in order to rent specific brands that can help them communicate their desired identity. This suggests that psychological ownership may be able to replace actual ownership when it comes to sharing services (Wei et al., 2022).

Engaging as users in the sharing economy enables consumers to access a plethora of materialistic goods, including expensive or special high-end items such as a luxurious apartment or car (Akbar et al., 2016). This mode of consumption may be particularly attractive to materialistic consumers because it enables them to satisfy their need for diverse material objects while respecting potential financial restrictions. Thus, are materialistic consumers prone to engage in the sharing economy if such behavior enables them to maximize their access to possessions? Despite traditional consumer theories, on closer examination it can be proposed that the sharing economy holds the potential to offer both a short-term material experience of the accessed good as well as its usage and benefits.

While prior research has begun to investigate the linkage between sharing and materialism, some call for additional research to better understand the relationship (Lawson et al., 2016). The authors aim to contribute to the current debate. Specifically, this chapter provides an investigation into the materialistic consumer's participation intentions based on their role as a user versus as a provider. In doing so, it contributes to prior literature on materialism and CC by providing a novel perspective into the dual roles that consumers can play, which enriches the literature on the topic.

The present chapter examines the linkage between materialism and the sharing economy by introducing an investigation that focuses on the perspectives of both the user and the provider. We propose that materialistic consumers are more likely to participate in CC as users because this participation will maximize their access to material goods. On the other hand, we also suggest that materialism will decrease consumers' participation as providers in CC because this will minimize their access to material goods. In other words, we suggest that materialism, as an individual consumer trait, will have a distinct effect on the role of the participant as a user versus a provider:

Hypothesis 1: Materialism will have a positive effect on consumer participation in CC as a user.
Hypothesis 2: Materialism will have a negative effect on consumer participation in CC as a provider.

RESULTS FROM AN EXPERIMENTAL STUDY

Based on the authors' theorizing, quantitative data was collected in order to elucidate in more detail the engagement of materialistic consumers in the sharing economy. The preliminary experimental study investigates the materialistic consumer's likelihood of participating in the sharing economy, and whether there is a potential difference in participation intentions based on their role in the sharing scheme (user vs. provider). In particular, consumer-to-consumer sharing schemes enable the consumer to act as the user of others' possessions, or as the provider of one's own possessions to peers. Based on existing theory, it is expected that materialistic consumers may be eager to use others' possessions in a way that extends their access to material goods (Habibi et al., 2016; Hawlitschek et al., 2016), while also being reluctant to offer their own belongings for sharing. Therefore, this study examines the individual's intention to use (vs. provide) another's (vs. their own) possessions in two different sharing scenarios: sharing an apartment or sharing clothes.

RESULTS

An online survey was administered to consumers to collect data on the hypotheses suggested above. Specifically, we collected survey data from 395 respondents through the online data collection platform CrowdFlower to obtain preliminary insights into the proposed relationships. Respondents were randomly assigned to two conditions – User vs. Provider – and were presented with a hypothetical scenario involving a peer-to-peer sharing scheme for either apartments (similar to Airbnb) or clothes (similar to Tulerie). They had the option of participating in a scheme in which they could use (vs. provide) an apartment or clothes. Next, their likelihood of participating and their personal level of materialism were measured.

The respondents' level of materialism was measured using six items, with each response captured on a seven-point Likert scale (Richins & Dawson, 1992). Their intention to participate in the sharing scheme was measured on a seven-point Likert scale from 1 ("very unlikely") to 7 ("very likely"). To test our predictions, we conducted a moderated regression on sharing inten-

tions, with materialism, sharing role (dummy-coded following a median split
into two groups; provider = 1 vs. user = 2), and their interaction used as the
independent variables. In line with our theorizing, the results show a marginal
interaction effect between materialism and sharing role (b = 0.457, t(391) =
1.77, p = .07). Post-hoc analysis shows that materialism has no significant
effect on participation intention in the provider condition (b = −0.117, t(91)
= −0.650, p = .52). However, materialism has a marginal positive influence
on intention to share in the user condition (b = 0.340, t(391) = 1.84, p = .06).
Findings were consistent for both product categories and were indexed. The
results are illustrated in Figure 4.1.

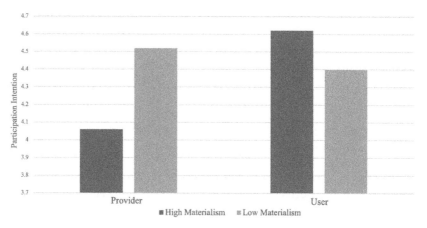

Figure 4.1   *Mean differences for providers' and users' participation*
             intention

While observing effects in line with previous studies, the preliminary results
indicate no significant difference between materialistic and nonmaterialistic
consumers in terms of using other consumers' possessions in a peer-to-peer
sharing scheme. This is a slight difference from Hypothesis 1. It should be
noted that other factors outside the scope of this study, such as product involvement and lack of financial mobility, may have contributed to our findings as
they could also lead consumers to be more reluctant to provide. However, the
data show that materialistic consumers are more reluctant to provide their own
possessions for sharing. Thus, the hypotheses are partly supported by demon-
strating the negative effect of materialism on consumers' participation in CC
as a provider. This finding extends previous research on the linkage between
materialism and the sharing economy by adding a preliminary quantitative
element that suggests a distinction between the role of user and provider.

CONCLUSION

The theorizing and empirical findings presented in this chapter add to the current understanding of the interplay between materialism and the consumer's participation intentions in CC based on their role as a user versus a provider. While prior studies have examined the effect of materialism on CC participation intentions, there are limited works on this from the perspectives of the user and the provider.

Although previous work has explained the marketing of products in an ownership context (White et al., 2011), little is known about how companies can market CC schemes effectively and foster consumers' participation intentions in CC. For marketing scholars, it is therefore pivotal to fill the existing research gap and suggest empirically quantified and validated ways to position CC schemes in the highly competitive market. As such, we suggest that future research develop and test marketing messages specifically targeted to materialistic consumers.

Specifically, the authors illustrate that, for the tested hypothetical scenarios, materialistic consumers are inclined to participate in sharing as a user. Thus, targeted marketing communication could be utilized for materialistic consumers in order to increase their engagement in the sharing economy as a user and in favor of the environment. This finding contributes to the prior literature on materialism and CC by providing a novel perspective on the two roles that consumers can play, and it enriches the literature on the topic.

Contributions and Theoretical Implications

This chapter contributes to prior literature examining the relationship between materialism and the sharing economy by investigating the distinct roles of user and provider in peer-to-peer sharing schemes. The results have important theoretical implications and add a preliminary quantitative perspective to the research on materialism as a personality trait and its role in CC.

First, we extend literature on CC and anti-consumption practices (Lee et al., 2009; Schaefers et al., 2016) by investigating the nature of peer-to-peer sharing as opposed to business-to-consumer sharing schemes. Our research complements existing literature (Lindblom et al., 2018) by further elucidating the unexpected role of material traits in sharing and CC (Belk, 2010; Richins & Dawson, 1992; Twenge & Kasser, 2013).

Second, we extend the stream of literature on materialism and CC (Albinsson et al., 2019; Lindblom et al., 2018; Wei et al., 2022) by examining the role of materialism in CC schemes that do not involve a transfer of ownership but instead include a user and a provider. Thus, by focusing on the distinct roles of provider and user, we contribute to the literature that connects the constructs of sharing and materialism (Akbar et al., 2016; Davidson et al., 2018) and extend prior findings to the provider perspective.

Third, our findings extend the study of consumer behavior in the post-ownership economy era. In this new era, consumers can operate not only as users (buyers) of products but also as providers (sellers). While prior research suggests that materialism has broadened to adapt to non-ownership centrality in novel consumption contexts, we find that, particularly in peer-to-peer schemes, the providing consumer who owns the material object and grants others access to its usage has to be investigated separately from consumers engaging in CC as users.

Practical Implications

With urbanization continuously progressing over recent decades (Allen & You, 2002), institutions and public policy makers must satisfy citizens' need for mobility, home appliances, and tools, while respecting environmental and spatial limitations. A report published by the World Bank (2023) highlights that 56 percent of the world's inhabitants (4.4 billion) live in cities. Regarding future mobility, CC innovations such as car- or bike-sharing can potentially disrupt the traditional paradigm of ownership and provide attractive mobility solutions that also favor the environment (Meyer & Shaheen, 2017). The shift from car ownership to service usage is another example of CC that can lead to long-term sustainability (Prettenthaler & Steininger, 1999). That is, car sharing represents a promising way to fulfill consumers' needs for mobility without car ownership. Unlike exclusive ownership, consuming collaboratively is more sustainable, holds the potential to decrease environmental damage, and reduces original material consumption.

Our study further offers implications for managers and public policy prac-titioners by providing new insights into individual characteristics that must be respected when nudging consumers to engage in CC. As noted earlier, fostering materialistic consumers' engagement in CC has important environ-mental, financial, and social advantages. As such, public policy makers may want to pay special attention to consumers' individual traits when attempting to shift consumers' consumption behavior toward a more sustainable and CC. Our study further suggests that targeted outreach initiatives may be needed for peer-to-peer schemes that involve the distinct roles of users and providers, as individual traits will impact participation likelihood differently for those two roles. Overall, shifting materialistic consumers to CC can help establish long-term sustainability and reduce environmental harm by reducing material purchases and overconsumption (Burroughs et al., 2013; Richins, 2011).

Second, associations and boards that aim to educate vulnerable consumer groups about debt and the reliance on credit in order to purchase material goods, may want to consider the unexpected link between materialism and the sharing economy. Among materialistic youth and adult groups, a tendency remains to carry excessive debt loads and to engage in borrowing to fulfill the desire for material status symbols (Richins, 2011; Watson, 2003). Individuals can reduce their financial burdens by shifting from ownership to access of material goods while still fulfilling their need for material objects and luxury goods. As noted, this study and prior literature suggest that materialistic consumers participate in access-fee-based CC schemes to fulfill their desire for materialistic goods. However, we find that this may not apply to the role of the providing consumer.

Third, fostering consumers' engagement in CC schemes is further relevant to society as a whole. For example, Ozanne and Ozanne (2011) find that toy libraries provide infants with tools that are crucial for their social development, and research has demonstrated that CC mobility solutions improve the well-being and quality of life of citizens in urban areas and megacities. Thus, our research provides additional insights that are of interest to stakeholders such as educators, public policy officials, and parents in order to rethink the possibility of attracting material consumers to share rather than own.

REFERENCES

Absolute Reports. (2023, March 15). 32 percent growth in sharing economy market by 2023–2028: Analyzing views and position in global competition. *Globe News Wire*. https://www.globenewswire.com/en/news-release/2023/03/15/2627768/0/en/32-Growth-in-Sharing-Economy-Market-by-2023-2028-Analyzing-Views-and-Position-in-Global-Competition.html

Akbar, P., Mai, R., & Hoffmann, S. (2016). When do materialistic consumers join commercial sharing systems. *Journal of Business Research, 69*(10), 4215–4224.

Albinsson, P. A., Perera, B. Y., Nafees, L., & Burman, B. (2019). Collaborative consumption usage in the US and India: An exploratory study. *Journal of Marketing Theory and Practice, 27*(4), 390–412.

Allen, A., & You, N. (2002). *Sustainable urbanisation: Bridging the green and brown agendas.* University College Press.

Atanasova, A., & Eckhardt, G. M. (2021). The broadening boundaries of materialism. *Marketing Theory, 21*(4), 481–500.

Balderjahn, I., Peyer, M., Seegebarth, B., Wiedmann, K. P., & Weber, A. (2018). The many faces of sustainability-conscious consumers: A category-independent typology. *Journal of Business Research, 91*, 83–93.

Bäro, A., Toepler, F., Meynhardt, T., & Velamuri, V. K. (2022). Participating in the sharing economy: The role of individual characteristics. *Managerial and Decision Economics, 43*(8), 3715–3735.

Belk, R. (1983). Wordly Posessions: Issues and Criticisms. *Advances in Consumer Research, 10*, 514–519.

Belk, R. (2010). Sharing. *Journal of Consumer Research, 36*(5), 715–734.

Belk, R. (2014). You are what you can access: Sharing and collaborative consumption online. *Journal of Business Research, 67*(8), 1595–1600.

Burroughs, J. E., Chaplin, L. N., Pandelaere, M., Norton, M. I., Ordabayeva, N., Gunz, A., & Dinauer, L. (2013). Using motivation theory to develop a transformative consumer research agenda for reducing materialism in society. *Journal of Public Policy & Marketing, 32*(1), 18–31.

Davidson, A., Habibi, M. R., & Laroche, M. (2018). Materialism and the sharing economy: A cross-cultural study of American and Indian consumers. *Journal of Business Research, 82*, 364–372.

Delhey, J. (2010). From materialist to post-materialist happiness? National affluence and determinants of life satisfaction in cross-national perspective. *Social Indicators Research, 97*, 65–84.

Eckhardt, G. M., & Bardhi, F. (2015a). The sharing economy isn't about sharing at all. *Harvard Business Review*, pp. 2–4.

Eckhardt, G. M., & Bardhi, F. (2015b). Liquid Consumption. *Journal of Consumer Research, 44*(3), 582–597.

Frenken, K., & Schor, J. (2017). Putting the sharing economy into perspective. *Environmental Innovation and Societal Transitions, 23*, 3–10.

Habibi, M. R., Kim, A., & Laroche, M. (2016). From sharing to exchange: An extended framework of dual modes of collaborative non-ownership consumption. *Journal of the Association for Consumer Research, 1*(2), 277–294.

Hawlitschek, F., Teubner, T., & Gimpel, H. (2016, January). Understanding the sharing economy: Drivers and impediments for participation in peer-to-peer rental. In *Proceedings of the 49th Hawaii International Conference on System Sciences* (pp. 4782–4791). IEEE.

Kasser, T., & Ahuvia, A. (2002). Materialistic values and well-being in business students. *European Journal of Social Psychology, 32*(1), 137–146.

Lang, C., & Armstrong, C. M. J. (2018). Collaborative consumption: The influence of fashion leadership, need for uniqueness, and materialism on female consumers' adoption of clothing renting and swapping. *Sustainable Production and Consumption, 13*, 37–47.

Lastovicka, J. L., & Sirianni, N. J. (2011). Truly, madly, deeply: Consumers in the throes of material possession love. *Journal of Consumer Research, 38*(2), 323–342.

Lawson, S. J., Gleim, M. R., Perren, R., & Hwang, J. (2016). Freedom from ownership: An exploration of access-based consumption. *Journal of Business Research, 69*(8), 2615–2623.

Lee, M. S., Fernandez, K. V., & Hyman, M. R. (2009). Anti-consumption: An overview and research agenda. *Journal of Business Research, 62*(2), 145–147.

Lindblom, A., Lindblom, T., & Wechtler, H. (2018). Collaborative consumption as C2C trading: Analyzing the effects of materialism and price consciousness. *Journal of Retailing and Consumer Services, 44*, 244–252.

Meyer, G., & Shaheen, S. (Eds.). (2017). *Disrupting mobility: Impacts of sharing economy and innovative transportation on cities.* Springer.

Ozanne, L. K., & Ozanne, J. L. (2011). A child's right to play: The social construction of civic virtues in toy libraries. *Journal of Public Policy & Marketing, 30*(2), 264–278.

Prettenthaler, F. E., & Steininger, K. W. (1999). From ownership to service use lifestyle: The potential of car sharing. *Ecological Economics, 28*(3), 443–453.

Richins, M. L. (2011). Materialism, transformation expectations, and spending: Implications for credit use. *Journal of Public Policy & Marketing, 30*(2), 141–156.

Richins, M. L. (2013). When wanting is better than having: Materialism, transformation expectations, and product-evoked emotions in the purchase process. *Journal of Consumer Research, 40*(1), 1–18.

Richins, M. L., & Dawson, S. (1992). A consumer values orientation for materialism and its measurement: Scale development and validation. *Journal of Consumer Research, 19*(3), 303–316.

Schaefers, T., Wittkowski, K., Benoit, S., & Ferraro, R. (2016). Contagious effects of customer misbehavior in access-based services. *Journal of Service Research, 19*(1), 3–21.

Twenge, J. M., & Kasser, T. (2013). Generational changes in materialism and work centrality, 1976–2007: Associations with temporal changes in societal insecurity and materialistic role modeling. *Personality and Social Psychology Bulletin, 39*(7), 883–897.

Van Boven, L., & Gilovich, T. (2003). To do or to have? That is the question. *Journal of Personality and Social Psychology, 85*(6), 1193–1202.

Watson, J. J. (2003). The relationship of materialism to spending tendencies, saving, and debt. *Journal of Economic Psychology, 24*(6), 723–739.

Wei, X., Jung, S., & Choi, T. M. (2022). Share it or buy it? Exploring the effects of product brand attachment on commercial sharing services. *Journal of Business Research, 153*, 115–127.

White, K., MacDonnell, R., & Dahl, D. W. (2011). It's the mind-set that matters: The role of construal level and message framing in influencing consumer efficacy and conservation behaviors. *Journal of Marketing Research, 48*(3), 472–485.

World Bank (2023). *Urban development.* https:// www .worldbank .org/ en/ topic/ urbandevelopment/

5. Self-regulating a collaborative engagement platform: case REKO

Hanna Leipämaa-Leskinen, Elina Närvänen, and Hannu Makkonen

INTRODUCTION

Collaborative consumption (CC) can be characterised as a set of resource circulation schemes in which consumers take more active roles in both receiving and providing valuable resources or services through direct interaction with other consumers or through an intermediary (Ertz et al., 2019, p. 32). To elaborate the conceptual basis of CCs further, a few recent discussions have explicated different types of CCs, addressing issues such as the consumer's ability to switch roles from receiver to provider and vice versa (Ertz et al., 2019; Hofmann et al., 2017). For instance, Hofmann et al. (2017) distinguish between business-to-consumer, peer-to-consumer, and self-regulating CC communities, highlighting how the market logic and managerial orientation differ in these types of communities. To emphasise the differences, they argue that business-to-consumer CCs are legislated and managed by a professional service provider, while the two other types of CCs operate on a less regulated and often non-profit basis. In the latter two models, the peer consumers or the communities themselves are the organising providers, acting without legal regulation (Hofmann et al., 2017).

The dual roles of consumers have been acknowledged especially in discussions on hybrid economies (Mamali et al., 2018; Scaraboto, 2015), access-based consumption (Bardhi & Eckhardt, 2012), and consumption communities (Schau et al., 2009). Scholars have highlighted that consumers take roles in initiating, self-organising, and maintaining their respective community (Mamali et al., 2018) as well as engage in embedded entrepreneurship and collaborate to produce and access resources (Scaraboto, 2015). Some recent studies have introduced the idea of collaboration between consumers and producers as a driver in developing and maintaining CC initiatives (Leipämaa-Leskinen et al., 2022). This idea that the consumer and provider members have collaborative and equal roles goes hand-in-hand with the idea of having less formalised regulation, which is realised through the participation of all the members in organising their CC communities (Fehrer et al., 2018). However, how such initiatives are regulated in practice remains an understudied problem.

In this chapter, we elaborate further on the issue of regulation and self-regulation in the context of CC communities. We approach CC through the construct we refer to as a *collaborative engagement platform* (CEP). Building on our previous work, we define a CEP as a self-organised constellation of physical and virtual touchpoints designed to provide institutional support for the mutual exchange and integration of resources for value co-creation (Leipämaa-Leskinen et al., 2022, p. 27; Breidbach et al., 2014). In Hofmann et al.'s (2017) typology, it represents a self-regulating CC community. According to Fehrer et al. (2018, p. 866), engagement is a central governance mechanism for CC that articulates the particular suitability of the concept of CEP for synthesising the community and regulation perspectives into a unified analysis in our study.

Our empirical illustration focuses on a local food platform called REKO (abbreviated from '*rejäl konsumtion*', which means 'fair consumption'), which we studied in our ethnographic longitudinal research from its establishment in 2013 until the end of 2020. REKO is a consumer-driven response to the increasing demand for local food in Finland. It consists of local nodes that engage three member types: consumers, food producers, and voluntary administrators. On REKO, local food products are traded weekly at physical locations where consumers buy products directly from local producers. Besides face-to-face exchanges, REKO nodes are organised in closed Facebook groups in which producers announce their offerings and consumers pre-order food items (Leipämaa-Leskinen, 2021). Thus, the REKO platform operates on both physical (food delivery) and virtual (Facebook) touchpoints (Breidbach et al., 2014). Since its introduction, the REKO platform has grown exponentially. Today in Finland there are more than 200 local REKO nodes with over 280 000 members, and increasing activity in Sweden, Norway, Italy, Ireland, and Canada.

Because it involves consumers who strive for alternative ways of consumption (Leipämaa-Leskinen, 2021), REKO represents a marketplace that hinges on community building and shared values between consumers and producers such as sustainability (Albinsson & Perera, 2012; Ertz et al., 2019), but which is still run according to market logic. Similarly, Ranieri et al. (Chapter 13, this book) also discuss the impact of CC on sustainable supply chains. Therefore, by using REKO as an illustrative case study, we demonstrate how REKO members collaborate to implement its vision and strengthen shared community consciousness while safeguarding the livelihoods of farmers. More precisely, we aim to illuminate the mechanisms and processes that manifest how the various understandings, emotional engagements, and goals of heterogeneous members are negotiated and reconciled in a collaborative platform (Breidbach & Brodie, 2017; Schau et al., 2009; Närvänen et al., 2019). Our specific research question is: what kinds of collaborative practices are being created and applied in a self-regulated CC community?

The findings show that the REKO members engage in five types of collaborative practices: facilitating, mutual learning, recruiting, bonding, and socialising, which are used as soft regulation mechanisms in the platform. Furthermore, we discuss the identified practices as soft regulation mechanisms and classify them in a framework based on their objectives and the focus of the regulation. This chapter puts forward a nuanced analysis and conclusions concerning collaborative practices as an alternative to centralised regulation of CC communities. Furthermore, this research has implications for building theory on collaborative engagement, especially its regulation and governance, as well as for practitioners working in the field of CC.

THEORETICAL UNDERPINNINGS

It is often argued that business models and initiatives based on CC differ from traditional marketplace exchange, as there are often less formal and explicit rules and regulations in place (Marth et al., 2020). Instead, regulation and governance in general are more reliant on technology (platforms, algorithms, and AI) and engagement (Fehrer et al., 2018). However, as CC models are very heterogeneous, the nature and extent of regulation also varies. Regulation in communities can basically be divided into two types: formal and informal (or harsh and soft; Marth et al., 2020), where formal refers to explicit rules, monitoring, and sanctions, and informal refers to more implicit control that is based on social aspects such as fostering a collective identity and shared social norms (Luedicke et al., 2017). For business models controlled by a single company, the creation of formal regulation is simpler than for community-based models as communities often resist external control (Goulding et al., 2013; Närvänen et al., 2019).

There is no agreement in the literature on which kind of regulation would be more appropriate for CC. Hartl et al. (2016) investigated how consumers themselves react to formal control mechanisms in a CC context. In their experimental study, participants imagined they were members of a tool library that enabled them to lend tools with or without formal regulatory mechanisms in place. They found that in this context, the vast majority of consumers supported the introduction of formal regulation, especially when their level of trust in other people was low. Thus, this study concluded that people favour regulation when they lack trust in the other members of a community – the stronger the community members' trust in each other, the less need there is for explicit and formal regulation. Indeed, trust or the lack of it has been commonly suggested as the key explanatory factor in the success or failure of sharing economy initiatives (Hofmann et al., 2017; Räisänen et al., 2021). The presence of soft regulation reduces the level of perceived risk and encourages people to join sharing communities (Marth et al., 2020). The context has a significant influence here; another study on a peer-to-peer accommodation sharing platform found that the introduction of formal regulation instead of soft trust-building mechanisms decreased the perceived risk by consumers (Marth et al., 2022). However, there is still a need to engage in further study of regulation in different CC contexts. Specifically, no studies have investigated how regulation is performed in the CC context through member interactions. Such research would be very relevant for gaining an understanding of the way CC communities develop regulation mechanisms in the absence of a single provider or host organisation.

Soft regulation is commonly present in self-organised consumption and brand communities that gather around lifestyles or consumption interests both offline and online. These represent self-regulating communities in which no provider can wield power over their members (Hofmann et al., 2017). For instance, consumption communities share common rules and norms that are negotiated and reinforced through interaction between the members (Närvänen et al., 2013; Muñiz & O'Guinn, 2001). These individuals feel normative pressure to follow the community rules and norms (Algesheimer et al., 2005) and gradually learn to do so through participation (Goulding et al., 2013). Typically, more experienced members have more decision-making and rule-setting power (Mamali et al., 2018; Luedicke et al., 2017). Essentially, the regulation of the consumption community takes place through a process of aligning participants' interests and values rather than through top-down, hierarchical control (Närvänen et al., 2019; Järvensivu & Möller, 2009).

While traditional consumption communities may operate effectively with just informal rules, the need for governance arises often when these social collectives transform into something more. For instance, Mamali et al. (2018, p. 522) detail how in the process of a community becoming a formal organisa-tion, the 'members' ability to play by their own rules becomes restricted and the doctrines governing previously amateur organising practices are subject to change'. This is also because consumption communities generally operate based on a non-market logic (e.g. solidarity, reciprocity) whereas organisations and business models operate based on a market logic where resource exchange is mediated by the market (Scaraboto, 2015). Bardhi and Eckhardt (2012) have found that business models based on CC, such as car sharing, sometimes struggle to combine market and non-market logics. On the one hand, the busi-ness is responsible for setting the rules for the exchange and sanctioning users for misbehaving. On the other hand, the business model as a whole depends largely on consumer-to-consumer interaction and thus would benefit from informal governance mechanisms like trust and shared identity. However, due to market logic, users are not encouraged to create and reinforce such informal mechanisms. Scaraboto's (2015, p. 173) example of Zipcar nicely illustrates this: 'For instance, a Zipcar user is unlikely to feel compelled to clean the car after use as a "thank you" to the company or to other users when it is widely known that Zipcar rewards users with a US$15 discount for cleaning the cars themselves'. Sometimes, the simultaneous existence of multiple modes of exchange results in hybrid economies where multiple logics may coexist and members' roles become blurred (Scaraboto, 2015). However, the particular mechanisms or practices through which these logics are reconciled in order to regulate a self-regulated CC have not been previously identified.

METHOD

This study adopts an ethnographic research design (Hammersley & Atkinson, 2007) that is implemented through a longitudinal case study covering a seven-year period from the end of 2013 to 2020 (Yin, 2009). The actual data collection began in 2014 and was completed in 2020. We focused on several REKO nodes – the largest was REKO Vaasa and the other four were located in the Pirkanmaa region (Kangasala, Nokia, Pirkkala, and Hervanta). We started from REKO Vaasa, which was established in 2013. The node comprised more than 13 000 Facebook members in May 2020. The other four nodes were launched between 2014 and 2015, comprising around 1800 to 3800 Facebook members in October 2020.

The authors started data collection by making observations from the REKO Facebook group discussions. These data provided us with a preliminary under-standing of the virtual touchpoints of the platform. We took the role of observ-ers and acted as ordinary consumer members who followed the Facebook discussions and placed occasional pre-orders for food items. We also collected observations of the physical touchpoints by visiting the food deliveries in the different REKO nodes. Contrary to assuming a more passive role in the online discussions, we were more actively engaged with REKO's operations by pre-ordering food items and then fetching them to gain first-hand customer experience. In both online and on-site observations, the period 2014–2016 was the most intensive, during which the authors documented their shopping expe-riences and Facebook discussions in their field notes. Overall, the observa-tional data provided us with a tacit cultural knowledge of the research context, revealing the doings, sayings, rules, and norms that are specific to REKO.

Second, we generated interview data that included 34 interviews with 20 consumers, 10 producers, and four administrators. Again, the period between 2014 and 2016 was the most intensive in terms of data gathering: consumer

interviews were conducted during the years 2014 and 2016, producer interviews in 2015 and 2016, and the administrator interviews over the period
between 2014 and 2015. The consumer informants were recruited from the
REKO Facebook groups and their ages varied between 23 and 58 years. The
producers and administrators were contacted directly by email or phone. The
interviews took place either in the parking lot right after the food delivery
event or in a commonly agreed public space, such as a cafeteria or library.
The duration of the interviews ranged from 30 to 90 minutes. All of them were
recorded and transcribed afterwards, resulting in 500 pages of text.

The data were analysed by applying a practice-based approach (Schatzki,
2001). According to Schatzki (2001), practices represent the primary entities
of the social world, and society itself is a field of practices. Thus, the unit of
analysis is not the individual members' experiences, but the practices which
people engage in to make sense of the social order. In our study, practices indicate how the REKO members make sense of the collaboration. The analysis
started by searching for data extracts that described any type of collaboration or
sharing resources (material, knowledge, skills, social, symbolic, etc.) between
the REKO members. Then, all the codings were collated to show what kinds
of collaborative practices the REKO members engaged in when operating in
the platform. The final phase of the analysis was to identify how the practice
entities operated as soft regulation mechanisms in REKO. Next, we elaborate
the practice entities in the findings section and then we theorise them further in
relation to regulation in the discussion section.

FINDINGS

Our analysis resulted in five collaborative practices: facilitating, mutual learning, recruiting, bonding, and socialising. *Facilitating* is a collaborative practice
that includes all the activities that support the existence and functionality of
the CEP. This practice is characteristic of CEPs as the members typically share
a common purpose for their actions (Leipämaa-Leskinen et al., 2022), and are
thus motivated to help other members in order to strengthen the whole community. In the current data, facilitating often took place between two REKO
producers; if a producer was unable to attend a REKO event, another producer
could deliver the other producer's products to the consumers:

> I was at Teisko [a REKO event], and there I met a honey producer who is based in
> Teisko. The Orivesi event [another REKO event] was set to be held directly after
> this Teisko event, and the honey producer had only a few jars of honey to deliver
> to Orivesi, so *I took care of it by taking the jars with me to Orivesi. We took care of
> the matter between the two of us.* [The honey producer] was an older fellow, so he
> was reluctant to drive there in the dark, so he was pleased that I took them. (T31,
> Producer, REKO Pirkanmaa)

Similarly, many consumer members reported that they sometimes picked up products for their friends who were not able to attend the delivery event. Moreover, administrators sometimes acted as mediators between the producers and consumers, for instance, by helping a producer collect the orders placed via Facebook:

> There is one producer of organic grain in our REKO who is over 70 years old, and I've been their loyal customer for a long time. I think that their product is very good, and it must absolutely be available at REKO, *so I've been acting as their so-called 'mediator' – I open the customer orders on Facebook and then send them to the producer by email.* So they [the producer] are not members of Facebook, but they of course come to the REKO event and meet consumers face-to-face there. ... And I also know that *there are some producers who open the order chat on Facebook on behalf of another producer.* (T34, Administrator, REKO Pirkanmaa)

The second practice is *mutual learning,* which covers all the activities in which the members familiarise themselves with the rules and procedures of the new platform. Our data showed that mutual learning was a multidirectional process: consumers learned to shop in REKO, producers learned to market in REKO, and administrators learned to manage REKO. The following observation note describes how a consumer needs to learn where to find the pre-ordered products and how to act at the delivery event:

> At first, it was a bit difficult to find the products I'd ordered, and I had to ask for advice. People were happy to help and tell me what they were queuing up for' (Observation, REKO Pirkanmaa).

A typical example of mutual learning was related to pricing of the products. While retail store prices are something that consumers and producers are familiar with, setting up a commonly accepted price level in REKO demands learning and open discussion. The following quotes show how an administrator and a consumer advised producers to set higher prices for their products:

> I just told the other guy [selling flour at REKO] that you should raise your prices. I thought that I'd have done so myself, but they said that the prices are good, they won't raise them. I said that he won't get any profit for himself unless he increases the prices. *I think that if somebody is selling their goods too cheaply, they can hurt the whole thing.* (T31, Producer, REKO Pirkanmaa)
>   Well, *I've said that some prices could even be higher.* For example, I've discussed with [producer name] that they should raise their prices. In my opinion, their vegetable prices are too low – that said, I haven't compared them with supermarket prices. (T2, Consumer, REKO Vaasa)

Thus, the practice of mutual learning is grounded in the tacit cultural understanding of the value of locally produced food and the explicit rules and principles of fair exchange. The overall aim of the practice is to ensure that the CEP works in a way that is mutually beneficial to all the group members.

The third collaborative practice is labelled as *recruiting*. It includes various kinds of activities to obtain more members and to better engage the existing members in the platform. Our data showed that both consumer members and producer members were recruited primarily by word of mouth. All members engaged in recruiting activities, as exemplified below:

> *Especially at the beginning there was a lot of recruiting* [of new customers and producers]. And *many consumers brought a producer with them.* These consumers are the kind of people who are very aware of these issues – they have been used to sourcing products directly from a producer for a long time. So, they gave us a lot of tips that they know a good producer and a product that they suggested we could then invite to the REKO group. (T34, Administrator, REKO Pirkanmaa)

The practice of recruiting is thus related to practical know-how on where and how to recruit new members. The data showed that this was an ongoing challenge because the number of ordering consumers decreased over the data gathering period, and there was much discussion on how to get more paying customers for the local nodes.

Fourth, the *bonding* practice involves the emotional support that the members give to and receive from other members of the platform. This is a particularly important collaborative practice in the CEP, which is based on a shared vision and values between the heterogenous members. The current data revealed many examples of members providing emotional support to each other, such as liking Facebook comments and using smileys in these discussions. Moreover, many informants described that they sense emotional connection in the delivery events, as one female consumer tells below:

> *Sometimes, you can just feel it.* And then in the queue you can chat while waiting for your own products ... you start chatting, and some of the people are really nice, and you get new information from them. It's not like [at a traditional grocery store] ... you're not just another customer. [At a supermarket,] *you don't get such a feeling of being similar, having the same kind of values. Then it's just another human being, and that's it.* (T7, Consumer, REKO Vaasa)

As the quote shows, the bonding practice is connected to the emotional engagements that originate from meeting other people face-to-face and sensing the community spirit among the members.

The fifth practice, *socialising,* includes doings and sayings that support and strengthen the informal and low-threshold communication between the REKO members. Thus, while bonding is related to emotional connection, socialising includes all kinds of interactions. Typical examples of the socialising practice were consumers asking producers for more information about their products.

Also, the observation notes included several entries about how people social-
ised with friends at delivery events. The administrators had a significant role in
this practice. They monitored the Facebook groups, accepted members to the
groups, and thus ensured that people felt safe discussing and sharing ideas on
Facebook, as shown in the quote below:

> [As administrators] we are always on the job … we keep the group closed because
> our aim is to give room for a community to grow, so *we cannot let just anyone read
> those posts.* It's a big thing that people order products by themselves – outsiders
> must not be able to spy on what this and that family is eating. And then of course
> *people can discuss other things like good recipes and other stuff around the topic.*
> So, it's a kind of community. (T34, Administrator, REKO Pirkanmaa)

Often REKO was described as an 'old-style' marketplace where consumers
and producers get to know each other. To exemplify this, one of the producers
describes the overall atmosphere of the weekly event, highlighting the good
spirit and equal standing of all the producers:

> *There's a really good cooperative spirit.* Here, I've been able to meet great produc-
> ers who I haven't even heard about before and also their products at the same time.
> … It's normal of course to have some competition in a market economy, but here,
> it's conducted in a good spirit, and basically everyone has an equal standing. So the
> atmosphere is really nice here. (T14, Producer, REKO Vaasa)

When it comes to the more specific ways and roles of how REKO consumers,
producers, and administrators participate in each of the collaborative practices,
we can identify that the administrators are the key members in terms of regulating the whole CEP. Thus, they take key roles in facilitating, mutual learning,
and recruiting. They set up the Facebook groups, organise the pick-ups, and
keep the activities ongoing. Second, the producers' main responsibility is to
implement fair selling and marketing activities, thus they are also actively
involved in the practice of facilitating. Besides that, the producers are involved
in the practices of socialising and bonding, for example, by providing more
transparent information about their farming methods for the consumers.
Finally, the analysis showed that the consumer members' roles extend from
ordinary customer roles to covering the regulation mechanisms of the CEP in
a versatile manner. That is, the consumer members advise producers in their
business decisions and recruit new members, besides being active in socialising and bonding practices.

DISCUSSION

Figure 5.1 presents our theorisation of the practice entities with regard to soft regulation mechanisms. The figure positions the collaborative practices in terms of the *objective* and *focus* of regulation within a self-regulated CEP. The bottom half of the framework depicts the practices that seek to maintain the CEP whereas the upper half illustrates the practices that seek to expand the CEP. Similarly, the left-hand side of the framework demonstrates the exchange-related and the right-hand side the community-related practices.

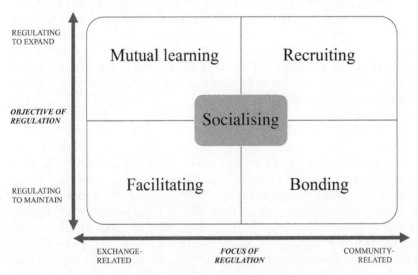

Figure 5.1   Collaborative practices in a self-regulated CEP

In terms of the *objective of regulation*, facilitating and bonding take place when the members seek to *maintain* the CEP. To safeguard the continued viability of the CEP, it is important that the members engage in facilitating (i.e. helping each other and moderating the activities within the platform). Similarly, the practice of bonding helps maintain the CEP through strengthening the sense of belonging between the members. On the other hand, if the CEP seeks to *expand* and scale up its operations, the members need to learn new activities, such as marketing, pricing, and packaging decisions and strategies. It is also essential that the platform acquires more members and therefore the practice of recruiting new members is crucial. While previous studies on self-regulated consumption communities have highlighted similar kinds of practices (e.g. learning new skills, bonding with other members, and recruiting new members; Goulding et al., 2013; Närvänen et al., 2019), our analysis integrates them more explicitly into the soft regulation mechanisms and identifies how they situate in relation to the objective of soft regulation.

In terms of the *focus of regulation*, the practices of mutual learning and facilitating appear *exchange-related*, being connected to the market logic of the CEP. They enable the CEP to apply a business model that ensures that all resource exchange is cost-effective and profitable. The practices of bonding and recruiting, however, are *community-related*, reinforcing the experienced communality between the members. Indeed, our analysis highlights that the exchange-related and the community-related focuses appear equally important in a CEP. Thus, we agree with the previous discussions, which have revealed that the different CC models combine, and often struggle with, the market and non-market logics in their operations (Bardhi & Eckhardt, 2012; Scaraboto, 2015; Mamali et al., 2018). But we also bring forward a more nuanced classification of these practices in a self-regulated CEP to reconcile these two logics and their underlying values and purposes.

Finally, the practice of *socialising* is depicted in the middle of the matrix, addressing its central role in the CEP and how it is connected to all other collaborative practices. Thus, our analysis emphasises the importance of informal interactions that act as a glue between the members and increase the sense of trust in the community. In fact, the practice of socialising appears inevitable in a self-regulated CEP, and all the members are involved in it, although some members more intensively than others. This is also highlighted in previous research which has identified that both consumers and producers often participate in CCs because of social motives (Benoit et al., 2017), and that the sense of trust between the members is one of the key explanatory factors in the success of CC initiatives (Hofmann et al., 2017; Räisänen et al., 2021; Marth et al., 2022). Therefore, we can conclude that it is crucial to ensure that there are enough touchpoints between the members to encourage more socialising activities (Breidbach et al., 2014).

CONCLUSIONS

This chapter has focused on REKO to demonstrate a self-regulated CEP featuring soft regulation mechanisms (Marth et al., 2020; Luedicke et al., 2017) that are based on engagement. We identified five kinds of collaborative practices – *facilitating*, *mutual learning*, *recruiting*, *bonding*, and *socialising* – that illustrate the mechanisms that help the members to negotiate and reconcile the various understandings, emotional engagements, and goals of a collaborative platform. Our analysis further positioned the practices in terms of the *objective* and *focus* of soft regulation mechanisms within a self-regulated CEP.

In line with the logic of case research strategy (Yin, 2009), this study aims at providing conceptual, not empirical, generalisation. The classification of the objective and focus of regulation and the five practices theorised thereon, provide a basis for further research on collaborative practices in a self-regulated CEP. Further studies may use these conceptualisations as a structure that provides guidelines for research and also allow the researcher to find ways for inductive insights to emerge. In this regard, the framework may need empirical specifications regarding the context of the study. That is, we assume that the general idea of our classification and proposed practices hold, but the empirical realities and properties regarding them are likely to vary and thus require respective operationalisation.

In conclusion, the current analysis has highlighted that the CEP members engage in varied types of collaborative practices to overcome the lack of formal regulation in the CCs. Our analysis reveals how CC members may be encouraged to take responsibility for informal regulation in the absence of formal rules that govern the community. These practices are often employed intuitively by the members, but it would be beneficial to organise them more systematically. Our conceptual analysis provides CC practitioners with tools to identify which practices are needed in different phases of CEP development, thereby further helping them choose what to focus on.

REFERENCES

Albinsson, P. A., & Perera, B. Y. (2012). Alternative marketplaces in the 21st century: Building community through sharing events. *Journal of Consumer Behaviour, 11*(4), 303–315.
Algesheimer, R., Dholakia, U. M., & Herrmann, A. (2005). The social influence of brand community: Evidence from European car clubs. *Journal of Marketing, 69*(3), 19–34.
Bardhi, F., & Eckhardt, G. M. (2012). Access-based consumption: The case of car sharing. *Journal of Consumer Research, 39*(4), 881–898.
Benoit, S., Baker, T. L., Bolton, R. N., Gruber, T., & Kandampully, J. (2017). A triadic framework for collaborative consumption (CC): Motives, activities and resources & capabilities of actors. *Journal of Business Research, 79*, 219–227.
Breidbach, C. F., & Brodie, R. J. (2017). Engagement platforms in the sharing economy: Conceptual foundations and research directions. *Journal of Service Theory and Practice, 27*(4), 761–777.
Breidbach, C., Brodie, R., & Hollebeek, L. (2014). Beyond virtuality: From engagement platforms to engagement ecosystems. *Managing Service Quality: An International Journal, 24*(6), 592–611.
Ertz, M., Durif, F., & Arcand, M. (2019). A conceptual perspective on collaborative consumption. *AMS Review, 9*, 27–41.
Fehrer, J. A., Benoit, S., Aksoy, L., Baker, T. L., Bell, S. J., Brodie, R. J., & Marimuthu, M. (2018). Future scenarios of the collaborative economy. *Journal of Service Management, 29*(5), 859–882.

Goulding, C., Shankar, A., & Canniford, R. (2013). Learning to be tribal: Facilitating the formation of consumer tribes. *European Journal of Marketing, 47*(5/6), 813–832.

Hammersley, M., & Atkinson, P. (2007). *Ethnography: Principles in practice.* Routledge.

Hartl, B., Hofmann, E., & Kirchler, E. (2016). Do we need rules for 'what's mine is yours'? Governance in collaborative consumption communities. *Journal of Business Research, 69*(8), 2756–2763.

Hofmann, E., Hartl, B., & Penz, E. (2017). Power versus trust: What matters more in collaborative consumption? *Journal of Services Marketing, 31*(6), 589–603.

Järvensivu, T., & Möller, K. (2009). Metatheory of network management: A contingency perspective. *Industrial Marketing Management, 38*, 654–661.

Leipämaa-Leskinen, H. (2021). Practicing mundane consumer resistance in the REKO local food system. *Qualitative Market Research: An International Journal, 24*(3), 341–357.

Leipämaa-Leskinen, H., Närvänen, E., & Makkonen, H. (2022). The rise of collaborative engagement platforms. *European Journal of Marketing, 56*(13), 26–49.

Luedicke, M. K., Husemann, K. C., Furnari, S., & Ladstaetter, F. (2017). Radically open strategizing: How the premium cola collective takes open strategy to the extreme. *Long Range Planning, 50*(3), 371–384.

Mamali, E., Nuttall, P., & Shankar, A. (2018). Formalizing consumer tribes: Towards a theorization of consumer-constructed organizations. *Marketing Theory, 18*(4), 521–542.

Marth, S., Sabitzer, T., Hofmann, E., Hartl, B., & Penz, E. (2020). The influence of regulation on trust and risk preference in sharing communities. *Frontiers in Psychology, 11*, 1369.

Marth, S., Hartl, B., & Penz, E. (2022). Sharing on platforms: Reducing perceived risk for peer-to-peer platform consumers through trust-building and regulation. *Journal of Consumer Behaviour, 21*(6), 1255–1267.

Muñiz, A. M., & O'Guinn, T. C. (2001). Brand community. *Journal of Consumer Research, 27*(4), 412–432.

Närvänen, E., Kartastenpää, E., & Kuusela, H. (2013). Online lifestyle consumption community dynamics: A practice-based analysis. *Journal of Consumer Behaviour, 12*(5), 358–369.

Närvänen, E., Koivisto, P., & Kuusela, H. (2019). Managing consumption communities. *Journal of Strategic Marketing, 27*(5), 388–404.

Räisänen, J., Ojala, A., & Tuovinen, T. (2021). Building trust in the sharing economy: Current approaches and future considerations. *Journal of Cleaner Production, 279*, 123724.

Scaraboto, D. (2015). Selling, sharing, and everything in between: The hybrid economies of collaborative networks. *Journal of Consumer Research, 15*, 152–176.

Schatzki, T. R. (2001). Introduction: Practice theory. In T. R. Schatzki, K. Knorr Cetina, & E. von Savigny (Eds.), *The practice turn in contemporary theory* (pp. 10–23). Routledge.

Schau, H. J., Muñiz, A. M., & Arnould, E. J. (2009). How brand community practices create value. *Journal of Marketing, 73*(5), 30–51.

Yin, R. K. (2009). *Case study research: Design and methods.* Sage.

PART III

Grassroots and community efforts

6. Repair cafés: exploring collaborative repair

Lucie K. Ozanne

INTRODUCTION

Electronic and textile waste are challenging municipalities across the world (Degenstein et al., 2021). Approaches to reducing these forms of waste include designing products that last longer or that can be mended or repaired. Increasing product lifespans is one of the most effective environmental strategies. Consequently, repair is a part of a circular economy approach that aims to keep products and materials in use for a longer period (Jaeger-Erben et al., 2021; Laitala et al., 2021). However, many impediments currently frustrate consumers' ability to repair the products they own (Svensson et al., 2018). Specifically, they need access to parts, tools, diagnostics, schematics, and repair documentation. In addition, consumers need the right to repair without invalidating product warranties (Ozanne et al., 2021).

Around the world, consumers are increasingly demanding the right to repair their belongings (Hielscher & Jaeger-Erben, 2020), with growing consumer movements supporting repair and advocating for the "right to repair" through legislation (Harrabin, 2021; Hernandez et al., 2021; Madon, 2022; WasteMINZ, 2020). For instance, in New Zealand, policy advocates call for products to be more repairable, to be labelled with a repairability index, and for retailers to offer spare parts and repair services to enable self and commercial repair (Repair Café Aotearoa New Zealand [RCANZ], 2022). A recent survey in the UK showed that an overwhelming majority (81 per cent) of consumers support the right to repair electronics, including design for repair and access to spare parts and repair documentation (Restart, 2021). Along with legislation, self-repair is also supported by a number of initiatives including online fixing sites (e.g., American, https:// www .ifixit .com), social enterprises, Restart parties (e.g., UK-based, The Restart Project), non-governmental organizations (e.g., Consumer New Zealand), and recent television programmes (e.g., UK produced *The Repair Shop*; Ahnfelt, 2016; Charter & Keiller, 2016; Graziano & Trogal, 2017).

Consumer research conceptualizes repair as a spectrum of interventions through which people seek to affect the capacities of objects in ways that correspond to their material readiness to enable routinized patterns of action (Godfrey et al., 2022). However, a sociological view considers repair as fundamentally relational in nature rather than consumers simply working on an object to ensure its function (Niskanen et al., 2021). From this perspective, repair encompasses relationships within communities, and is often expressed through collaborative forms of repair (McLaren, 2018).

A recent survey of consumers in Norway found that a large share of repairs are conducted by consumers in the home through self-repair. The main barrier hampering repair is the low price of new products, which means consumers are more likely to buy new rather than repair current products (Laitala et al., 2021). Using practice theory, Jaeger-Erben and colleagues (2021) found that the behavioural and financial costs for repair are perceived as high and that social and material settings are more likely to impede than to enable repair. They also found that novelty-seeking is an important predictor for non-repair. In clothing repair, self-repair was found to be the most common form of repair, with women being more highly engaged in self-repair practices, which increases with age (McQueen et al., 2022).

Because of the challenges to repair, and the challenges and impediments to self-repair in particular, the repair café movement began as an approach to help consumers repair their possessions, and as a practical approach to prevent unnecessary waste (Charter & Keiller, 2016; Meißner, 2021). It is estimated that there are now over 2000 repair cafés around the world. By making repair visible, repair cafés help transform the social norms around this practice, making it more acceptable, accessible, and mainstream (Madon, 2022).

Repair cafés are a form of collaborative consumption where consumers with items in need of repair work with volunteers who have repair skills to repair their broken belongings (Charter & Keiller, 2016). Repair cafés usually take the form of community events which may meet regularly or as pop-ups. Visitors are often asked for a small donation in return for the assistance provided. Some repair cafés encourage visitors to fix or mend their own goods with the guidance of experts on hand to assist (Ahnfelt, 2016; Repair Café, 2021; Rosner, 2013). In New Zealand, the site of this study, most community repair cafés are part of the RCANZ association, which supports organizers with marketing assistance and enables them to adopt best practices and share expertise. RCANZ is part of the International Repair Café movement (RCANZ, 2023).

In a survey of repair cafés, the most common items brought for repair include small kitchen appliances, lighting, clothing, bicycles, and DVD/CD players (Charter & Keiller, 2014). Participants are motivated to participate in repair cafés to keep items out of the waste stream, to support the local community, and to meet others who care about the local community (Charter & Keiller, 2016). A recent review found that visitors to repair cafés want to prolong the lifespan of their existing products in order to avoid buying new items and to reduce waste (Moalem & Mosgaard, 2021).

Despite the recent interest in repair and repair cafés, repair is overlooked in the literature (Niskanen et al., 2021; Moalem & Mosgaard, 2021), and in consumer research in particular (Godfrey et al., 2022). There has been little research examining experts who volunteer and offer their skills and time at repair cafés. In addition, limited research explores how repair cafés are organized and marketed to facilitate collaborative repair. As part of a larger project on repair cafés, this qualitative study aims to address these gaps using Tronto's theory of care with the following research questions:

- What motivates expert volunteers and what benefits do they receive from participating in repair cafés?
- What are the impediments to collaborative repair at repair cafés?
- How do organizers facilitate collaborative repair at repair cafés?

An understanding of the motivations, benefits, and challenges experienced by volunteers and organizers, and how they enact the phases of care at repair cafés, is necessary to recruit suitable and skilled participants. Doing so ensures safe and successful events, and allows organizers to successfully market repair cafés as a form of collaborative consumption.

BACKGROUND AND CONCEPTUAL MODEL

Care has been suggested as an ethic to guide repair work (McLaren, 2018), and has been used to identify the elements that are cared for at repair cafés (Meißner, 2021). However, there is a lack of empirical research examining care in the context of consumption (Shaw et al., 2017). This research extends previous repair research. It also contributes to consumer research by using Tronto's feminist ethic of care to understand the experiences of repair volunteers and how collaborative repair is facilitated by repair café organizers.

Care is acknowledged to be universal and omnipresent in society. It comprises caring about (something/someone) and caring for (taking responsibility for; Tronto, 2015). Care is conceptualized as "a species activity that includes everything that we do to maintain, continue, and repair our world so that we can live in it as well as possible. That world includes our bodies, ourselves, and our environment, all of which we seek to interweave in a complex, life-sustaining web" (Fisher & Tronto, 1990, p. 40). Thus, caring work can involve caring for the self, caring for others, and caring for the world (Nguyen et al., 2017). As conceived by Fisher and Tronto (1990), caring is seen as a complex process with four phases identified in the processes of delivering care:

1. Caring about. During this first phase, someone or some group notices unmet caring needs.
2. Caring for. Once needs are identified, someone or some group has to take responsibility to make certain that these needs are met.
3. Caregiving. The third phase of caring requires that the actual caregiving work be done.
4. Care receiving. Once care work is done, there will be a response from the person, thing, group, animal, plant, or environment that has been cared for. Observing that response and making judgements about it. (Tronto, 2013, p. 21)

Subsequently, Tronto (2013) added a fifth phase of care:

5. Caring with. This final phase of care requires that caring needs and the ways they are met need to be consistent with democratic commitments to justice, equality, and freedom for all. (Tronto, 2013, p. 23)

Further, Tronto (2013) identifies five moral qualities that align with the five phases of care. These ethical qualities are attentiveness, responsibility, competence, responsiveness, and plurality (p. 34).

In this research, the five phases of care are utilized to understand how expert volunteers consider and undertake their work at repair cafés, what impediments they experience in undertaking the care, and how the phases of care are facilitated by organizers.

METHOD

To address these gaps and undertake this research, a qualitative approach was used that included semi-structured interviews and participant observation. Nineteen expert volunteers were interviewed from seven repair cafés across New Zealand. The RCANZ played a pivotal role in introducing the author to the repair café community, which enabled access to both volunteers and organizers. The interviews occurred between November 2021 and December 2022. Given COVID restrictions in New Zealand at the time, the interviews were conducted in both face-to-face and online settings (i.e., Zoom). A semi-structured interview guideline was prepared in advance to minimize misunderstandings due to the mixed face-to-face and online approaches, and to allow participants to elaborate on their experiences of offering repair at repair cafés. The interviews ranged from 35 to 90 minutes in length. The interviews were audio-recorded and transcribed. Also, nine individuals involved in starting and running repair cafés were interviewed to understand their motivations for starting repair cafés and the operational challenges they face, especially in recruiting expert volunteers. Interviews with organizers were often more informal and most took place while the repair café was running; however, three organizers participated in a formal interview (Ed, Ming, and Ann). Participant observation was utilized to better understand how the repair cafés operate and the challenges expert volunteers face repairing items. Interview transcripts were systematically coded, sorted, and analysed with the aim of identifying common patterns, themes, and subthemes both within and across the interviews in a thematic analysis. Participants' names have been anonymized to protect their identity. This analysis was conducted manually to facilitate greater immersion in the data when compared to computer-based analysis tools (Shaw et al., 2017; Wood & Kroger, 2000).

RESULTS

Expert volunteers with differing levels of participation were interviewed (1 to 10+ sessions) to capture a variety of experiences. Of the 19 expert volunteers, ten were male and nine were female. Participants ranged in age from 23 to 74 years old. Eight of the participants were retired. Participants brought a range of skills including woodworking, sewing, bicycles, small appliances, computers, and electrical. Of the organizers, seven were female and two were male. We now turn to how the five phases of care are manifest in repair cafés, supported by quotes from the data and a graphical representation of the results (Figure 6.1).

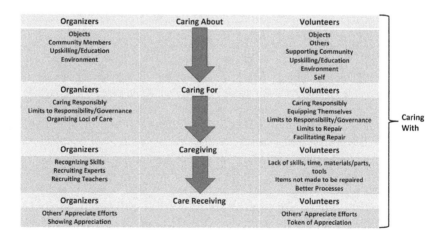

Figure 6.1   Phases of care in collaborative repair

CARING ABOUT

In the first phase of care, an unmet need in the community must be recognized (Tronto, 2013). Both organizers and volunteers must suspend their own self-interest and become attentive to others' needs or the care needs of objects (Tronto, 2013). During this phase, we see that organizers and volunteers consider multiple caring needs and requirements of different stakeholders including objects, self, family, community, and the environment. This means they juggle a range of concerns (Shaw et al., 2017).

Organizers recognize that broken objects are in need of care to ensure that they can maintain their capacity and continue to function (Godfrey et al., 2022). Ming, who is involved in a community group that supports expatriates, sees the repair café as more than caring for objects; it is also an extension of her work to care for and support the needs of members in this organization. Consequently, she started a repair café to give her mostly elderly members a way to use their skills and feel valued. As Ming elaborated: "I want our members to use their skills to help people. You see their happiness on their face. It's quite rewarding. So my motive is to let our members, mostly seniors, do something for the community" (Ming, 72).

Like Ming, Ann (45) found that as she held more events, many women in her local community needed care and support. So, the repair café became a method for fixing their objects and imparting skills to the women to empower them to do their own repair work. The organizers also believed that the role of the repair café was to train and educate visitors to enable them to undertake repair at home. In this way, they could meet the educational needs of community members with regard to repair, so that "they can be repeated themselves" (Ed, 27). Finally, all of the organizers articulate a strong concern for the needs of the natural environment, which motivates them to organize and run repair cafés.

Expert volunteers also recognize various unmet needs in the community, which further motivates them to participate. Many recognize a need to care for both the functional and sentimental values of the objects brought in for repair (Meißner, 2021). Providing this care enables them to care for the needs of the individuals who bring these items to the café for repair, as Hazel (42) described: "And I just make people happy when I make things work for the people who care about their belongings". They also provide repair expertise to be part of supporting the needs of the wider community (Meißner, 2021). Some volunteers see giving their time and expertise as a small way to offer assistance to the organizers of the repair café. For instance, John (62) described himself as "an ardent reuse person", and wanted to support the organizers in their efforts to hold the community event. Volunteers also recognize and support the educational needs of individuals by teaching them repair skills. Almost all the repairers recognized broader societal needs as a reason why they participate in repair cafés. These include minimizing waste, protecting the environment, and supporting a circular economy (Meißner, 2021; Niskanen et al., 2021). For instance, Linda (70) discussed her feelings in this way: "I get a lot of personal pleasure from having a small footprint". Thus, repair allows them to meet their own personal needs of living a more sustainable lifestyle. Finally, participation in the repair café enables volunteers to care for themselves by participating in something they are good at and enjoy doing, as well as experiencing the positive feelings when they bring an item back to life. This supports Houston and colleagues' argument that people who repair objects consider the act of repairing as having value (Houston et al., 2016).

CARING FOR

In the second phase of care, someone or some group has to take responsibility to make certain that identified needs are met (Tronto, 2013). Organizers bear a large responsibility to organize the repair events, staff them with skilled volunteers, and ensure events run smoothly and safely, among other tasks. To ensure the safe operation of events, it is necessary that appropriately qualified volunteers be present. Most of the organizers try to ensure that there are certified electricians at each event, but this is something they often struggle to find. Ming (72) discussed her desire to continue running the repair cafés during the COVID pandemic, as well as the changes made to protect the volunteers and run events responsibly. Organizers also have to place boundaries on the level of care that can be offered at each repair event, as they are constrained by time considerations, limited tools and equipment, parts and other supplies, and the skills of the volunteers. Thus, they often specify through their marketing initiatives (e.g., flyers, Facebook, advertisements) the number of items that can be repaired, the fact that new items cannot be brought to the events, and that visitors should bring necessary parts or supplies (e.g., zips, buttons, batteries). For instance, Ming (72) noted, "Another thing we have to mention is that they don't bring new clothing in (for hemming) … because that's asking for cheap labour". A key consideration is arranging for the loci of care. Organizers often consider partnering with like-minded organizations and offering other amenities (e.g., coffee, kids' entertainment) to encourage and make it easy for visitors to attend the repair event.

In taking on the responsibility to offer their skills, volunteers equip themselves to ensure they have the proper tools and a range of items that may be needed (e.g., spare fabric, patches, thread) to perform the repair responsibly. Some of the volunteers also see that it is necessary to indicate limits around the use of their time and skills. They do this by only working during the allotted time of the event, not taking items home with them, and indicating when they do not have the necessary time, skills, equipment, or parts. For instance, Fran (68) described her regret at not adhering to these limits when she agreed to make an item for a repair café visitor: "We don't make things. We repair. But the visitor asked, 'but you could make it, couldn't you?'" Volunteers also appreciate that the events are governed by certain rules to ensure their repair work stays within these rules (e.g., not taking things home to fix). As Ian (42) explained, "There's very clear boundaries. I'm available at this time". A key service volunteers perceive they offer is to indicate when items cannot be repaired. Thus, they give permission to visitors to throw these items out, and free themselves from the need to repair their item because there are limits to what is capable of being repaired. For instance, Rob (69) described his interaction with a visitor when he told them, "You can throw this away. You know, we can't fix it". Finally, if volunteers are not able to fix an item, they are often able to provide information about how and where it may be fixed, thus facilitating possible future repair.

CAREGIVING

The third phase of care requires that the actual caregiving work be done (Tronto, 2013). However, the exercise of giving care is subject to potentially extensive challenges such as time and resource constraints, socialization norms, and/or conflict as to which caring needs to address (Black & Cherrier, 2010). To ensure the care work of repair is able to occur, organizers have to ensure repairers have the competence or necessary skills. Ming (72) developed a repair café focusing only on sewing and mending as she recognized those skills existed in her community. She also became attuned to the levels of competence among her repairers, and recruited Claire to run the industrial sewing machine because Claire had worked as a tailor before retiring. Surprisingly, most of the organizers find that volunteers are happy to come for a one-off event, and with the exception of electricians, they do not struggle to find volunteers. However, for those repair cafés where repair education is key, finding repairers who are able and want to teach repair skills can be more difficult.

For the volunteers, a number of impediments frustrate their ability to ensure the care work can be given during events. Volunteers point to not having sufficient skills, time, materials and parts, and tools to undertake the repair. Claire (72) discussed her frustration at not always being able to fix things well under the constraints present at the repair café. For instance, some volunteers feel they are not always competent to do the repair work in this setting (Gregson et al., 2009; Dant, 2010; Hielscher & Jaeger-Erben, 2021). This was described by Mel (49) as, it's "above the skills that I've got. I'm a good amateur, smart sewer, but I'm not a tailor". A large number of the volunteers described frustration with modern manufacturing in terms of products not being repairable. As noted by Luke (38), products are "cheap enough to be functional for a while, but they are not built to be taken apart ... they are either glued together or they're clipped together in such a way that they are never designed to be opened or opening them is destructive". A small number of volunteers suggest that processes at the repair café could be altered to improve how things are run, such as managing visitor expectations and directing visitors to the appropriate tables. However, most indicate these impediments are minor annoyances that do not overly detract from their experience or mean that they will not participate again.

CARE RECEIVING

In the fourth phase of care, the care work is done and there may be a response from the person, thing, group, or other entity that has been cared for (Tronto, 2013). It is important to note that responsiveness is not always possible or likely in some circumstances (Shaw et al., 2017). Although the care receiver may be the one who responds, this may not always be the case, and others in any particular care setting may also be in a position to assess the effectiveness of the caring act(s) (Tronto, 2013). For instance, during the repair event, organizers often have the opportunity to assess the repair or the response of the visitors who have their item repaired. Organizers also believe that they have the responsibility to be responsive and show their own appreciation to the repair volunteers. They do this by offering a coffee or petrol voucher, providing food during the event or organizing a shared lunch after the event, or by providing a certificate to honour the volunteers' work. Ming (72) discussed how she shows appreciation for volunteers: "So what we do is that every time after the sewing repair café cause... we have a lunch gathering ... We give a certificate of appreciation, and then we invite the local board chair or someone to present it".

Because data have not yet been collected from visitors, we do not have evidence of their actual response. However, the data reflects how the volunteer repairers feel about the response of visitors. Generally, volunteers are very grateful when visitors are responsive and acknowledge their repair work with gratitude and appreciation. Many discuss how positive it makes them feel to have their efforts acknowledged, as enthused by Erin (23): "She was so engaged and thankful and expressive about the fact that the service even exists in the first place then she was really engaged in learning about how to mend". When asked if they would like to be paid for their repair work at the repair café, none of the volunteers interviewed indicated that they would. Most feared that this would dramatically change the experience for them. In essence, they suggested that it would take repair cafés from a community event to a paid service, where visitors would have much higher expectations and it would feel more like work. A word of thanks and an occasional gesture from the organizers was sufficient to acknowledge their time and expertise.

CARING WITH

The fifth phase of care is less a stage of care and more of an approach to providing care throughout the other phases. Caring with describes how care should be provided among a group or organization. As described by Tronto (2013), the final phase of care requires that caring needs and the ways in which they are met should be consistent with democratic commitments to justice, equality, and freedom for all. The qualities that align with this phase of care are plurality, communication, trust, respect, and solidarity (Tronto, 2013). In particular, internal solidarity may be created during the process of mobilization through care work (Santos, 2020). Organizers describe feelings of being supported by the community, and they are very enthusiastic that community connections have been forged during the repair events. While expert volunteers describe a supportive community atmosphere, the ability to meet other like-minded community members and participate in repair cafés allows them to contribute to a community effort. Finally, Linda (70) described how the repair café events are different from other community events, as they encourage a sense of gratitude and respect from the visitors, which she appreciates.

CONCLUSIONS

The results show that repair occurring at repair cafés can be considered a form of care that takes place across five phases (Tronto, 2013). By utilizing this framework, this research identified the motivations and benefits experienced by organizers and volunteers, the impediments to providing repair, and the tasks that organizers must pursue to successfully run and market this form of collaborative consumption. Through those care phases, care needs are identified and responsibility is assumed by organizers and volunteers to meet those care needs. Loci of care are arranged and staffed with appropriately qualified repairers, and processes are developed to deliver care. Volunteers ensure that they are properly equipped with tools and materials to undertake care during the repair events. To acknowledge the care work, organizers provide appreciative responses to volunteers who in turn indicate their appreciation for these gestures. During these care events a sense of solidarity is built among organizers, volunteers, and often with members of the community more broadly (Santos, 2020).

Like other forms of collaborative consumption, repair cafés provide a number of individual and collective benefits. As the needs of objects, individuals, and the community are identified, responsibility can be assumed and care can be provided. For instance, organizers discuss meeting the needs of individuals in their community by providing them a venue to offer their skills, thus acknowledging their capacities and allowing them to continue to be involved and valued (Ozanne & Ozanne, 2016). Because they provide care to objects by repairing their functional and sentimental values, repair volunteers appreciate that they provide care to the owners of those objects. In addition, as objects are cared for through repair, the life of the objects is extended, minimizing waste, and contributing to the care needs of the wider natural environment. In addition, as educational needs are identified and met in the community, repair cafés build repair skills that contribute to the development of visitors' self-efficacy (Ozanne & Ozanne, 2021). As repairers practise their repair skills, they also build their own skills and feelings of self-efficacy (Niskanen et al., 2021; Ozanne & Ozanne, 2021). In addition, as social links are forged among repair community members and a sense of solidarity is built as group members practise working together on repair projects, community efficacy is developed (Ozanne & Ozanne, 2016).

However, repair cafés also confront the limits of care that can be offered at repair cafés and the repair of products more broadly. Because they are infrequent community events staffed by volunteers, repair cafés are limited by time, tools, equipment, materials, and the skills of volunteers. Thus, it is critical that organizers govern these events and communicate with visitors what can be brought, what items are likely to be repairable, what materials they should supply, and other expectations (e.g., whether items can be left, or that items will not be taken home by repairers). Because repair volunteers juggle a range of care concerns, they may be subject to conflicting care relations across multiple levels (Chatzidakis & Shaw, 2018; Shaw et al., 2017). Therefore, organizers should create rules to help volunteers negotiate those conflicts. Volunteers should be equipped to indicate the limits of their repair skills, the limits of the repair café settings in terms of time, tools and equipment, and the limits of what can actually be repaired. While volunteers may be able to direct visitors to other repair services, they often are confronted with the limitations of what can currently be repaired.

Care through repair of household items is not always possible as modern manufacturing practices have led to products that are currently irreparable. For instance, planned product obsolescence, with the goal of stimulating replacement buying by consumers, can occur by designing for limited repair, which can have detrimental environmental consequences as these items end up in landfills (Guiltinan, 2009). However, the increased interest in, and support of repair through repair cafés creates opportunities for both marketers and policy makers to facilitate repair. Marketers can provide access to help desks, repair videos, and improve distribution of replacement parts/tools, or enable and support retail channels to provide repair (Ozanne et al., 2021). Policy makers should support repair networks by providing spaces, tools and materials, and by promoting community events such as repair cafés.

Repair cafés exist to help facilitate repair and keep still usable products out of the waste stream. They rely on volunteer experts who offer their skills for free to care for and fix other peoples' belongings. Without an understanding of the motivations, benefits, and challenges experienced by these individuals and the way they enact the phases of care at repair cafés, organizers may struggle to recruit their help, which is likely to thwart the development of this growing collaborative form of consumption. The findings of this research may also be useful to other organizations who depend on expert volunteers to offer their service, for instance docents at museums, coaches in community sports, or retired individuals who offer their skills in various education settings (e.g., University of the Third Age).

ACKNOWLEDGEMENTS

The author would like to thank Repair Café Aotearoa New Zealand for their support with this research.

REFERENCES

Ahnfelt, K. A. (2016). *Community repair within a circular economy – An outdated practice or prefiguration of the future?* [Unpublished master's thesis]. University of Oslo.

Black, I. R., & Cherrier, H. (2010). Anti-consumption as part of living a sustainable lifestyle: Daily practices, contextual motivations and subjective values. *Journal of Consumer Behaviour*, *9*(6), 437–453.

Charter, M., & Keiller, S. (2014). *Grassroots innovation and the circular economy: A global survey of repair cafés and hackerspaces.* Centre for Sustainable Design, University of the Creative Arts.

Charter, M., & Keiller, S. (2016). *The repair café WIKI.* http://repaircafe.shoutwiki.com/wiki/Main_Page

Chatzidakis, A., & Shaw, D. (2018). Sustainability: Issues of scale, care and consumption. *British Journal of Management*, *29*(2), 299–315.

Dant, T. (2010). The work of repair: Gesture, emotion and sensual knowledge. *Sociological Research Online*, *15*(3), 97–118.

Degenstein, L. M., McQueen, R. H., & Krogman, N. T. (2021). "What goes where?" Characterizing Edmonton's municipal clothing waste stream and consumer clothing disposal. *Journal of Cleaner Production*, *296*, 126516.

Fisher, B., & Tronto, J. (1990). Toward a feminist theory of caring. In E. Abel & M. Nelson (Eds.), *Circles of care* (pp. 35–62). SUNY Press.

Godfrey, M. D., Price, L. L., & Lusch, R. F. (2022). Repair, consumption, and sustainability: Fixing fragile objects and maintaining consumer practices. *Journal of Consumer Research*, *49*(2), 229–251.

Graziano, V., & Trogal, K. (2017). The politics of collective repair: Examining object relations in a postwork society. *Cultural Studies, 31*(5), 634–658.

Gregson, N., Metcalfe, A., & Crewe, L. (2009). Practices of object maintenance and repair: How consumers attend to consumer objects within the home. *Journal of Consumer Culture, 9*, 248–272.

Guiltinan, J. (2009). Creative destruction and destructive creations: Environmental ethics and planned obsolescence. *Journal of Business Ethics, 89*, 19–28.

Harrabin, R. (2021, March 10). "Right to repair" law to come in this summer. *BBC.* https://www.bbc.com/news/business-56340077

Hernandez, R., Constanza, M., & Julian, G. (2021). Empowering sustainable consumption by giving back to consumers the "Right to Repair." *Sustainability, 12*(3), 850.

Hielscher, S., & Jaeger-Erben, M. (2021). From quick fixes to repair projects: Insights from a citizen science project. *Journal of Cleaner Production, 278*, 123875.

Houston, L., Jackson, S. J., Rosner, D., Ahmed, S. I., Young, M., & Kang, L. (2016). *Values in repair* [Paper presentation]. CHI'16 ACM, San Jose, CA, USA.

Jaeger-Erben, M., Frick, V., & Hipp, T. (2021). Why do users (not) repair their devices? A study of the predictors of repair practices. *Journal of Cleaner Production, 286*, 125382.

Laitala, K., Klepp, I. G., Haugrønning, V., Throne-Holst, H., & Strandbakken, P. (2021). Increasing repair of household appliances, mobile phones and clothing: Experiences from consumers and the repair industry. *Journal of Cleaner Production, 282*, 125349.

Madon, J. (2022). Free repair against the consumer society: How repair cafés socialize people to a new relationship to objects. *Journal of Consumer Culture, 22*(2), 534–550.

McLaren, D. (2018). In a broken world: Towards an ethic of repair in the Anthropocene. *Anthropocene Review, 5*(2), 136–154.

McQueen, R. H., McNeill, L. S., Huang, Q., & Potdar, B. (2022). Unpicking the gender gap: Examining socio-demographic factors and repair resources in clothing repair practice. *Recycling, 7*(53), https://doi.org/10.3390/recycling7040053

Meißner, M. (2021). Repair is care? Dimensions of care within collaborative practices in repair cafés. *Journal of Cleaner Production, 299*, 126913.

Moalem, R. M., & Mosgaard, M. A. (2021). A critical review of the role of repair cafés in a sustainable circular transition. *Sustainability, 13*, 12351.

Nguyen, T. N., Zavoretti, R., & Tronto, J. (2017). Beyond the global care chain: Boundaries, institutions and ethics of care. *Ethics and Social Welfare, 11*(3), 199–212.

Niskanen, J., McLaren, D., & Anshelm, J. (2021). Repair for a broken economy: Lessons for circular economy from an international interview study of repairers. *Sustainability, 13*, 2316. https://doi.org/10.3390/su13042316

Ozanne, L. K., & Ozanne, J. L. (2016). How alternative consumer markets can build community resiliency. *European Journal of Marketing, 50*(3/4), 330–357.

Ozanne, L. K., & Ozanne, J. L. (2021). Disaster recovery: How ad hoc marketing systems build and mobilize social capital for service delivery. *Journal of Public Policy & Marketing, 40*(3), 372–388.

Ozanne, L. K., Stornelli, J., Luchs, M. G., Mick, D. G., Bayuk, J., Birau, M., Chugani, S., Fransen, M. L., Herziger, A., Komarova, Y., Minton, E. A., Reshadi, F., Sullivan-Mort, G., Trujillo, C., Bae, H., Kaur, T., & Zuniga, M. (2021). Enabling and cultivating wiser consumption: The roles of marketing and public policy. *Journal of Public Policy & Marketing, 40*(2), 226–244.

Repair Café. (2021). *About*. https://repaircafe.org/over/

Repair Café Aotearoa New Zealand (RCANZ). (2022). *Make it our right to repair*. https://www.repaircafeaotearoa.co.nz/_files/ugd/a5ef56_d8d69abe35ec46ecacda71 3c0762d86e.pdf

Repair Café Aotearoa New Zealand (RCANZ). (2023). *Our story*. https:// www .repaircafeaotearoa.co.nz/our-story

Restart. (2021, November 3). *Poll: Overwhelming support for a university right to repair in Great Britain*. The Restart Project. https:// therestartproject .org/ news/ overwhelming-support-right-to-repairbritain/?utm_source=newsletter-nov21&__s= vvvo700rdm0fz6nlgo1v

Rosner, D. (2013). Making citizens, reassembling devices: On gender and the development of contemporary public sites of repair in Northern California. *Public Culture*, *26*(1), 51–77.

Santos, F. G. (2020). Social movements and the politics of care: Empathy, solidarity and eviction blockades. *Social Movement Studies*, *19*(2), 125–143.

Shaw, D., McMaster, R., Longo, C., & Özçağlar Toulouse, N. (2017). Ethical qualities in consumption: Towards a theory of care. *Marketing Theory*, *17*(4), 415–433.

Svensson, S., Richter, J., Maitre-Ekern, E., Pihlajarinne, T., Maigret, A., & Dalhammar, C. (2018). *The emerging "Right to Repair" legislation in the EU and the U.S.* [Paper presentation]. Going Green Care Innovation, Vienna.

Tronto, J. C. (2013). *Caring democracy: Markets, equality, and justice*. New York University Press.

Tronto, J. C. (2015). *Who cares? How to reshape a democratic politics*. Cornell University Press.

WasteMINZ. (2020). *Pathways for Right to Repair in Aotearoa New Zealand*. https://www.wasteminz.org.nz/wp-content/uploads/2020/09/Pathways-for-right-to -repairin-Aotearoa-New-Zealand

Wood, L. A., & Kroger, R. O. (2000). *Doing discourse analysis: Methods for studying action in talk and text*. SAGE.

7. Sustainability in alternative consumer networks: understandings and expectations

Birgit Teufer

INTRODUCTION

A comprehensive reduction and shift in energy and material consumption is necessary to address the global challenges we face today (Intergovernmental Panel on Climate Change [IPCC], 2022). While collaborative consumption has the potential to facilitate more sustainable consumption, it (and related concepts like the collaborative economy or sharing economy; for an overview see Mahmuda et al., 2021) is highly criticized for focusing on financial benefits (e.g., Geissinger et al., 2021), problems like discrimination (Piracha et al., 2021), and the circumvention of labor laws (e.g., Ahsan, 2020). Initiatives that remain true to their original ideas and values of promoting sustainable development are often community oriented (Geissinger et al., 2021; Perera et al., Chapter 1, this book). While there are different types of community-based approaches to collaborative consumption (Ertz et al., 2016), some go beyond the sharing or swapping of goods and services to provide embeddedness in a social network. These types of alternative consumer networks (ACNs) are typically characterized by a non-profit and long-term orientation and a strong social character.

Although there has been growing interest in such community-based ACNs in recent decades (e.g., Albinsson et al., 2021; Forssell & Lankoski, 2015), they are a niche phenomenon. Furthermore, it is unclear if such networks really contribute to sustainable development (Forssell & Lankoski, 2015), whether they can have undesirable effects (Buhalis et al., 2020), and whether those effects can be measured. Given the aforementioned criticisms and research gaps, this chapter examines the following research questions (RQ):

1. How do members of ACNs understand the concept of sustainability?
2. How can sustainability be measured in such networks?
3. What do members of ACNs expect from their networks?
4. Which barriers have to be overcome for ACNs to generate impact?

Answering these questions will result in a better understanding of the complex construct of "sustainable development" in ACNs. This, in turn, will enable ACNs to assess their level of sustainability and help disseminate such social innovations.

THEORETICAL BACKGROUND: THE COMPLEXITY OF SUSTAINABLE DEVELOPMENT

Given that sustainability and sustainable development are among the most important issues facing our world, the scientific community has focused intensely on these concepts over the past few decades. However, developing a comprehensive definition of those terms has been challenging. Although the origins of the words can be traced to the field of forestry during the early 1800s, intensive study of sustainability as an ideal for social, environmental, and economic conditions began in the late 1970s (Caradonna, 2014). In 2015, the United Nations adopted Agenda 2030 as "a plan of action for people, planet and prosperity" (United Nations, 2015, p. 3), which addressed the three dimensions of sustainability: social, environmental, and economic. This concept is also called the triple bottom line approach and is rooted in various scientific disciplines such as political science, economics, and ecology, among others (see Caradonna, 2014, for an overview of the history of "sustainability"). Though there is no rigorous theoretical description of the three dimensions (social, environmental, and economic), the sustainability concept is ubiquitous and widely accepted in the literature (Purvis et al., 2019). Agenda 2030 further details the concept by defining 17 Sustainable Development Goals (SDGs), including the elimination of poverty and hunger, ensuring health and equality for all, securing clean water and energy, fighting climate change, and ensuring peace and justice (United Nations, 2015). These goals are not only interlinked but can create trade-offs and goal conflicts. This leads to the need for a holistic approach that considers the complexity of sustainable development (Fu et al., 2019). According to de Vries and Petersen (2009), taking into account people's value orientations and their understanding of sustainability is necessary for an appropriate operationalization of sustainable development in a particular social-ecological system.

COMMUNITY-BASED COLLABORATIVE CONSUMER NETWORKS

If implemented correctly, one way to contribute to sustainability is through collaborative consumption. For example, Ranieri, Tregua, and Di Bernardo (Chapter 13, this volume) show that different stages of food supply chains, from farming to production to retail, can contribute to achieving the SDGs through collaboration. However, defining or delineating collaborative consumption may be as difficult as finding a universally accepted definition for sustainability. According to Belk (2014b), "collaborative consumption is people coordinating the acquisition and distribution of a resource for a fee or other compensation" (p. 1597). This definition excludes sharing activities without compensation but includes sharing economy activities based on profit goals. In contrast, Belk (2014a) separates sharing from pseudo-sharing based on the existence of profit motives and the lack of a sense of community, among others. Moreover, there are terms like collaborative economy or sharing economy, which refer to similar concepts (see Mahmuda et al., 2021, for an overview). Many of the initiatives operating under these terms have been criticized for moving away from the original goal of collaborative consumption (reducing environmental and social problems), and focusing on financial benefits. This may also be due to the fact that it is often not at all clear what stands behind these terms. Geissinger et al. (2021) found that community-oriented initiatives are more likely to stay committed to their initial goal of promoting sustainable development. Still, there is no single definition of community-based approaches to collaborative consumption (Ertz et al., 2016). Many community-based approaches to collaborative consumption that deal with food (distribution) also fall under various definitions of alternative food networks. The term "alternative food network" is not limited to community-based initiatives such as food co-ops or community gardens. It is also used to refer to very different food production and distribution systems, such as farmers' markets, farm stores, and even organic farming and fair trade (Renting et al., 2003). This can bring the term "network" into question.

Based on past research suggesting that community-oriented initiatives mostly adhere to their values about sustainable development (Geissinger et al., 2021), this research examines how sustainability can be measured in community-based collaborative consumer networks or what this research refers to as "alternative consumer networks" (ACNs). It also examines what can be expected from such networks. To do so, a definition of what entails an ACN is needed. To identify characteristics that permit consideration of different types of ACNs while distinguishing them from other types of food networks and other forms of collaborative consumption, this research builds upon prior conceptualizations shared in the extant literature (Celata & Sanna, 2019; Ertz et al., 2016; Ozcan, 2004; Preiss et al., 2017; Venn et al., 2006; Volpentesta et al., 2013; Watts et al., 2005).

The following key features for defining an ACN were elaborated: alternativeness, network, and collaboration. Alternativeness is defined by economic interactions that transcend the boundaries of profitability which are used to differentiate the ACN from the conventional economic and for-profit sharing economy systems. To underline the network character, continuous social interaction must take place, which means longer-term relationships between consumers or between consumers and producers. Furthermore, there must be some kind of shared risks and responsibilities between consumers or consumers and producers which can be formalized or created through a formal arrangement such as membership in associations or long-term contracts. Unpacking the definition of an ACN was needed prior to addressing the research questions using in-depth qualitative research as described in the following section.

METHOD

For this research, a total of 29 persons were interviewed in semi-structured focus groups (FG) with consumers and in individual interviews with producers and experts. The sample consisted of 17 consumers (14 female, 3 male) from selected ACNs in Austria (FoodCoops, timebanking, community gardens, and community-supported agriculture initiatives). Also in the sample were six producers (three female, three male) defined as suppliers of FoodCoops or operators of community-supported agriculture initiatives, and six experts (two female, four male) defined as persons active in researching and/or teaching in topics related to responsible consumption and production.

"Purposive sampling" (Bryman, 2016) was used to select participants based on their ability to provide answers to the research questions. The focus groups included participants from diverse ACNs, acknowledging possible overlaps between networks. For example, members of a FoodCoop could also be members of a community-supported agriculture initiative or members of a timebanking organization collectively operated as a FoodCoop, and so on. However, these overlaps were welcomed as they allowed insights from different perspectives, especially from participants with experience in multiple ACNs. Moreover, certain ACNs, such as exchange associations and community gardens, intentionally blur the boundaries between consumers and producers and are known as "prosumers." Farmers can be producers in FoodCoops, but also consumers. As a result, this study did not aim to separate opinions based on consumer or producer roles, as multiple informants represented both roles.

Interview guides were developed based on a comprehensive literature review. Questions were intentionally open-ended to encourage participants to freely express their thoughts.

Due to COVID-19 social distancing restrictions, interviews and focus groups were conducted in German between November 2021 and February 2022, mostly using videoconferencing software. Participants were provided information about the study's objectives, procedures, data protection, and privacy. The conversations were recorded and transcribed verbatim following Dresing and Pehl's (2020) recommendations.

Reflexive thematic analysis (Braun & Clarke, 2022) was used to analyze the transcribed data to gain a detailed understanding of the topics discussed in the following chapter. It is crucial to note that the interpretation of the study's data does not claim to be objective because fully qualitative research does not strive for objectivity. Instead, the study provides readers with insightful, detailed descriptions of the data supporting the researchers' interpretations and conclusions, accompanied by translated quotes from the original German.

ANALYSIS AND DISCUSSION

This section summarizes the three key themes that were developed from the data. The first theme, "The understanding of sustainability in ACNs," which addresses RQ 1, shows that, although the interpretation of sustainability is quite different among members of ACNs, a comprehensive and complex understanding of the relationships is acknowledged. In addressing RQs 2 and 3, the second theme ("What is expected from ACNs and how can this be measured?") highlights that ACNs can be strongly active in the field of knowledge transfer and can support resilience, but only on a regional level. Measurement must be specified individually for each network and relative improvement is more important than absolute achievement. Finally, the theme "How ACNs can become impactful" addresses RQ 4. It discusses possible opportunities and challenges that ACNs face including limited diversity, lack of resources for public relations, and goal conflicts between growth and the maintenance of social embeddedness. Each theme is accompanied by relevant sub-themes *highlighted in italics* and illustrated by quotes. These themes are discussed and considered in relation to the extant literature.

THE UNDERSTANDING OF SUSTAINABILITY IN ACNS

The term "sustainability" is too abstract and vague. Although the informants acknowledged the need for sustainable development, they noted that the terms "sustainability" or "sustainable" are sometimes used in a misleading way. For instance, Producer 5 noted that they are "simply used to describe something that is not really great, as if it were a good thing," meaning that the terms are used for greenwashing. The term sustainability is "inflationary and so vague, because the whole world uses it," and could be understood as "everything and nothing [without further explanation of parameters and benchmarks]" (Participant FG1). Despite intensive discussion around the term, solutions that would address the roots of the world's problems are still far away. This aligns with de Vries and Petersen's (2009) reasoning that sustainability and sustainable development are at risk of becoming "buzzwords with a lifespan of a decade" (p. 1006) without appropriate operationalizations. However, those operationalizations will be hard to find considering the complexity described next.

Sustainability requires a comprehensive and complex understanding. Many of our participants noted that the concept of sustainability is difficult to understand and is therefore even harder to measure or assess. Sustainability should not only include ecological aspects because "it also includes the economy and social aspects" (Participant FG2). Assessment must be done on several levels, reflecting the interplay of ecological, economic, and social criteria (Le Blanc, 2015). Although the data reflected different perspectives on how sustainability should be understood, a comprehensive and complex understanding of the concept was present among the majority of the participants. According to Fu et al. (2019), such a comprehensive and complex understanding is necessary because sustainable development "can only be achieved through a holistic societal approach" (p. 388). However, a holistic view does not necessarily imply that all sustainability dimensions should be given equal importance, as will be discussed next.

Equality of the three dimensions is criticized. Although most of our participants felt that sustainability must include the triple bottom line perspective (i.e., the ecological, economic, and social aspects), they doubted that these three dimensions were equal. While some people felt that the ecological dimension must have priority over the other two, others found the social dimension much more important for ACNs. This disagreement about which of the dimensions is most important has also been shown in previous research. For example, whether health outcomes, other social outcomes, or environmental impact were rated most important in food co-ops depended on the region in the UK (Caraher et al., 2015). Although the economic dimension was rated the least important in our research, good working conditions and fair wages for (small) producers were seen as very important. In this context, the overlap and interplay of the dimensions can be seen, because good working conditions and fair wages can be counted among the social aspects, while at the same time they impact the economic aspect of the business or organization. In this regard, one participant of FG1 illustrated that "a good life for all that would be a great benchmark," not economic growth, which is in contrast to the prevailing consumption-oriented Western social paradigm (Kilbourne, 2006).

Further, it was seen as "problematic when you start to trade these dimensions with each other" (Expert 4), giving as an example the possibility of monetary offsetting of ecological factors (e.g., CO_2 certificates). This reflects a long-standing scientific debate on whether the concept of strong sustainability (meaning that existing natural capital has strict borders and cannot be replaced by other means of capital) is preferable to the concept of weak sustainability, where natural capital can be substituted by man-made capital (see Neumayer, 2003, for a discussion of the two concepts). Building on this diverse understanding of sustainability, the following sections elaborate on the accompanying expectations placed on ACNs.

WHAT IS EXPECTED FROM ACNS AND HOW CAN THIS BE MEASURED?

ACNs can create local effects. ACNs are seen as part of the global sustainability movement that can become active in their own local environment. This is in accordance with Kessari et al. (2020) who identified the concept of territory as a major issue when defining sustainability for alternative food networks. On the other hand, this limited geographic reach may hinder potential participants from joining (as the case studies show in Ranieri et al., Chapter 13, this book). Regionality can nevertheless be seen as an important proxy for all three dimensions of sustainability. "A certain localization, or regionalization, or small scale of agriculture is certainly important," though Expert Informant 1 pointed out that local production does not necessarily have to be good or sustainable, per se: "It depends on which criterion I select here." Still, "local" is used as a proxy for many other sustainability criteria. For example, local production and consumption would lead to savings in transportation and thus increase environmental sustainability. Economic sustainability would be achieved through local consumption, resulting in value and job creation within the region. The social dimension can also be covered by local production and consumption, as it leads to a stronger local identity and culture. Although "buying local" can be questioned as a good proxy for other sustainability goals (Young, 2022), short food supply chains are considered very important for rural development (Renting et al., 2003). Not only does the territorial scope of ACNs determine their sustainability impact, but also their thematic focus, as shown in the next section.

ACNs have their own area of expertise, but all can contribute through knowledge transfer and role model effect. The analysis of the interview data shows that a single network cannot achieve everything, and that its success can only be measured by its own goals. This means that ACNs are encouraged to focus on their own area of expertise, whether it is providing healthy food, repair skills, or community building: "Not every network has to achieve sustainability in a global galactic perspective, but as long as we think at least relatively, every network makes a small contribution" (Expert 3). To measure sustainability, a set of appropriate criteria would need to be defined for each ACN individually, which reflects de Vries and Petersen's call (2009) for incorporating people's values and beliefs when defining sustainability outcomes. This was, for example, implemented by Munté-Pascual et al. (2022) defining social impact indicators in a Roma community.

Although different ACNs have different areas of expertise and objectives, "empowerment, knowledge transfer, talent development, I think this is one of the main priorities" (Participant FG 2). Knowledge and competence transfer is essential for sustainable development, as diverse behavioral shifts rely on relevant expertise and skills. Furthermore, networks have a role model effect because "they can have a very practical and exemplary effect and can inform and inspire people" (Producer 4), which cannot be measured. People's engagement in their communities, which can lead to further activities, was considered the most important social impact of cooperatives in a study by Caraher et al. (2015). This strong connection to the community and region is further reflected in the following section.

ACNs strengthen the resilience and autonomy of regions, consumers, and suppliers through small-scale production. Our participants pointed out that the state or "politics" would be responsible for ensuring a high degree of self-sufficiency of regions, which was equated with resilience. However, the current situation is seen critically, as a dependence on large corporations and a close interconnection of international supply chains is observed. As an example, supply shortages in times of the COVID-19 pandemic were mentioned, which showed the vulnerability of these international supply chains: "We have felt it a bit in the last two years, how dependent we are internationally because of the Corona crisis, some people have become aware of how valuable it is that we are so well supplied regionally" (Producer 4). Sales in ACNs increased dramatically because they "always work, unlike the big ones, which have already failed" (Participant FG3). Such greater environmental awareness and increased spending on environmentally sustainable products during the COVID-19 pandemic was noticed in further research studies (e.g., Severo et al., 2021).

However, autonomy and self-sufficiency were becoming increasingly important even before the pandemic. Autonomy is seen as the ability of members to take part in decision-making and to shape their own lives, which is strengthened by close contact with each other and with suppliers. Through ACNs, suppliers gain more autonomy via greater freedom of action, for example, in terms of what they grow and how prices are set. Flora and Bregendahl (2012) demonstrated these financial advantages for producers through participation in ACNs. According to our informants, this not only improves the well-being of the producers but also enables sustainable operations, which aligns with Flora and Bregendahl's findings (2012) that producers' greatest benefits include their contribution to environmental health.

Furthermore, since climate change is considered a threat to reliable supply in small-scale agriculture, regional supply is seen as a necessary solution because those farms would be more flexible and better able to adapt to climatic conditions: "Predominantly, the small-structured farms look more at ecological balance" (Producer 1). Although the superiority of small farms over large agribusiness in terms of climate change effects has been shown in individual studies (e.g., Lin et al., 2011), these results can potentially be put into perspective by negative effects. Similar controversies can be found for organic farming where positive environmental impact may be questioned when considering reduced efficiency (e.g., Seufert & Ramankutty, 2017), and for short food supply chains where reported effects are highly context dependent (Kiss et al., 2019). This trade-off is also evident in the next section when it comes to relative vs. absolute goals.

Relative improvement is more realistic than achieving absolute sustainability. Absolute sustainability, understood as the simultaneous pursuit of all SDGs while operating within environmental planetary boundaries, is seen as a desirable target state. However, because Western countries are so far away from this in terms of consumption, achieving this state is seen as illusory. Networks can facilitate positive changes, and in the best case scenarios, they should also be evaluated on a regular basis to see whether they are on a path of sustainable development. However, some informants regarded this approach critically, stating that when people "think about sustainable consumption, they often think about other consumption, ... that's just somehow not sufficient in total, as long as we have such massive overconsumption" (Expert 3). The debate on how to measure sustainability – absolute vs. relative, which means better than before or better than others – is also prevalent in the scientific literature (e.g., Mori & Christodoulou, 2012). Even absolute measures are not uncontroversial (Guinée et al., 2022). Furthermore, some noted that "doing something" would be more important than measuring actual impact, since "as soon as I decide for myself that I do something in that direction, then it is a contribution" (Producer 5). However, this can be viewed critically, because numerous research shows that the mechanism of moral licensing can be effective here, where people justify climate- or environmentally damaging or unethical behavior in some areas by showing ethical, climate- or environmentally friendly behavior in others (e.g., Burger et al., 2022; for an overview, see Blanken et al., 2015). This often leads to a massive overestimation of the contribution made and thus to an overall negative effect (Brudermann, 2022). Nevertheless, most networks and their members truly want to create an impact, and the following section discusses ways to achieve this.

HOW ACNS CAN BECOME IMPACTFUL

Should the network grow or stay small? Some producers noted that a stronger growth of the networks would be desirable because the current sales volumes would either not be financially rewarding or it would be difficult to acquire and retain members. However, some producers pointed out that besides the financial aspect, their participation in ACNs is also driven from an idealistic point of view based on social and human values, as Producer 1 illustrates: "What I like so much about the cooperation with the FoodCoops is that there is a high level of commitment, almost a soulfulness behind it ... That's something that makes me feel, yes, it's a pleasure for me as a producer to work together with them." This aligns with previous findings from Flora and Bregendahl (2012) who found that although financial benefit was the primary driver, producers' participation was also driven by their values.

According to our informants, networks that grow faster and stronger can be beneficial for their members because they promote sustainable consumption, economic advantages, and possibly exert stronger influence at the systemic level such as (local) politics and market structures. On the other hand, ACNs should remain rather small in order to avoid losing the advantages of local production and consumption. In addition, participants view growing too large negatively because they fear that social aspects will be lost in larger networks. If networks grow bigger, social embeddedness could disappear as "the greater the number of members, the less willing they are to get involved and the less they need to communicate with each other" (Producer 1). Kessari et al. (2020) support these arguments. They identified fluid communication between members as a crucial factor for the sustainability of networks and found that a (sufficiently small) group size ensures this communication. On the other hand, not all members of ACNs show motivation for social interactions and community building, as studies on community-supported agriculture showed (e.g., Brehm & Eisenhauer, 2008; Cone & Myhre, 2000).

A solution to gain advantages of bigger organizations, such as political relevance, without needing the individual networks to grow could be the emergence of more regional initiatives and a stronger network among them, possibly with a superordinate platform. In general, stronger collaboration with other initiatives was identified as an important success factor, as is illustrated next.

Collaboration with other institutions creates greater impact. ACNs should network and cooperate with other institutions, e.g., other regional initiatives and schools, but also local or municipal political institutions. This could lead to stronger social cohesion in the region and to a multiplier effect, since all these institutions can reach different target groups to some extent. ACNs could be a platform for other emerging community-building projects. Furthermore, this "political institutional and economic embedding ... can also ensure the viability of the initiatives in the long term" (Expert 6). This is supported by Kiss et al. (2019), who state that political support or resistance greatly affects short food supply chains. Political support may be achieved through better promotional efforts, but this proves difficult, as shown in the next section.

Networks need more public relations. ACNs would need stronger public relations and "a person who can deal with it professionally" (Expert 5) to grow and achieve stronger influence over the community and political conditions. Indeed, Kessari et al. (2020) identified a lack of communication with relevant stakeholders about the mission, and a lack of marketing activities as reasons why networks are not able to reach sustainability. Similarly, Ranieri et al. (Chapter 13, this book) conclude that there is a need to raise awareness of the results that can be achieved through such networks. However, such initiatives are mostly run on a volunteer basis and lack not only time and financial resources for more outreach, but also knowledge of how good public relations work, as illustrated by Producer 5: "How are people who haven't learned to do that, who don't do that are supposed to do that? ... how are they supposed to advertise on the Internet in a really good way, ... or how are they supposed to come up with a concept, how do I get the politicians involved?"

The difficulty with many ACNs being built on volunteerism is reflected not only in a lack of resources for promotional activities, but also in the fact that some people find it requires too much effort to participate, as illustrated in the next section.

Participation in ACNs takes effort. In general, the desire for convenience deters many people from behaving more sustainably, which therefore represents a barrier to ACN membership. Individuals' participation starts with understanding the need for sustainability and how to engage in an ACN. Membership itself involves a certain amount of effort, or more effort than simply shopping in a supermarket. Not only shopping can be more time-consuming. Numerous networks can only exist because members actively participate and take on organizational tasks "because we're not a supermarket, if that's what you want, and because of that you also have to discuss the logistical availability" (Participant FG1). Participants also noted that some people ask why a higher price should be paid if purchasing through these networks involved additional effort. Indeed, previous research showed that one of the main reasons for community-supported agriculture participants leaving such programs is the higher level of effort required for purchases (Flora & Bregendahl, 2012). On the other hand, Cone and Myhre (2000) showed that higher participation fosters the commitment to the network over the long term. Participants mentioned partnerships between networks and delivery services and offering those who actively collaborate additional benefits for their engagement as a potential remedy for increasing convenience. However, these suggestions are in strong contrast to other statements contending that convenience should not be prioritized as it prevents sustainable development, and that such a goal is also contrary to the idea of networks and cooperation based on solidarity. Either way, higher prices and additional efforts required could deter various consumer groups from joining ACNs.

ACNs are (often) not inclusive. Many ACNs are somewhat of a "well-intentioned bubble" (Participant FG3) in that they are not inclusive.

Only people who already have a sustainable mindset become members. In principle, all people would be welcome in the networks, but they often appeal exclusively to the social middle class because they are the only ones "who can afford it ... who have the time to deal with it, and are interested in it" (Expert 4). While inclusivity is considered as being important, it is not easy for the networks to achieve. Although collaborative consumption is often regarded as offering financial benefits for consumers, this is not true for all ACNs. Community-supported agriculture and FoodCoops, for example, provide organic foods that are typically more expensive than conventionally grown foods. Some participants regarded membership fees as a potential barrier to inclusivity in terms of attracting diverse collaborators. Indeed, previous research not only confirms this bubble in alternative food networks that stems from socioeconomic backgrounds (e.g., Macias, 2008); it also highlights that social inclusiveness and achieving other sustainability goals can conflict with each other in such settings (Fourat et al., 2020).

CONCLUSION AND IMPLICATIONS

Although the understanding of sustainability is quite diverse among ACN members, a more comprehensive and complex understanding is recognized. When determining goals for the network, ACN managers (e.g., board members, founders) should take their members' different understandings and interpretations of sustainability into account and attempt to find a common ground through good communication and coordination. Thus, developing appropriate metrics and evaluation methods can help in assessing the network's impact and communicating its value to stakeholders.

This diverse understanding of sustainability is partly reflected in members' expectations toward ACNs. However, most participants recognize that such networks can be very active in knowledge transfer in terms of helping people to behave sustainably, but their effectiveness can only unfold on a local level. ACN managers should highlight and facilitate knowledge-sharing initiatives within the network to promote sustainable practices among members. ACNs can strengthen the resilience and autonomy of regions, consumers, and suppliers by supporting local producers, encouraging sustainable sourcing practices, and empowering consumers to make informed choices. They can focus their efforts on increasing the network's influence and impact in the local community by maintaining close relationships with local stakeholders such as regional institutions, businesses, and community organizations. To expand beyond regional effectiveness, ACNs need good socioeconomic embeddedness and collaboration with other institutions. Thus the networks should look for opportunities to collaborate with broader networks, government organizations, and larger sustainability initiatives. Building partnerships can enhance the network's ability to address sustainability issues on a larger scale. Conflicts arise between (1) the desire for social embeddedness, which only works as long as these networks remain relatively small, and (2) greater effectiveness in addressing sustainability issues, for which these networks would need to grow. A certain mindset and financial ability are preconditions for membership, which may create a bubble that is not socially inclusive. Finding ways to make the network accessible to a wider range of individuals can foster growth and diversify its impact. However, networks should carefully balance the need for inclusivity and growth with the desire to keep social embeddedness. Further, in close consultation with members, a good balance must be found between convenience for members and necessary social engagement that leads to greater embeddedness and social impact. In conclusion, this research contributes to the discussion about measuring sustainability in community-based collaborative consumer networks. It highlights the importance of considering the values, beliefs, and expectations of individuals within these networks when determining sustainability. Furthermore, the goals and measurements of sustainability should be derived accordingly, based on these factors. In addition, while ACNs can generate impact through close collaborations with other initiatives, they must overcome barriers such as balancing the need for inclusivity and growth with the desire to keep social embeddedness and engagement in order to help such social innovations spread.

REFERENCES

Ahsan, M. (2020). Entrepreneurship and ethics in the sharing economy: A critical perspective. *Journal of Business Ethics*, *161*(1), 19–33.

Albinsson, P. A., Perera, B. Y., & Griffiths, M. A. (2021). Overcoming scarcity through efficient consumption: Innovative sharing initiatives. In T. Sigler & J. Corcoran (Eds.), *A modern guide to the urban sharing economy* (pp. 55–70). Edward Elgar Publishing.

Belk, R. (2014a). Sharing versus pseudo-sharing in Web 2.0. *The Anthropologist*, *18*(1), 7–23.

Belk, R. (2014b). You are what you can access: Sharing and collaborative consumption online. *Journal of Business Research*, *67*(8), 1595–1600.

Blanken, I., Van De Ven, N., & Zeelenberg, M. (2015). A meta-analytic review of moral licensing. *Personality and Social Psychology Bulletin*, *41*(4), 540–558.

Braun, V., & Clarke, V. (2022). *Thematic analysis: A practical guide*. SAGE.

Brehm, J. M., & Eisenhauer, B. W. (2008). Motivations for participating in community-supported agriculture and their relationship with community attachment and social capital. *Journal of Rural Social Sciences*, *23*(1), 5.

Brudermann, T. (2022). *Die Kunst der Ausrede: Warum wir uns lieber selbst täuschen, statt klimafreundlich zu leben*. Oekom Verlag.

Bryman, A. (2016). *Social research methods*. Oxford University Press.

Buhalis, D., Andreu, L., & Gnoth, J. (2020). The dark side of the sharing economy: Balancing value co-creation and value co-destruction. *Psychology & Marketing, 37*(5), 689–704.

Burger, A. M., Schuler, J., & Eberling, E. (2022). Guilty pleasures: Moral licensing in climate-related behavior. *Global Environmental Change, 72,* 102415.

Caradonna, J. L. (2014). *Sustainability: A history.* Oxford University Press.

Caraher, M., Smith, J., & Machell, G. (2015). To co-op or not to co-op: A case study of food co-ops in England. *Journal of Co-operative Studies, 47*(2), 6–19.

Celata, F., & Sanna, V. S. (2019). A multi-dimensional assessment of the environmental and socioeconomic performance of community-based sustainability initiatives in Europe. *Regional Environmental Change, 19*(4), 939–952. https://doi.org/10.1007/s10113-019-01493-9

Cone, C., & Myhre, A. (2000). Community-supported agriculture: A sustainable alternative to industrial agriculture? *Human Organization, 59*(2), 187–197.

de Vries, B. J., & Petersen, A. C. (2009). Conceptualizing sustainable development: An assessment methodology connecting values, knowledge, worldviews and scenarios. *Ecological Economics, 68*(4), 1006–1019.

Dresing, T., & Pehl, T. (2020). Transkription. In G. Mey & K. Mruck (Eds.), *Handbuch qualitative Forschung in der Psychologie* (pp. 835–854). Springer.

Ertz, M., Durif, F., & Arcand, M. (2016). Collaborative consumption: Conceptual snapshot at a buzzword. *Journal of Entrepreneurship Education, 19*(2), 1–23.

Flora, C. B., & Bregendahl, C. (2012). Collaborative community-supported agriculture: Balancing community capitals for producers and consumers. *International Journal of Sociology of Agriculture and Food, 19*(3), 329–346.

Forssell, S., & Lankoski, L. (2015). The sustainability promise of alternative food networks: An examination through "alternative" characteristics. *Agriculture and Human Values, 32*(1), 63–75.

Fourat, E., Closson, C., Holzemer, L., & Hudon, M. (2020). Social inclusion in an alternative food network: Values, practices and tensions. *Journal of Rural Studies, 76,* 49–57. https://doi.org/10.1016/j.jrurstud.2020.03.009

Fu, B., Wang, S., Zhang, J., Hou, Z., & Li, J. (2019). Unravelling the complexity in achieving the 17 sustainable-development goals. *National Science Review, 6*(3), 386–388.

Geissinger, A., Pelgander, L., & Öberg, C. (2021). The identity crisis of sharing: From the co-op economy to the urban sharing economy phenomenon. In T. Sigler & J. Corcoran (Eds.), *A modern guide to the urban sharing economy* (pp. 40–54). Edward Elgar Publishing.

Guinée, J. B., de Koning, A., & Heijungs, R. (2022). Life cycle assessment-based Absolute Environmental Sustainability Assessment is also relative. *Journal of Industrial Ecology, 26*(3), 673–682.

Intergovernmental Panel on Climate Change. (2022). *Mitigation of climate change. Contribution of Working Group III to the Sixth Assessment Report of the Intergovernmental Panel on Climate Change.* CU Press.

Kessari, M., Joly, C., Jaouen, A., & Jaeck, M. (2020). Alternative food networks: Good practices for sustainable performance. *Journal of Marketing Management, 36*(15–16), 1417–1446.

Kilbourne, W. E. (2006). The role of the dominant social paradigm in the quality of life/environmental interface. *Applied Research in Quality of Life, 1*(1), 39–61.

Kiss, K., Ruszkai, C., & Takács-György, K. (2019). Examination of short supply chains based on circular economy and sustainability aspects. *Resources, 8*(4), 161.

Le Blanc, D. (2015). Towards integration at last? The sustainable development goals as a network of targets. *Sustainable Development, 23*(3), 176–187.

Lin, B. B., Chappell, M. J., Vandermeer, J., Smith, G., Quintero, E., Bezner-Kerr, R., Griffith, D. M., Ketcham, S., Latta, S. C., & McMichael, P. (2011). Effects of industrial agriculture on climate change and the mitigation potential of small-scale agro-ecological farms. *CABI Reviews, 2011*, 1–18. https:// doi .org/ 10 .1079/ PAVSNNR20116020

Macias, T. (2008). Working toward a just, equitable, and local food system: The social impact of community-based agriculture. *Social Science Quarterly, 89*(5), 1086–1101. https://doi.org/10.1111/j.1540-6237.2008.00566.x

Mahmuda, S., Sigler, T., Corcoran, J., & Knight, E. (2021). What is the sharing economy? Origins and precedents. In T. Sigler & J. Corcoran (Eds.), *A modern guide to the urban sharing economy* (pp. 11–26). Edward Elgar Publishing.

Mori, K., & Christodoulou, A. (2012). Review of sustainability indices and indicators: Towards a new City Sustainability Index (CSI). *Environmental Impact Assessment Review, 32*(1), 94–106.

Munté-Pascual, A., Khalfaoui, A., Valero, D., & Redondo-Sama, G. (2022). Social impact indicators in the context of the Roma Community: Contributions to the debate on methodological implications. *International Journal of Qualitative Methods, 21.* https://doi.org/10.1177/16094069211064668

Neumayer, E. (2003). *Weak versus strong sustainability: Exploring the limits of two opposing paradigms.* Edward Elgar Publishing.

Ozcan, K. (2004). *Consumer-to-consumer interactions in a networked society: Word-of-mouth theory, consumer experiences, and network dynamics.* University of Michigan Press.

Piracha, A., Sharples, R., & Dunn, K. (2021). Discrimination in the urban sharing economy. In T. Sigler & J. Corcoran (Eds.), *A modern guide to the urban sharing economy* (pp. 282–295). Edward Elgar Publishing.

Preiss, P., Charão-Marques, F., & Wiskerke, J. S. (2017). Fostering sustainable urban–rural linkages through local food supply: A transnational analysis of collaborative food alliances. *Sustainability, 9*(7), 1155.

Purvis, B., Mao, Y., & Robinson, D. (2019). Three pillars of sustainability: In search of conceptual origins. *Sustainability Science, 14*(3), 681–695. https://doi.org/10.1007/ s11625-018-0627-5

Renting, H., Marsden, T. K., & Banks, J. (2003). Understanding alternative food networks: Exploring the role of short food supply chains in rural development. *Environment and Planning A, 35*(3), 393–411.

Seufert, V., & Ramankutty, N. (2017). Many shades of gray: The context-dependent performance of organic agriculture. *Science Advances, 3*(3), e1602638.

Severo, E. A., De Guimarães, J. C. F., & Dellarmelin, M. L. (2021). Impact of the COVID-19 pandemic on environmental awareness, sustainable consumption and social responsibility: Evidence from generations in Brazil and Portugal. *Journal of Cleaner Production, 286*, 124947. https://doi.org/https://doi.org/10.1016/j.jclepro .2020.124947

United Nations. (2015, September 15). *Transforming our world: The 2030 Agenda for Sustainable Development.* United Nations.

Venn, L., Kneafsey, M., Holloway, L., Cox, R., Dowler, E., & Tuomainen, H. (2006). Researching European "alternative" food networks: Some methodological consider-ations. *Area, 38*(3), 248–258.

Volpentesta, A. P., Ammirato, S., & Della Gala, M. (2013). Classifying short agrifood supply chains under a knowledge and social learning perspective. *Rural Society, 22*(3), 217–229.

Watts, D. C. H., Ilbery, B., & Maye, D. (2005). Making reconnections in agro-food geography: Alternative systems of food provision. *Progress in Human Geography, 29*(1), 22–40. https://doi.org/10.1191/0309132505ph526oa

Young, C. (2022). Should you buy local? *Journal of Business Ethics, 176*(2), 265–281.

8. Collaborative consumption after community tragedies: public space for communal healing

Amy Greiner Fehl and Marlys Mason

INTRODUCTION

Marketplaces unite consumers. Shared, communal consumption spaces are embedded in our lives. They are the foundation by which we collectively carry out mundane, routine consumption acts, gather to socialize and engage with others, and come together to celebrate and experience special events. However, during such shared consumption, violence can strike suddenly and fracture the communal coexistence of these spaces. This violence may take many forms, from the shootings at a supermarket in Buffalo, New York, in May 2022, to the bombing at the Ariana Grande concert in December 2018 in Manchester, England, or the terrorist attacks at cafes in November 2015 in Paris, France. In all these cases, the marketplace itself was the target of the violence and the victims were unknowing consumers engaging in collective consumption in shared spaces. When marketplaces are struck by these deliberate acts of violence that cause collective trauma, the once uniting public space is literally torn asunder. Collaborative consumption offers a path to healing.

Marketing scholars recognize that collaborative consumption is a source of meaningful connections, interactions, and interdependency between consumers who share consumption experiences and spaces in cooperation with one another (Arnould et al., 2021; Belk, 2010; Cova et al., 2007; Muniz & O'Guinn, 2001). In addition to the experience of consumption, shared participation in rituals and traditions, shared consciousness, and a sense of moral responsibility to each other reinforce a sense of community among consumer and brand collectives (Muniz & O'Guinn, 2001). In fact, community is both reinforced and newly built through sharing events and moments together, which provide a framework for meaning-making and identity building (Albinsson & Perera, 2012) beyond the abstract contemplation of group similarities. In contrast, when marketplace violence occurs, consumers are thrust together and bonded by a violent act and trauma rather than by positive communal experiences. When such collective trauma occurs (Alexander, 2012; Hirschberger, 2018), meaningful community responses are needed. The wounds following market violence are communal and thus consumers and the marketspace are likely to require communal, collaborative, and shared activities for consumer and community healing and transformation.

Hirschberger (2018) defines collective trauma as "a cataclysmic event that shatters the basic fabric of society," leading to a "crisis of meaning" (p. 1). While marketing scholars, through existing research, are beginning to understand the role of consumption after trauma, much is left to be explored. We know that shared consumption experiences after natural disasters lead to a shared sense of vulnerability and this vulnerability is a key social process leading to lasting change (Baker et al., 2007). Scholars have also found that on an individual level, consumption choices during and after health crises can pave the way for adaptation and resilience (Pavia & Mason, 2004, 2012; Pounders & Mason, 2018). On a macro level, market activities can provide a catalyst for lasting social changes subsequent to violent conflict (Barrios et al., 2016). Extant literature highlights the importance of consumption to trauma recovery and how trauma can lead to liminal states and transformative consumer experiences. What is less well understood is how collaborative consumption can be the conduit for community healing and curative practices following marketplace violence – which is the focus of this chapter. To better illuminate its importance in this context, we define collaborative consumption as individuals consuming together in a cooperative manner with a shared purpose. In the case of marketplace violence, the shared purpose is the healing and restoration of the affected community and individuals. Collaborative consumption is thus one type of collective or group-based consumption. As noted in previous research, "the notion of community is at the core of collaborative consumption" where exchanges among community members, either monetary or not, provide the basis for positive change (Albinsson & Perera, 2012).

In this chapter we explore the nature of consumers sharing communal space, action, and reflection to heal collective trauma as a response to heinous targeted acts of violence. Specifically, we describe three central facets of collaborative consumption in the marketplace that facilitate individual and community healing and restoration: (1) physicality of consumption in the shared space, (2) reaffirmation of the common identity through meaningful consumption, and (3) ritualized expressions of grief (Figure 8.1).

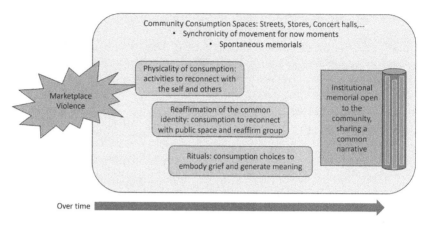

Figure 8.1   Collaborative consumption for communal healing

HEALING TRAUMA BY RECONNECTING TO THE PHYSICAL SELF THROUGH THE COMMUNAL SPACE

From the start, traumatic events cause a physical reaction resulting from the apparent disconnect between what is happening and what individuals in the community are able to understand (Van der Kolk, 2015). To start moving forward, community members need to reconnect to present reality and ground themselves by establishing a tangible link to their surroundings. Consumption choices offer the opportunity to soothe oneself with comforting consumption choices, such as hot chocolate (Luomala, 2002), and to remind oneself of life before the trauma by engaging in mundane consumption activities, such as going to buy basic necessities. The place of consumption provides literal space for healing.

Contrary to the Western Cartesian conception of the mind as separate from the body and thus controllable through force of will and training (Forstmann et al., 2012), trauma literature explains that separating oneself from one's body or dissociation in fact causes trauma and can lead to posttraumatic stress disorder (PTSD) if it is not treated (Van der Kolk et al., 1996). Emotions are not abstract but rather physical reactions to events that the brain then tries to understand by layering meaning onto the body's sensations (De Waal, 2019). Dissociation results from the failure to comprehend a stressful event and one's reaction to it because the brain shuts down and disconnects from the body, which is the source of information inputs. In other words: "what makes memories traumatic is a failure of the central nervous system to synthesize the sensations related to the traumatic memory into an integrated semantic memory" (Van der Kolk,

2000, p. 16). But how does the brain integrate the unimaginable, such as when one's neighborhood grocery store becomes the scene of a mass shooting?

The person must have a physical space to occupy to process what has happened and start healing from the trauma. While thinking about what has happened and connecting with loved ones can be helpful, it is often not sufficient to heal and move past the traumatic experience. As explained by Van der Kolk (2000), "Traumatized individuals need to have experiences that directly contradict the emotional helplessness and physical paralysis that accompany traumatic experiences" (p. 19). Furthermore, it is generally not enough to simply talk about what happened – often, people need to act, and this is where consumption choices can allow individuals to begin to heal. They are concrete, action-oriented, and purposeful. Consumption choices move people out of their heads and into their bodies through tangible expressions of grief, self-soothing choices, or a simple return to consumption patterns practiced before the trauma. As explained in extensive marketing literature, consumption choices are extensions of the self (Belk, 1988) and a way to realize a transcendent or sacred experience in daily life (Belk et al., 1989).

Furthermore, sharing in consumption is a critical part of these extensions of self and meaning-laden experiences (Belk, 2010). Consumers have a desire to feel unity and a communal sense of self, thus, they share. This sharing may be of physical spaces, of events, or of objects, leading to collaborative consumption co-created with others with a clear purpose. Such sharing connects one with others, often in powerful, emotional ways that unite and bond (Belk, 2010). As such, consuming in the public space has the benefit of consuming with others, known and unknown, and offers the opportunity for healing to many persons due to low barriers to participation.

In fact, consuming with others can be very low cost – such as the price of a coffee – or even free, such as reading on a bench in a park. The same consumption choice may have different meanings for different individuals, but consuming together lessens the individual load and increases the healing impact of meaningful consumption choices. When consuming in public spaces, individuals may or may not share directly when consuming, but they all share the space. They may collaborate explicitly or tacitly, but either way they ultimately share the same consumption experience. Specifically, the individual "shares in" the communal space because ownership of the space is common (Belk, 2010).

After marketplace violence, this "sharing in" the communal space and consuming together offer a unique opportunity for healing through collaborative consumption because moving in concert with others literally calms the central nervous system and helps re-integrate the body and the brain (Classen et al., 2021). The synchronicity of movement as a group allows individuals to experience "now moments" – being present and not stuck in the trauma – because shared movement brings individuals literally and symbolically away from the trauma and toward healing (Dworkin & Errebo, 2010). The synchronicity of movement in a public space through consumption choices, where each comes to the same spot and follows the same motions to leave a memento commemorating what was lost or raise a glass, for example, likewise generates a synchronicity of emotions leading to curative connection (Páez et al., 2015). These acts represent collaborative consumption – consuming together with the purpose of healing and restoration. We find a similar mechanism for communal healing in therapeutic systems of consumption. For example, in Malawi (Friedson, 1996), individuals who choose to participate in ritual dance to heal themselves and support others demonstrate the power of collaborative consumption. Another example is the emotional healing that may occur in therapeutic servicescapes in which consumers collaboratively engage in pilgrimages laden with ritualistic communal performative consumption, such as visits to Lourdes (Higgins & Hamilton, 2019).

REAFFIRMATION OF THE COMMON IDENTITY THROUGH MEANINGFUL COLLABORATIVE CONSUMPTION

Importantly, when marketplaces have been attacked, the damage extends beyond the individual – shared consumption identities have been threatened or destroyed leading to collective trauma (Hirschberger, 2018). Communities thus seek to reaffirm communal identity, establish a common narrative about what happened and how the community will move forward, and determine who is responsible (Alexander, 2016). Communities must physically take back the public spaces and develop their story of resilience. We can trace these through popular press articles and images (Cross et al., 2017) and through the community outpouring in public spaces and social media that addresses emotional bonds, coming together, and themes of collective identity (Eriksson, 2016). Prior research has demonstrated that finding novel ways for communities to come together in the wake of crises, such as natural disasters, can build resilience at the community level and protect the most vulnerable members (Ozanne & Ozanne, 2016).

In recovering from collective trauma, the collectivity must reestablish a sense of we-ness and reaffirm the core values that comprise the shared identity. In fact, communities are defined by what they have in common and what they do together – which is the basis of collective identity (Albinsson & Perera, 2012). Consumption choices in particular confirm identity and core values and are then reinforced through the often public nature of the choices (McAlexander et al., 2002). Moreover, individuals are motivated to construct and strengthen group identities because of the meaning they provide. A need to belong to a community drives participation in collaborative consumption, generating new meaning and new layers of community (Albinsson & Perera, 2012). Certainly, the meaning one finds through social identity underscores why people search for identity and renegotiate the meaning of the collective with others and the self (Vignoles et al., 2006). This meaning needs to be reestablished after a collective trauma since the incomprehensible can seemingly erase how one understood the world and one's place in it (Hirschberger, 2018).

Many individuals turn to some form of ritual to find meaning and connection to a common identity. Rituals establish and renew shared identity through the concert of action of individuals and the confirmation of core beliefs. Rituals are not limited to sacred spaces; rather, "ritual is to be found everywhere that humans live together if we look in the right places" (Bellah, 2005, p. 200). Collective trauma from outside aggression (Hirschberger, 2018) disrupts these everyday rituals and severs community bonds, perhaps especially when the marketplace is the target of the aggression. Individuals may feel cut off from others in consumption spaces and unmoored in the marketplace. Returning to previous consumption rituals provides the opportunity for healing and reconnection to the collective because of the way in which they are by nature collaborative.

MEMORIALS: RITUALIZED EXPRESSIONS OF GRIEF

Spontaneous memorials in public spaces have become a type of ritual that, on the one hand, follows the general pattern of collaborative consumption and, on the other hand, responds to the specific needs of the individuals and the community following marketplace violence. Examining how the community uses spontaneous memorials allows us to explore both the need for concrete expressions of grief and the rebuilding of collective identity. Memorials of marketplace violence form at the scene of the violence, offering a space for collaborative consumption and sharing that removes personal boundaries (Belk, 2010) and literally intermingles pieces left by community members. As individuals collaborate to develop a mosaic of responses, working together, this intermingling heals both individual and communal wounds.

Each memorial uniquely embodies the violent event, but we also find patterns across memorials: candles, pictures, notes left for the victims, and other representations of what was lost. These "spontaneous shrines" (Grider, 2001) have become crucial modern-day rituals that allow communities to come together and experience common emotion (Durkheim, 1912/1961) through collaborative consumption. They merge both the sacred and the profane literally (Belk et al., 1989) by including spiritual items, such as candles and prayers written on paper, with profane objects, such as stuffed animals and balloons. Communities clearly come together to collaborate on the memorial, resulting in an embodiment of collaborative consumption, and some community members even anoint themselves as guardians of the memorial, removing dead flowers and arranging items for maximum impact (Antichan, 2020).

More precisely, the ritualized collaborative consumption we observe in spontaneous memorials for marketplace violence combines the two previous facets of community responses to trauma explored in this chapter. First, the rituals feature a physical, concrete aspect: sharing the public space to experience the memorial and even contributing an item to it. Allowing oneself to experience the embodiment of emotion as a group disperses the trauma and provides a path for meaning-making, particularly with ritualized elements (Dworkin & Errebo, 2010). The physicality of visiting and adding to a memorial allows the individuals to physically process what has happened and connect with others who have gone through the same steps – embodied common grief. Second, the items left at the memorial tell a meaningful story of what aspects of the collective identity were threatened and need to be reaffirmed (Cross et al., 2017).

Looking at popular press images of memorials from around the world, we can see common themes and common items left; in fact, the pictures of these shrines are eerily and sadly similar. One consistently sees words of love and connection, flowers to honor the deceased (Drenten et al., 2017), and candles to symbolize hope and the sacred (Sherry & Kozinets, 2004). Many memorials for marketplace violence include stuffed animals, even in the absence of children among the victims. Community members also leave personal pieces of themselves, such as drawings, notes to the individuals who lost their lives, and personal belongings. As documented extensively in marketing literature, possessions are extensions of the self, thus, people who leave drawings, postcards, or favorite items are literally leaving a piece of themselves in the community space (Belk, 1988). For example, following the attack on the LGBTQ nightclub in Colorado in November 2022, photos of the memorials show pieces of the self and representations of a common identity left there: names of loved ones lost written by hand, photos, pride flags and rainbow-themed objects representing a shared identity, cellophane-wrapped flowers, and manifestos for peace and acceptance to confirm shared values (Akaka et al., 2014).

By participating in this collaborative consumption ritual of spontaneous memorials, community members experience healing through common emotion. They find a shared purpose in confirming collective identity via the themes expressed by the individual items as well as the strength of the collaborative response overall. The common emotion experienced while participating in rituals was first described by Durkheim (1912/1961) as "collective effervescence." More recently, research in the sciences has shown that quantitatively strong emotions are experienced by those participating in rituals as a group (Xygalatas et al., 2011). Durkheim originally explained that collective effervescence arises from people gathering together: "When they are once come together, a sort of electricity is formed by their collecting" (Durkheim, 1912/1961, p. 247). Durkheim further explains that this need to come together is heightened during calamitous times: "There are periods in history, when under the influence of some great collective shock, social interactions have become much more frequent and active. Men look for each other" (p. 241).

One evocative repository of how communities come together in the ritual of spontaneous memorials after marketplace violence is the Paris Archive's work to digitize items left by community members at the different locations of the November 2015 Paris terrorist attacks (Archives de Paris, 2022). Even in their sanitized and digitized form, the images of the items left are electric and moving. They show expressions of grief and hope, pictures of loved ones lost, hand-written notes to the deceased, collective identities, and many drawings of shared consumption activities, such as wine glasses, bread, and music notes.

We can see in the items left that the we-ness of the community is expressed through shared consumption values, such as enjoying the pleasures in life ("*joie de vivre*"), bars and restaurants, café tables, and so on. As shown in Figure 8.2, the items left at the memorials illustrate the three collaborative consumption themes described here. The physicality of the memorial is shown by the pair of shoes that have been decorated with the colors of the French flag and the motto for Paris: "*Fluctuat nec mergitur*" (rocked by the waves but does not sink). The owner of the shoes left a piece of herself to both commemorate the atrocity and to leave it behind (Marcoux, 2017). A reaffirmation of the common identity can be seen in one drawing that depicts a table with bread, cheese, and wine and the note: "*Paris est une fete et le restera*" (Paris is a celebration and will remain one). Another beautiful image not shown in the figure is that of a watercolor portraying a couple sitting at a table at a café with shipping tape depicting the word "FRAGILE" bordering the painting. These images underscore how certain consumption acts symbolize the Parisian identity. Finally, we find ritualized grief and a search for meaning in the drawing that shows the Eiffel Tower, a woman crying, a candle, and the words "Pray for Paris."

Accordingly, the memorials for marketplace violence exemplify the collaborative consumption of rituals within a ritual: the daily consumption rituals depicted in the ritual of leaving items to memorialize what was lost in the violence that targeted the marketplace. Over time, recurring rituals of healing at the anniversary of community tragedy also keep the memory alive and reaffirm relationships (Bonsu & Belk, 2003). Rituals are living memories. Rituals by their nature represent collaborative consumption even when performed alone because they connect to what others have done, are doing in the present, and will continue to do in the future, and in that way are always collaborative in nature.

Physicality of consumption	Reaffirmation of the common identity	Ritualized grief and meaning-making

Shoes left at the memorial with the French flag and the motto of Paris	"Paris is a party and will remain one"	"Pray for Paris"

Source: Images can be accessed at https://archives.paris.fr/r/137/hommages-aux-victimes-de s-attentats-de-2015/.

Figure 8.2   Healing themes from collaborative consumption at the Paris Memorials

CONCLUSION

The three central facets of community responses following marketplace violence that are explored here are: (1) the physicality of consumption in collective space, (2) the reaffirmation of the common identity through meaningful consumption, and (3) the ritualized expressions of grief. They illustrate how collaborative consumption can heal communal wounds and restore individuals and communities. Collaborative consumption can strengthen collectives by allowing for different types of exchanges that build meaning, create a sense of community (Albinsson & Perera, 2012), and engender resilience (Ozanne & Ozanne, 2016).

We also see in Figure 8.1 the importance of institutional or governmental support in the wake of marketplace violence. Immediately following the violence, governments and local institutions provide much-needed financial and substantive support (Christensen et al., 2013). Accordingly, institutions can further reinforce the three aspects of collaborative consumption for community recovery after marketplace violence by, first, providing the necessary space for grieving and, over time, dedicating permanent memorials (Milošević, 2018) such as the Oklahoma City National Memorial and Museum, which honors all those affected by the 1995 bombing. In fact, institutionalized or permanent memorials play many roles once the immediacy of the marketplace violence has passed and communities have started the healing process by coming together. Official memorials create a permanent space for grieving to continue what was started by the ephemeral memorials. If emotions are physical and our need to comfort others and ourselves is visceral (De Waal, 2019), then we need both connection and a place to connect to restore ourselves, express our emotions, and work together to heal through collaborative consumption.

Furthermore, official memorials help individuals and communities understand that the traumatic event is part of history and no longer a part of the current moment, which is a key aspect of trauma recovery (Van der Kolk, 2000, p. 19). Dedicating time, such as setting aside an annual day of remembrance, is another key way that institutions can provide space – here, temporal space – to reflect on the violent act that shook the marketplace and honor the victims (Milošević & Truc, 2021).

Additional research on the themes explored in this chapter would lead to a better understanding of collaborative consumption and healing activities in the wake of marketplace violence. Importantly, more research would improve community and national responses to these increasingly common occurrences. Specifically, future research could focus on the different roles played by community members engaging in collaborative consumption following marketplace violence: business owners who provide a space for people to come together, individuals contributing items to spontaneous shrines, those who are there simply to bear witness, the role of children, and the different types of institutional support that may be provided. Furthermore, research is needed on the importance of institutionalized memorials to help victims heal, tell their stories, and provide collaborative consumption opportunities: Who should be allowed to contribute to these memorials? How does the general public consume these narratives during a visit and then share the story more broadly with others, thus co-creating the history of the event? Finally, which concrete aspects of collaborative consumption are most helpful to individuals recovering from a community tragedy: consuming with friends vs. unknown community members? Reviving everyday consumption rituals or creating new ones? Such future research can highlight the role that collaborative consumption plays in collective healing following traumatic, violent marketplace acts.

REFERENCES

Akaka, M. A., Corsaro, D., Kelleher, C., Maglio, P. P., Seo, Y., Lusch, R. F., & Vargo, S. L. (2014). The role of symbols in value cocreation. *Marketing Theory*, *14*(3), 311–326.

Albinsson, P. A., & Perera, B. Y. (2012). Alternative marketplaces in the 21st century: Building community through sharing events. *Journal of Consumer Behaviour*, *11*(4), 303–315.

Alexander, J. C. (2012). *Trauma: A social theory.* Polity Press.

Alexander, J. C. (2016). Culture trauma, morality and solidarity: The social construction of "Holocaust" and other mass murders. *Thesis Eleven, 132*(1), 3–16.

Antichan, S. (2020). Les mémoriaux post-attentats et leurs publics. In S. Gensburger & G. Truc (Eds.), *Les mémoriaux du 13 novembre* (pp. 62–83X). Éditions de l'EHESS.

Archives de Paris. (2022). *Hommages aux victimes des attentats de 2015.* https://archives.paris.fr/r/137/hommages-aux-victimes-des-attentats-de-2015/

Arnould, E. J., Arvidsson, A., & Eckhardt, G. M. (2021). Consumer collectives: A history and reflections on their future. *Journal of the Association for Consumer Research, 6*(4), 415–428.

Baker, S. M., Hunt, D. M., & Rittenburg, T. L. (2007). Consumer vulnerability as a shared experience: Tornado recovery process in Wright, Wyoming. *Journal of Public Policy & Marketing, 26*(1), 6–19.

Barrios, A., de Valck, K., Shultz, C., Sibai, O., Husemann, K., Maxwell-Smith, M., & Luedicke, M. (2016). Marketing as a means to transformative social conflict resolution: Lessons from transitioning war economies and the Colombian coffee marketing system. *Journal of Public Policy & Marketing, 35*(2), 185–197.

Belk, R. W. (1988). Possessions and the extended self. *Journal of Consumer Research, 15*(2), 139–168.

Belk, R. W. (2010). Sharing. *Journal of Consumer Research, 36*(5), 715–734.

Belk, R. W., Wallendorf, M., & Sherry Jr, J. F. (1989). The sacred and the profane in consumer behavior: Theodicy on the odyssey. *Journal of Consumer Research, 16*(1), 1–38.

Bellah, R. N. (2005). Durkheim and ritual. In J. C. Alexander & P. Smith (Eds.), *The Cambridge companion to Durkheim,* (pp. 183–210). Cambridge University Press.

Bonsu, S. K., & Belk, R. W. (2003). Do not go cheaply into that good night: Death-ritual consumption in Asante, Ghana. *Journal of Consumer Research, 30*(1), 41–55.

Christensen, T., Lægreid, P., & Rykkja, L. H. (2013). After a terrorist attack: Challenges for political and administrative leadership in Norway. *Journal of Contingencies and Crisis Management, 21*(3), 167–177.

Classen, C. C., Hughes, L., Clark, C., Hill Mohammed, B., Woods, P., & Beckett, B. (2021). A pilot RCT of a body-oriented group therapy for complex trauma survivors: An adaptation of sensorimotor psychotherapy. *Journal of Trauma & Dissociation, 22*(1), 52–68.

Cova, B., Kozinets, R. V., & Shankar, A. (Eds.). (2007). *Consumer tribes.* Butterworth-Heinemann.

Cross, S. N., Harrison, R. L., & Gilly, M. C. (2017). The role of marketing in ritual evolution. *Journal of Macromarketing, 37*(4), 460–478.

De Waal, F. (2019). *Mama's last hug: Animal emotions and what they tell us about ourselves.* W. W. Norton & Company.

Drenten, J., McManus, K., & Labrecque, L. I. (2017), Graves, gifts, and the bereaved consumer: A restorative perspective of gift exchange. *Consumption Markets & Culture, 20*(5), 423–455.

Durkheim, E. (1961). *The elementary forms of religious life.* Free Press. Original work published 1912.

Dworkin, M., & Errebo, N. (2010). Rupture and repair in the EMDR client/clinician relationship: Now moments and moments of meeting. *Journal of EMDR Practice and Research, 4*(3), 113–123.

Eriksson, M. (2016). Managing collective trauma on social media: The role of Twitter after the 2011 Norway attacks. *Media, Culture & Society, 38*(3), 365–380.

Forstmann, M., Burgmer, P., & Mussweiler, T. (2012). The mind is willing, but the flesh is weak: The effects of mind–body dualism on health behavior. *Psychological Science, 23*(10), 1239–1245.

Friedson, S. M. (1996). *Dancing prophets: Musical experience in Tumbuka healing.* University of Chicago Press.

Grider, S. (2001). Spontaneous shrines: A modern response to tragedy and disaster. *New Directions in Folklore, 5,* 12–18.

Higgins, L., & Hamilton, K. (2019). Therapeutic servicescapes and market-mediated performances of emotional suffering. *Journal of Consumer Research, 45*(6), 1230–1253.

Hirschberger, G. (2018). Collective trauma and the social construction of meaning. *Frontiers in Psychology, 9,* 1441.

Luomala, H. T. (2002). An empirical analysis of the practices and therapeutic power of mood-alleviative consumption in Finland. *Psychology & Marketing, 19*(10), 813–836.

Marcoux, J. S. (2017). Souvenirs to forget. *Journal of Consumer Research, 43*(6), 950–969.

McAlexander, J. H., Schouten, J. W., & Koenig, H. F. (2002). Building brand community. *Journal of Marketing, 66*(1), 38–54.

Milošević, A. (2018). Historicizing the present: Brussels attacks and heritagization of spontaneous memorials. *International Journal of Heritage Studies, 24*(1), 53–65.

Milošević, A., & Truc, G. (2021). (Un)shared memory: European Parliament and EU Remembrance Day for victims of terrorism. *Politique Européenne, 71*(1), 142–169.

Muniz, Jr, A. M., & O'Guinn, T. C. (2001). Brand community. *Journal of Consumer Research, 27*(4), 412–432.

Ozanne, L. K., & Ozanne, J. L. (2016). How alternative consumer markets can build community resiliency. *European Journal of Marketing, 50*(3/4), 330–357.

Páez, D., Rimé, B., Basabe, N., Wlodarczyk, A., & Zumeta, L. (2015). Psychosocial effects of perceived emotional synchrony in collective gatherings. *Journal of Personality and Social Psychology, 108*(5), 711–729.

Pavia, T. M., & Mason, M. (2004). The reflexive relationship between consumer behavior and adaptive coping. *Journal of Consumer Research, 31*(2), 441–454.

Pavia, T. M., & Mason, M. J. (2012). Inclusion, exclusion and identity in the consumption of families living with childhood disability. *Consumption Markets & Culture, 15*(1), 87–115.

Pounders, K., & Mason, M. (2018). Embodiment, illness, and gender: The intersected and disrupted identities of young women with breast cancer. In S. N. N. Cross, C. Ruvalcaba, A. Venkatesh, & R. W. Belk (Eds.), *Consumer culture theory. Vol. 19 of Research in Consumer Behavior* (pp. 111–122). Emerald Publishing.

Sherry, J. F., Jr., & Kozinets, R. V. (2004). Sacred iconography in secular space: altars, Alters and alterity at the Burning Man Project. In O. Cele & T. Lowry (Eds.), *Contemporary consumption rituals: A research anthology* (pp. 291–311). Lawrence Erlbaum.

Van der Kolk, B. A. (2000). Posttraumatic stress disorder and the nature of trauma. *Dialogues in Clinical Neuroscience, 2*(1), 7–22. https://doi.org/10.31887/DCNS.2000.2.1/bvdkolk

Van der Kolk, B. A. (2015). *The body keeps the score: Brain, mind, and body in the healing of trauma.* Penguin Books.

Van der Kolk, B. A., van der Hart, O., & Marmar, C. R. (1996). Dissociation and information processing in posttraumatic stress disorder. In B. A. Van der Kolk, A.

C. McFarlane, & L. Weisaeth (Eds.), *Traumatic stress: The effects of overwhelming experience on mind, body and society* (pp. 303–327). Guilford Press.

Vignoles, V. L., Regalia, C., Manzi, C., Golledge, J., & Scabini, E. (2006). Beyond self-esteem: Influence of multiple motives on identity construction. *Journal of Personality and Social Psychology, 90*(2), 308–333.

Xygalatas, D., Konvalinka, I., Bulbulia, J., & Roepstorff, A. (2011). Quantifying collective effervescence: Heart-rate dynamics at a fire-walking ritual. *Communicative & Integrative Biology, 4*(6), 735–738.

9. Hand-me-downs: the wallflower of pre-ownership and a special case for psychological ownership

Susanne Ruckelshausen and Bernadette Kamleitner

INTRODUCTION

Handing down things that one no longer needs to family and friends might be one of the oldest forms of collaborative consumption. Hand-me-downs are "things ... which have been used by someone else before you and which have been given to you for your use" (Collins, n.d.); the term also refers to the passing on of discarded (i.e., no longer needed or wanted) belongings to family members, friends, or acquaintances (Harper Collins, 1995). We thus define hand-me-downs as goods that one no longer needs that are passed down to people one knows in the absence of expected compensation. They represent a resource circulation system and can thus be classified as a form of collaborative consumption that "enable(s) consumers to both obtain, and provide, temporarily or permanently, valuable resources or services through direct interaction with other consumers" (Ertz et al., 2016, p. 15). Going beyond more narrow conceptualizations of collaborative consumption as the temporary fee-based access to products and services (e.g., Guo et al., Chapter 16, this book), hand-me-downs represent a practice in which goods, typically clothing or other personal possessions, are permanently transferred from one consumer to another. Instead of discarding or selling pre-owned goods, these items are given to others within a community or network often comprising family, friends, and peers. The practice of sharing hand-me-downs significantly differs from conventional market exchange because it balances the availability of resources over time, takes place within and fosters personal relationships, and is driven by reciprocity and community belonging (Lamberton, 2016).

Handing things down to someone else creates value through resource sharing and waste reduction. Distributing hand-me-downs increases product lifespans, reduces the need for new purchases, offers cost savings, makes essential goods more accessible, and potentially fosters social connections. It thus contributes to relational, commercial (low-cost), and resource-smoothing goals, such as sharing with others when possible, as set out in the goal-based framework of collaborative consumption (Lamberton, 2016).

This chapter zooms in on this rarely discussed private form of collaborative consumption, hence the title wallflower, and benchmarks it against its market equivalent, second-hand shopping. While we identify a number of features that distinguish the two practices, both hinge on the acceptance of pre-owned goods by new owners. We focus on the recipients of hand-me-downs and propose mechanisms that affect the appropriation of hand-me-downs in comparison to second-hand purchases. Our theoretical lens is that of psychological ownership (PO; Pierce et al., 2001). PO explains why and how we appropriate things and affects how sustainably these things are being used (Kamleitner & Rabinovich, 2010; Peck & Luangrath, 2023; Peck & Shu, 2018). In other words, the PO lens helps us to understand whether a variant of the circular economy is likely to fulfill its potential.

We start this chapter by providing an overview of the different "shades" of pre-ownership and identify the key distinctions between hand-me-downs and second-hand purchases. After a brief introduction to PO and its role in the sustainable use of products, we sketch the preconditions needed for its development. We next map features that are specific to hand-me-downs onto these preconditions and derive a set of testable propositions. Overall, this chapter offers unique insights on hand-me-downs and highlights the role of PO in collaborative consumption.

SHADES OF PRE-OWNERSHIP

The term second-hand, also called pre-owned, refers to products that are not new and have been owned by someone (Cambridge University Press, n.d.; Harper Collins, n.d.). Second-hand products have seen a steady increase in popularity. Macklemore and Ryan Lewis's song "Thrift Shop" pays testimony to the increasingly positive image of what has developed into a flourishing form of consumption and self-expression. Online second-hand stores and platforms to trade used products are seeing increasing success, and established brands increasingly recognize the business potential; this is occurring in fashion (e.g., thredUP or Vinted) and beyond (e.g., Rebuy in electronics and media). Second-hand purchases have become a fashionable way of obtaining pre-owned goods. These involve target groups beyond the particularly thrifty or those unable or unwilling to afford something else (Ferraro et al., 2016). Treasure hunters look for second-hand products because they are often so unique or special that they allow consumers to express their individuality or to bask in nostalgic feelings (e.g., Guiot & Roux, 2010; Turunen &

Leipämaa-Leskinen, 2015; Padmavathy et al., 2019). Influencers share thrift hauls on social media in the hope of sending desired signals about themselves. Consuming second-hand items can reflect personal ethical views and anti-consumption attitudes, and it can signal belonging to contemporary and eco-friendly consumer groups (e.g., Laitala & Klepp, 2018; Armstrong Soule & Sekhon, 2022). Consuming pre-owned goods pays into an increasing desire to consume sustainably (Guiot & Roux, 2010; Turunen & Leipämaa-Leskinen, 2015; Padmavathy et al., 2019). Reuse, especially of high-quality products, is one possibility to prolong a product's life cycle and to prevent waste. In addition, original, pre-owned items are appreciated for their authenticity (Turunen & Leipämaa-Leskinen, 2015). For example, early 2000s-inspired fashion has gained newfound popularity (McDowell, 2020) especially among millennials and members of Generation Z. Pre-owned goods tend to be transferred via methods and places of exchange that differ from those for new products (e.g., Guiot & Roux, 2010; Miller & Brannon, 2021). The phenomenon of second-hand purchasing is, however, only one way through which this happens. There are more shades to pre-ownership and not all of them have drawn equal attention. Table 9.1 summarizes and contrasts two key practices through which pre-owned goods are exchanged: second-hand markets and hand-me-downs. Most literature has focused on what we summarize as second-hand markets (i.e., the acquisition of second-hand products via second-hand, vintage, and thrift stores; flea markets; online platforms; or yard and garage sales; Guiot & Roux, 2010; Laitala & Klepp, 2018; Padmavathy et al., 2019). In these markets, buyers and pre-owners tend to not know each other, and goods are exchanged for money. This market facet has attracted much attention (e.g., Ferraro et al., 2016; Guiot & Roux, 2010; Styvén & Mariani, 2020; Yan et al., 2015). There is, however, also a non-market facet that has received significantly less attention.

Referring to it as non-monetary private exchange, Laitala and Klepp (2018) subsume practices such as swapping parties, giving away used goods online, and hand-me-downs. Given the difference between these practices in terms of relationship status and investments, this chapter focuses on the most prevalent form of non-monetary private exchange, hand-me-downs. Handing things down within a community may be the oldest form of collaborative consumption, and yet it appears to be a wallflower.

Like a wallflower, the practice of hand-me-downs has drawn little attention, but it is prevalent. In a Greenpeace (2015) study, a majority of participants said that they hand down prior belongings to friends or family, and data that we collected in a representative sample of the Austrian working population corroborate this (M.core, 2022). A majority of participants had already received pre-owned products as hand-me-downs, for example, used books (53 percent)

Table 9.1   *Structural differences between different ways of obtaining pre-owned products*

	Hand-me-downs	Second-hand market
Pre-owner	Known to and mostly connected with recipient	Mostly (previously) unknown to recipient
Compensation	None/for free	Monetary compensation
Initiation	Initiated by pre-owner	Self-initiated
Choice	Pre-selection by pre-owner, accept or reject	Personal choice from multiple offers by multiple parties
Examples	A bag given from an aunt to a niece or a toy given from an older to a younger sibling	A t-shirt bought at a flea market or a phone bought through an online platform for used electronics and other media (e.g., Rebuy)

and t-shirts (52 percent), while only a minority had bought these same (and other) products second-hand (34 percent books and 21 percent t-shirts).

Table 9.1 illustrates the key differences between second-hand purchases and hand-me-downs. First, the practice of giving hand-me-downs is characterized by freely sharing used goods among friends, family, and peers. This means that hand-me-downs and second-hand purchases differ with regard to (a) whether the pre-owner is known to the recipient and (b) whether any compensation is expected. Note that these points also distinguish hand-me-downs from, for example, swapping parties, which have been classified alongside second-hand purchases (Roux & Korchia, 2006) and hand-me-downs (Laitala & Klepp, 2018). Second, hand-me-downs (c) tend to be initiated by the pre-owner who (d) also tends to offer a limited choice of items at best. This leaves consumers less freedom of choice compared to other practices of reuse. Note, however, that initiation by the prior owner and severely limited choice are frequent characteristics of the practice of sharing hand-me-downs rather than part of its definition.

Both second-hand items and hand-me-downs are forms of collaborative consumption that can help address current societal issues by ensuring that existing resources are used to their fullest. Notably, they can only do so if people are willing to accept pre-owned products into their possession and if they then make use of those products. Whether this happens likely depends on whether consumers are able to think of something that used to belong to someone else as their own.

We next examine whether the differences between second-hand products and hand-me-downs are likely to play into this process of appropriation. We briefly sketch the conceptual underpinnings of PO before elaborating on how distributing hand-me-downs may affect the development of ownership feelings and, in turn, the consumption of objects that were handed down.

PSYCHOLOGICAL OWNERSHIP AS KEY TO SUSTAINABLE PRODUCT USE

PO has been defined as the state in which individuals feel that an object, or a part of that object, is theirs (Pierce et al., 2001, 2003). In other words, it describes the feeling of "that's mine" (Kamleitner, 2018, p. 112). PO can arise and exist in the absence of legal ownership (Pierce et al., 2003). A range of literature demonstrates that PO may be more predictive of people's behaviors than legal ownership status and that it can affect how we behave toward objects (Peck & Luangrath, 2023). The right-hand side of Figure 9.1 illustrates three related types of behaviors that can be fueled by PO. First, what we call acceptance refers to the fact that people are more likely to obtain what they already feel some sense of ownership for. For example, PO has been found to improve attitudes (Jussila et al., 2015) and increase object valuations (Brasel & Gips, 2014; Reb & Connolly, 2007) and willingness to pay for objects (Kamleitner & Feuchtl, 2015; Peck & Shu, 2009). Second, PO shapes what we summarize as people's attachment to objects so that they are more likely to keep objects for which they feel a sense of ownership, even if these have fallen out of fashion or are no longer like new. The more ownership one feels for a product, the harder it is to part with it (Baxter, 2017). Third, in what we summarize as attention, people tend to better focus on the needs of a product if they feel it is theirs. They behave more responsibly toward, protect, and care for objects they feel they own (Kamleitner & Rabinovich, 2010; Kirk et al., 2018; Peck & Luangrath, 2023; Pierce et al., 2001). PO thus plays an important role in whether a particular mode of consumption gains traction and contributes to sustainable product use or not. As a result of enhanced attachment and attention, PO can extend the life cycle of products. Figure 9.1 provides an overview of plausible connections between the characteristics of hand-me-downs, preconditions for the development of PO, and the three sketched effects of PO toward its targets.

THE DISTINCTIVE FEATURES OF HAND-ME-DOWNS AND THEIR EFFECT ON PO

Whether an object transforms from being *any* object to becoming *my* object depends on characteristics of that object and on the experiences people make with that object (Kamleitner & Mitchell, 2018; Peck & Luangrath, 2023; Pierce et al., 2001; see Figure 9.1). Drawing on prior PO research, Kamleitner and Mitchell (2018) distill three characteristics that objects need to have to

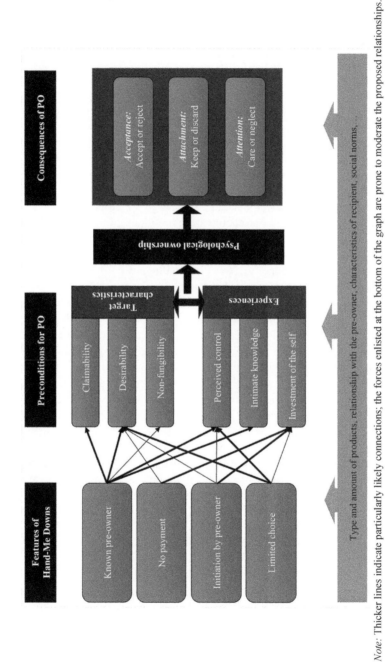

Note: Thicker lines indicate particularly likely connections; the forces enlisted at the bottom of the graph are prone to moderate the proposed relationships.

Figure 9.1   Proposed relationship between features of hand-me-downs and psychological ownership

become psychologically appropriated. People can only psychologically appropriate an object if (a) they feel they can claim it and make it theirs (claimable); (b) they desire the object and find it attractive or meaningful; and (c) they feel that it is or can be made into something that is unique to them, for example, because they can leave their own traces on the object (non-fungible).

Objects that are perceived as having these characteristics lend themselves to psychological appropriation. How strongly PO develops is, however, also a function of the experiences people have with an object. Pierce et al. (2003) indicated three partly interchangeable pathways that give rise to PO: intimate knowledge, investment of the self, and perceived control. Extant research since 2003 has found broad support for these "routes" to PO (Peck & Luangrath, 2023). The more knowledgeable one feels about an object, the more they feel they have invested into an object, and the more they perceive themselves as in control over an object, the more PO they feel for this object (Pierce et al., 2003). Figure 9.1 gives an overview of these preconditions and indicates how these may be affected by the specific features of hand-me-downs.

The distinctive features of hand-me-downs are likely to affect all of the preconditions for the development of PO and, thus, its consequences for object use. We theorize how this may happen and structure our analyses along the distinctive features of hand-me-downs.

Known Pre-Owner

Used products often elicit disgust or concerns regarding a lack of hygiene (Roux & Korchia, 2006). The mere knowledge of prior use can be a barrier to the development of PO (Baxter, 2017). Fraser (1922) argues that once an object has been owned by someone, this someone remains associated with it forever. Nemeroff and Rozin (1994) likewise argue that even by touching an object people transfer their essence and characteristics onto it. This phenomenon is described by the notions of contamination and contagion (Argo et al., 2006; Nemeroff & Rozin, 1994). In response, the recipient of a pre-owned object becomes connected not only to the object but also to its prior owner (Newman et al., 2011). Knowledge of prior owners may diminish an object's desirability and reduce the extent to which people feel that they can still claim the object. Knowing that another person interacted with an object may also diminish one's sense of intimate knowledge or perceived control over the object. At the same time, however, the actual or imagined traces of its pre-owner make pre-owned products one of a kind and non-fungible.

Generally, these influences apply to all pre-owned products. The case of hand-me-downs is, however, special in that recipients know and are often connected to the prior owner. This can equip recipients with additional information about both product and prior owner. Depending on who owned it before, people not only avoid (Rozin et al., 2015) but sometimes even desire pre-owned products. While the thought of strangers, as is common in second-hand markets, tends to raise concerns, the thought of someone one knows and trusts can buffer the sense of contagion (Nemeroff, 1995) and disgust (Bardhi & Eckhardt, 2012) that inhibit the psychological appropriation of pre-owned goods.

Targets that elicit a particularly strong sense of ownership tend to be meaningful for the person (Kamleitner & Mitchell, 2018) and have the power to anchor a person (Richins, 1994). Hand-me-downs can play a role in that because they solidify the connection between a recipient and pre-owner. For example, Belk (1988) invokes Lurie (1981), who studied adolescent girls swapping clothes. When girls do this, they share not only a friendship but also their identity. Products from close friends or relatives become meaningful because they facilitate identification with these previous owners (Roux & Korchia, 2006). This might be most apparent in heirlooms, which arguably constitute a special, intergenerational case of hand-me-downs. We thus propose: provided that the known pre-owner is perceived favorably, hand-me-downs facilitate perceptions of an object as desirable. Because people are prone to hold more knowledge about the peculiarities of an object and its prior owner, they likely also hold an advantage in terms of an object's perceived fungibility.

These potential advantages of hand-me-downs are, however, likely to meet an opposing force in the shape of diminished claimability. The fact that the object is imbued with its pre-owner may make it more special, but at the same time also limit the extent to which the object can become just "mine." We thus propose that people may find it harder to claim ownership for hand-me-downs than for second-hand purchases.

No Compensation

Getting an object for free is an objective advantage of hand-me-downs over second-hand purchases. Being free of cost, however, may also imply being free of investment and may hurt the development of PO. Paying for an object is a very salient investment (Kamleitner & Erki, 2013), and people tend to feel a stronger sense of personal ownership for things they have invested in (Kanngiesser et al., 2014). What is more, lack of payment characterizes not only hand-me-downs but also charitable giving, and the consumption of used products is already in danger of being perceived as a stigmatized and embarrassing sign of poverty (Laitala & Klepp, 2018). The parallel to receiving donations may thus detract from the desirability of the hand-me-down. We thus propose that lack of payment diminishes PO by lessening an object's desirability and claimability and by barring one experience of self-investment.

Initiation by Pre-Owner

The vast majority of theorizing about consumer behavior, including theorizing on collaborative consumption, maps onto what has often been called the consumption process. The common starting point is a person's need or desire, which then develops into the search for and acquisition of a product that may be capable of fulfilling this need or desire (Solomon, 2017). This also holds for second-hand purchases, but it does not hold for hand-me-downs (Laitala & Klepp, 2018). In the case of hand-me-downs, the person who would like to give away pre-selected products usually takes the initiative. The recipient of hand-me-downs merely has the chance to accept or reject. On the one hand, this may detract from an object's desirability. After all, a person's current needs add to the appeal of products capable of catering to that need. If no relevant need is salient, hand-me-downs may seem less attractive than they otherwise would. On the other hand, and potentially more importantly, being offered something without prior desire, search, or engagement eliminates relevant experiences in the process of appropriation. It bars recipients from initial self-investment and an experience of control via searching and finding an object (Kokkoris et al., 2020). We thus propose that initiation by the pre-owner diminishes PO by reducing self-investment and control experiences that precede acquisition and by reducing the desirability of the product in case this product does not answer to currently salient needs or desires.

Limited Choice

Pre-owners have full control over the range of products offered as hand-me-downs. Mostly, this range is at best small and at worst limited to one item that the recipient can accept or reject. This aggravates a known barrier to second-hand consumption: the lack of choice. In a representative survey of 500 people aged 12 to 19 years, a quarter of the respondents did not consider pre-owned clothing because they felt that second-hand offered too little choice (Greenpeace, 2015). In the case of hand-me-downs, these concerns are even more warranted. On the one hand, this may result in a reduced match of the product with a person's preferences, which lowers product attractiveness. On the other hand, this may impede the process of appropriation. Choosing a product represents an investment of the self and the exertion of control and can thus increase PO (Fuchs et al., 2010). We therefore propose that limited choice undermines psychological appropriation of hand-me-downs because it implies that the object is likely to be less desirable and because it means that recipients have less opportunity to invest themselves and take control over the process of object acquisition.

DISCUSSION

This chapter provides a new perspective on one of the oldest yet under-studied forms of collaborative consumption – the practice of passing on hand-me-downs. We highlight how hand-me-downs differ from second-hand markets as another key form of acquiring pre-owned goods. Through the lens of PO, we gauge the practice's potential contribution to a circular economy by asking whether people are likely to use handed-down resources sustainably. First and foremost, we offer a framework (see Figure 9.1) that displays how the distinctive features of hand-me-downs may affect the future use of objects by affecting psychological object ownership. Every arrow in this framework represents a theoretically grounded proposition that may inform future research on hand-me-downs. This framework centers on the specific distinction between hand-me-downs and second-hand markets. It can, however, also be of use to the study of other forms of collaborative consumption, such as swapping parties, that fall somewhere in between hand-me-downs and second-hand purchases.

A comprehensive range of propositions follows from this framework, and the bar on the bottom of Figure 9.1 indicates the likely importance of moderating contextual factors, such as the relationship between pre-owner and recipient (e.g., status difference, overall similarity, relationship quality), characteristics of the hand-me-down (e.g., product category, condition, pre-ownership duration), or characteristics of the recipient (e.g., economic need, sense of belonging). For example, one could ask whether it is easier to appropriate a handed-down jacket when the pre-owner has a similar vs. dissimilar style, when one has insufficient vs. sufficient economic means, when one feels inferior vs. equal or superior to the pre-owner, when it is in perfect condition vs. shows signs of wear and tear, or when any of those variations combine. In short, the framework sketches a rich field for future inquiry.

Our specific approach is, however, narrow. We only focus on the distinction between second-hand markets and hand-me-downs. Although this focus entails a corresponding narrowness in our propositions, the framework could easily be extended to accommodate distinctions between other modes of acquisition, for example, swapping parties, but also donations and gifts. For example, what is interesting about swapping parties is that pre-owners become compensated in a non-monetary manner and that consumers take more initiative and are offered more choice compared to receiving hand-me-downs. Individual choice gives consumers greater control (Fuchs et al., 2010) and the swap implies that they invest something of their own into the acquisition of something that is new to them. Thus, swapping parties allow for greater control and investment of the self, which suggests that they may facilitate psychological appropriation more than hand-me-downs do (Pierce et al., 2003).

Collaborative consumption has the potential to contribute to a more efficient use of resources. This, however, only manifests if consumers are willing to make the best use of resources. This also holds for hand-me-downs. Hand-me-downs can potentially overcome reservations arising from contagion, disgust, and mistrust that were often observed to hinder second-hand consumption. Yet, our analyses suggest that this potential may often fail to manifest. Most of the arrows in our framework point to influences that reduce the likelihood of psychological appropriation and thus also the likelihood that people actually accept these goods, feel attached, and attend to them.

The good news is that all preconditions of PO are subjective perceptions rather than objective facts. How people (are guided to) think about hand-me-downs determines whether they accept them and make good use of them or reject, hide, or (secretly) dispose of them. The handed-down jacket of one's uncle may be framed as a joyfully appropriated treasured gift and symbol of a relationship. It may, however, also be perceived as the embodiment of one's own inferiority and the uncle's eternal presence. Our hope is that the insights offered here will help pre-owners, recipients of hand-me-downs, and others to move the practice closer to its potential.

REFERENCES

Argo, J. J., Dahl, D. W., & Morales, A. C. (2006). Consumer contamination: How consumers react to products touched by others. *Journal of Marketing, 70*(2), 81–94.

Armstrong Soule, C. A., & Sekhon, T. S. (2022). Signaling nothing: Motivating the masses with status signals that encourage anti-consumption. *Journal of Macromarketing, 42*(2), 308–325.

Bardhi, F., & Eckhardt, G. M. (2012). Access-based consumption: The case of car sharing. *Journal of Consumer Research, 39*, 881–898.

Baxter, W. L. (2017). *Designing circular possessions: Exploring human–object relationships in the circular economy* [Unpublished dissertation]. Imperial College, London. https://spiral.imperial.ac.uk/bitstream/10044/1/52779/1/Baxter-W-2017-PhD-Thesis.pdf

Belk, R. (1988). Possessions and the extended self. *Journal of Consumer Research, 15*(2), 139–168.

Brasel, S. A., & Gips, J. (2014). Tablets, touchscreens, and touchpads: How varying touch interfaces trigger psychological ownership and endowment. *Journal of Consumer Psychology, 24*(2), 226–233.

Cambridge University Press. (n.d.). Pre-owned. In *Cambridge dictionary online.* Retrieved January 30, 2023, from https://dictionary.cambridge.org/de/worterbuch/englisch/pre-owned

Collins. (n.d.). Hand-me-down. In *Collins dictionary.* Retrieved January 30, 2023, from https://www.collinsdictionary.com/de/worterbuch/englisch/hand-me-down

Ertz, M., Durif, F., & Arcand, M. (2016). Collaborative consumption: Conceptual snap-shot at a buzzword. *Journal of Entrepreneurship Education, 19*(2), 1–23.

Ferraro, C., Sands, S., & Brace-Govan, J. (2016). The role of fashionability in second-hand shopping motivations. *Journal of Retailing and Consumer Services, 32*, 262–268.

Fraser, J. (1922). *The golden bough: A study of magic and religion*. Macmillan.

Fuchs, C., Prandelli, E., & Schreier, M. (2010). The psychological effects of empower-ment strategies on consumers' product demand. *Journal of Marketing, 74*(1), 65–79.

Greenpeace. (2015, March). *Saubere Mode hat's schwer: Repräsentative Greenpeace-Umfrage beleuchtet Modekonsum von Jugendlichen.* https:// www .greenpeace.de/sites/www.greenpeace.de/files/publications/mode-unter-jugendlichen -greenpeace-umfrage_zusammenfassung_1.pdf

Guiot, D., & Roux, D. (2010). A second-hand shoppers' motivation scale: Antecedents, consequences, and implications for retailers. *Journal of Retailing, 86*(4), 355–371.

Harper Collins. (1995). Hand-me-down. In *Harper Collins German dictionary* (2nd ed., p. 221). Harper Collins Publishers.

Harper Collins. (n.d.). Secondhand. In *Collins dictionary*. Retrieved January 30, 2023, from https://www.collinsdictionary.com/de/worterbuch/englisch/secondhand

Jussila, I., Tarkiainen, A., Sarstedt, M., & Hair, J. F. (2015). Individual psychological ownership: Concepts, evidence, and implications for research in marketing. *Journal of Marketing Theory and Practice, 23*(2), 121–139.

Kamleitner, B. (2018). Besitzend und Besessen – Konsum und Besitz vor dem Hintergrund bröckelnder Subjekt-Objekt-Grenzen. In P. Kenning & J. Lamla (Eds.), *Entgrenzungen des Konsums* (pp. 109–127). Springer.

Kamleitner, B., & Erki, B. (2013). Payment method and perceptions of ownership. *Marketing Letters, 24*(1), 57–69.

Kamleitner, B., & Feuchtl, S. (2015). "As if it were mine": Imagery works by induc-ing psychological ownership. *Journal of Marketing Theory and Practice, 23*(2), 208–223.

Kamleitner, B., & Mitchell, V.-W. (2018). Can consumers experience ownership for their personal data? From issues of scope and invisibility to agents handling our digital blueprints. In J. Peck & S. B. Shu (Eds.), *Psychological ownership and con-sumer behavior* (pp. 91–118). Springer.

Kamleitner, B., & Rabinovich, A. (2010). Mine versus our: Does it matter? In M. C. Campbell, J. Inman, & R. Pieters (Eds.), *Advances in consumer research* (Vol. 37, pp. 87–88). Association for Consumer Research.

Kanngiesser, P., Itakura, S., & Hood, B. M. (2014). The effect of labour on ownership decisions in two cultures: Developmental evidence from Japan and the United Kingdom. *British Journal of Developmental Psychology, 32*(3), 320–329.

Kirk, C. P., Peck, J., & Swain, S. D. (2018). Property lines in the mind: Consumers' psychological ownership and their territorial responses. *Journal of Consumer Research, 45*(1), 148–168.

Kokkoris, M. D., Hoelzl, E., & Kamleitner, B. (2020). Self-found, spellbound: The sense of own discovery shapes customer bonds with service venues. *Journal of Business Research, 113*, 303–316.

Laitala, K., & Klepp, I. G. (2018). Motivations for and against second-hand clothing acquisition. *Clothing Cultures, 5*(2), 247–262.

Lamberton, C. (2016). Collaborative consumption: A goal-based framework. *Current Opinion in Psychology, 10*, 55–59.

Lurie, A. (1981). *The language of clothes*. Random House.

M.core. (2022, February). *Im Fokus report*. Wirtschaftsuniversität Wien. https://www.wu.ac.at/fileadmin/wu/d/i/mcore/5_Forschung/4_Im_Fokus/ImFokus_Report_Februar_2022.pdf

McDowell, E. (2020, June 30). 8 fashion trends that Gen Z loves and Baby Boomers will never understand. *Insider*. https://www.insider.com/gen-z-fashion-trends-that-baby-boomers-will-never-understand-2020-6

Miller, R. J., & Brannon, L. A. (2021). Pursuing premium: Comparing pre-owned versus new durable markets. *Journal of Product & Brand Management, 30*(1), 2–16.

Nemeroff, C. J. (1995). Magical thinking about illness virulence: Conceptions of germs from "safe" versus "dangerous" others. *Health Psychology Journal, 14*, 147–151.

Nemeroff, C., & Rozin, P. (1994). The contagion concept in adult thinking in the United States: Transmission of germs and of interpersonal influence. *Ethos, 22*(2), 158–186.

Newman, G. E., Diesendruck, G., & Bloom, P. (2011). Celebrity contagion and the value of objects. *Journal of Consumer Research, 38*(2), 215–228.

Padmavathy, C., Swapana, M., & Paul, J. (2019). Online second-hand shopping motivation: Conceptualization, scale development, and validation. *Journal of Retailing and Consumer Services, 51*, 19–32.

Peck, J., & Luangrath, A. W. (2023). A review and future avenues for psychological ownership in consumer research. *Consumer Psychology Review, 6*(1), 52–74.

Peck, J., & Shu, S. B. (2009). The effect of mere touch on perceived ownership. *Journal of Consumer Research, 36*, 434–447.

Peck, J., & Shu, S. B. (Eds.). (2018). *Psychological ownership and consumer behavior*. Springer.

Pierce, J. L., Kostova, T., & Dirks, K. T. (2001). Toward a theory of psychological ownership in organizations. *Academy of Management Review, 26*(2), 298–310.

Pierce, J. L., Kostova, T., & Dirks, K. T. (2003). The state of psychological ownership: Integrating and extending a century of research. *Review of General Psychology, 7*(1), 84–107.

Reb, J., & Connolly, T. (2007). Ownership, feelings of ownership, and the endowment effect. *Judgment and Decision Making, 2*, 107–114.

Richins, M. L. (1994). Special possessions and the expression of material values. *Journal of Consumer Research, 21*(3), 522–533.

Roux, D., & Korchia, M. (2006). Am I what I wear? An exploratory study of symbolic meanings associated with secondhand clothing. *Advances in Consumer Research, 33*, 29–35.

Rozin, P., Haddad, B., Nemeroff, C., & Slovic, P. (2015). Psychological aspects of the rejection of recycled water: Contamination, purification and disgust. *Judgment and Decision Making, 10*(1), 50–63.

Solomon, M. R. (2017). *Consumer behavior: Buying, having, and being*. Pearson.

Styvén, M. E., & Mariani, M. M. (2020). Understanding the intention to buy secondhand clothing on sharing economy platforms: The influence of sustainability, distance from the consumption system, and economic motivations. *Psychology & Marketing, 37*, 724–739.

Turunen, L. L. M., & Leipämaa-Leskinen, H. (2015). Pre-loved luxury: Identifying the meanings of second-hand luxury possessions. *Journal of Product & Brand Management, 24*(1), 57–65.

Yan, R., Bae, S. Y., & Xu, H. (2015). Second-hand clothing shopping among college students: The role of psychographic characteristics. *Young Consumers, 16*(1), 85–98.

PART IV

CC platforms and branded efforts

10. Branded resale apparel programs: a response to collaborative consumption

Meegan Feori-Payne, Rebeca Perren, and Stephanie J. Lawson

INTRODUCTION

The resale of apparel has a long and well-established history. Driven by the pressures of changing fashions and styles and the inherent value of textiles, exchanges of secondhand clothes were common during the Renaissance and the 18th century (Tortola & Marcketti, 2021). These pressures continue in contemporary life, causing consumers to seek alternative means of acquiring clothing, including renting, swapping, or reselling (Park & Armstrong, 2017). This shift saw secondhand apparel overcoming negative perceptions and transforming from a stigmatized category into an expression of rebellion and individualism (Le Zotte, 2017). The ramifications of new owners' psychological ownership of pre-owned products are further examined by Ruckelshausen and Kamleitner (Chapter 9, this book). In today's digital age, those engaging in the resale of secondhand apparel have embraced new platforms like eBay and Depop, leading to a projected increase in potential resale revenue. Estimates suggest this market could grow from $15 billion in 2022 to $47 billion by 2025 (ThredUP, 2022). Brands not engaging in branded resale apparel programs risk missing out on significant gains.

In this evolving landscape, apparel brands have begun to explore several interrelated concepts, such as collaborative consumption and the circular economy, to enhance their business models. Collaborative consumption, as Belk (2014) articulates, involves "people coordinating the acquisition and distribution of a resource for a fee or other compensation" (p. 1597). This concept extends beyond mere peer-to-peer exchanges to include transactions between businesses and consumers and those facilitated by third-party platforms (Henninger et al., 2021; Perren & Kozinets, 2018). Arrigo's (2021) taxonomy in the fashion industry differentiates between consumer-led and business-led modes of collaborative consumption, considering compensation, consumption modes, and whether value arises from "utility-based" or "redistributed ownership."

Collaborative apparel business models, often viewed as innovative, are posited to support a circular economy—an economic system that aspires to minimize waste and optimize resource use (Dissanayake & Weerasinghe, 2022). These business models are viewed as more sustainable because they foster waste reduction by extending product use and preventing premature disposal (Henninger et al., 2021). In this context, branded resale apparel programs, where brands enable the resale of their secondhand items, incorporate elements of both collaborative consumption and the circular economy. However, we argue that these programs are primarily strategic responses to the burgeoning trend of collaborative consumption, aiming to maintain customer engagement, create new revenue streams, and adapt to market shifts. While motivations for consumers to divest clothing and acquire pre-owned fashion have been examined (e.g., Albinsson & Perera, 2009; Styvén & Mariani, 2020), a significant gap remains in research providing strategic guidance for apparel brands navigating the resale market.

This chapter explores the variations of branded resale programs within the apparel sector and proposes a typology of such offerings. We present our analysis of three key industry cases—Patagonia, Inc., Clare V., and Alexander McQueen—each of which illustrates a unique approach to resale channels. These cases represent different categories and price points: outdoor apparel, prêt-à-porter or ready-to-wear, and luxury, respectively. Patagonia, for instance, provides insights into how an outdoor apparel brand can leverage its commitment to sustainability in its resale program. Clare V. demonstrates how a ready-to-wear brand can engage its customer base through a peer-to-peer platform, while Alexander McQueen offers a perspective on how luxury brands can maintain their exclusivity while participating in the resale market. The chapter concludes with a discussion of the implications of our findings and suggestions for future research.

As brands seek to take advantage of the emerging resale trend, a better understanding of the business models in use, their opportunities, and challenges is essential. This study is significant not only for its potential to guide brands in capitalizing on the resale market but also for its implications for consumer behavior, such as encouraging sustainable consumption practices and the potential environmental benefits of extending the life cycle of apparel. Further research could build on our proposed typology of branded resale apparel programs and their critical factors by empirically examining the impacts of these programs on brand performance and sustainability metrics.

BACKGROUND

Resale Market and Challenges for Apparel Brands

Historically, apparel brands have hesitated to associate with resale market-places due to concerns over brand dilution, lack of control over the brand's representation, and the absence of resale profits (Berns et al., 2021). However, they have come to realize that, regardless of their stance, their merchandise will inevitably find its way into these resale markets. When customers opt for resale through third-party vendors or peer-to-peer transactions with no brand involvement, there is a risk of brand switching, product experimentation, and a potential loss of connection with the original brand. Yet, many brands that have introduced resale programs report increased conversion rates, enhanced customer loyalty, and improved control over their products (Verdon, 2022).

According to McKinsey and Business of Fashion (2022), the resale market presents an opportunity for apparel brands to offer consumers an affordable and responsible option. Resale marketplaces recognize the essential role of customer demand for authenticity in building trust and driving growth. With their ability to authenticate pre-owned products, brands have a distinct advantage in fostering this trust. Industry forecasts predict that the resale market will grow 11 to 16 times faster than the retail sector over the next three years (McKinsey and Business of Fashion, 2022; ThredUP, 2022). The number of branded resale apparel programs has proliferated, increasing from a handful in 2019 to over 100 in 2022 (ThredUP, n.d.). Despite these developments, apparel brands face unique challenges when entering the secondhand market, such as managing the receiving, tracking, and inventory of used clothing. Consequently, these brands are tasked with finding effective strategies to participate in the burgeoning resale market.

Resale-as-a-Service: A Solution for Brands

In response to these challenges and opportunities, a new group of technology companies has emerged, offering "Resale-as-a-Service" (RaaS) solutions. RaaS refers to a business model where technology companies provide mar-ketplace technology and services to help brands manage various aspects of the resale process, including receiving, tracking, and inventorying used clothing, among other logistics and fulfillment services (Owens, 2023).

RaaS solutions simplify fashion retail customers' process of reselling and recycling previously purchased garments. These platforms offer features that integrate resale with existing e-commerce, such as dynamic pricing (which adjusts prices based on market demand), listing review (which ensures the quality and authenticity of listed products), loyalty program integration (which rewards customers for their participation in the resale program), and bulk listing (which allows multiple products to be listed at once). Some also offer reverse logistics or fulfillment services. Most RaaS platforms provide a branded resale marketplace—an e-commerce site that embodies the brand's look and feel, often called a "re-commerce" site (Verdon, 2022). These marketplaces can be standalone or integrated into the brand's primary e-commerce site. They often facilitate peer-to-peer sales, where customers can list items on a custom storefront with pre-populated product information and images and ship directly to the buyer upon a sale.

Facilitating "take-back" programs for merchandise is another crucial aspect of RaaS platforms (Martin, 2022). These white-label technologies provide brands with pre-constructed apps for in-store or mail-in trade-ins of used products, enabling easy tracking and credit issuance for future purchases. Used items are sent to a fulfillment partner for resale preparation, which may also provide warehouse management systems to manage resale-specific SKU and inventory operations such as sorting, identification, cleaning, repair, photography, pricing, order fulfillment, and returns handling.

Brands seeking to enter the resale space can also benefit from additional services offered by RaaS providers. These services include integration with repair, upcycling, and recycling partners or collaborations with non-profit organizations to facilitate clothing donations. A prime example is the luxury e-commerce platform Farfetch. It partnered with ThredUP to allow consumers to donate their unworn clothes and shoes in exchange for Farfetch credits while supporting a charity (Edelson, 2022). In conclusion, the rise of the resale market presents both challenges and opportunities for apparel brands. RaaS platforms and other innovative solutions offer effective strategies for brands to participate in the resale market and reap its benefits. As the resale market grows, brands that adapt and innovate will be best positioned to succeed.

METHOD

To comprehensively analyze three critical cases of branded resale programs, we employed a netnographic case study approach (Hancock & Algozzine, 2017; Kozinets, 2002; Yin, 2009). Our exploration involved observing and analyzing these branded resale apparel programs, through which we discerned three principal strategies: centralized brand-owned resale programs, brand-hosted peer-to-peer platforms, and partnerships with third-party marketplaces. The sources of netnography included online user interactions, branding communications, and marketing efforts on these resale platforms. These data were supplemented with information from popular press features about the three branded resale programs.

The case selection was guided by the uniqueness of each brand's approach to resale programs and their representation of different market segments. This offered a comprehensive view of the branded resale landscape. Due to the evolving nature of these programs, an inductive qualitative approach was adopted. This approach, valuing adaptability and recognizing the "messiness" of research, focused on reflexive thinking and viewing research as an unbounded, fluid crafting process (Lugosi & Quinton, 2018).

Our analysis, informed by Thomas's (2011) case study typology, followed a multiple parallel case design. Comparing and contrasting the three resale programs during the analysis stage allowed us to identify recurring patterns and themes, thereby contributing to theory building. To ensure unbiased results, each author independently analyzed the data before comparing findings. Any discrepancies were thoroughly discussed until a consensus was reached, ensuring the robustness of our analysis.

FINDINGS AND DISCUSSION

No one resale model fits all brands. Within the typology of branded resale apparel programs, we observe three main approaches: centralized brand-owned resale programs, brand-hosted peer-to-peer platforms, and partnerships with third-party marketplaces. Centralized brand-owned resale programs deploy white-label technologies that integrate seamlessly with their e-commerce platforms. These branded storefronts integrate with existing channels and operations, and customers are virtually unable to distinguish whether they are dealing with the brand directly or with a provider that may be assisting with operational aspects of the resale, such as photography, item listing, packaging, storage, shipping, and so on. In contrast, branded-hosted resale platforms are transparent in that customers shop directly from other customers' belongings. Although the brand may offer some trust layers such as authentication, review, and handling of payment, these marketplaces often have features that embed humanity into the transactions, such as the ability to add commentary to posts (e.g., your favorite occasion to wear a dress or how your daughter loved to jump puddles in those rain boots). In this type of platform, resellers ship directly to the buyer, and the brand involvement is limited. Lastly, some luxury brands are partnering with third-party marketplaces and creating exclusively curated selections for shoppers. This model creates some distance between mainstream buyers and resale shoppers while preserving the sense of exclusivity. It can also be deployed selectively without "going all in" on resale. It has a feel of a pop-up shop—but more brands are signing up to test the waters. The next three cases that we present illustrate the typology of branded resale apparel programs.

Centralized Brand-Owned Resale Program Case: Worn Wear Program of Patagonia, Inc.

Patagonia, Inc., has pioneered the concept of branded resale. In 2005, Patagonia began its branded resale program, Worn Wear, as a standalone blog. The Worn Wear program has since evolved into a comprehensive effort that takes back, repairs, resales, and recycles products (Martin, 2022). It includes a digital re-commerce site, experiential events, and social media engagement. The program continues to grow in the face of challenges and opportunities, leading the way in branded resale. It is an exemplar of the business model we deem a centralized brand-owned resale program.

From the Patagonia e-commerce site, you are seamlessly redirected to the Worn Wear program re-commerce site. Trove is responsible for the site's logistics, technology, and program management while maintaining brand integrity (London, 2019). Worn Wear product offerings are currently seg-mented into three categories: ReCrafted Collection, Seconds Collection, and (Im)Perfectly Patched. The ReCrafted Collection consists of deconstructed apparel products that customers traded in and refashioned into unique remade products. It sells for more than an inline product due to its unique nature. The Seconds Collection offers a product with an aesthetic flaw, such as an inaccurate logo or wrong material color; however, functionality is not compro-mised. The bulk of the products sold on the Worn Wear site are (Im)Perfectly Patched—used Patagonia clothing traded in by mail or to retail locations (Worn Wear Patagonia, 2023). The Seconds Collection and (Im)Perfectly Patched sell for significantly less than an inline product. Worn Wear products can appeal to thrifty parents, aspiring customers who need help to afford new Patagonia items, and sustainably minded individuals (London, 2019).

Through its Worn Wear program, Patagonia fosters experiences and engagements with its brand, building a sense of community. The product can be traded in via mail or at Patagonia retail locations (Worn Wear Patagonia, 2023). Customers are encouraged to share their experiences with the item, an adaptation of Patagonia's Stories We Wear blog. The blog, hosted on Tumblr and pushed to other social platforms such as Instagram, details the adventures and antics of customers wearing, repairing, and passing garments to others. The themes within the blog (e.g., marking a turning point, expressing emotional attachment, and anthropomorphizing) offer rich user-generated content that is valuable for building marketing messages (Michel et al., 2019). Patagonia reinforces brand identity and fosters community through the mes-sages collected when trading in items and the blog. The re-commerce site and social engagement are augmented by experiential events where apparel items are repaired. Patagonia's Worn Wear program offers consumers a mediated collaborative consumption experience that furthers brand objectives.

Brand-Hosted Peer-to-Peer Platform Case: Clare V.

Clare V., a prêt-à-porter (ready-to-wear) brand founded by Clare Vivier in 2008, is known for its French-inspired design aesthetic with products ranging from $40 to $500 (Nachbar, 2019). The company's merchandise is manufactured in Los Angeles, California, and sold across multiple channels including online, department stores, and specialty boutiques (Clare V., n.d.). Clare V. shifted its retail strategy to meet the growing demand for resale by opening a brand-hosted peer-to-peer re-commerce site, "Le Resale," in February 2022. Recurate is the RaaS platform behind Clare V. Le Resale offers customized services, including peer-to-peer resale, take-back programs, and brand supply (e.g., returns, sales of imperfect items, and order fulfillment). Recurate partners with several brands, including Frye and Badgley Mischka, to facilitate branded resale programs that meet consumer demand and corporate sustainability efforts (Recurate, n.d.).

Presented as a "Peer-to-Peer Marketplace for Preloved Clare V.," consumers can purchase items from past seasons or trade in their pre-owned Clare V. products for 100 percent store credit. Le Resale items are shipped peer-to-peer. Unlike Patagonia's Worn Wear program, the brand does not collect, clean, or inspect for quality. All items are final sales, with customer service issues handled by Recurate's support team (Clare V., n.d.). "Preloved" items on the re-commerce site are listed with commentary from the product owners, such as "Absolutely love this hoodie, but I am parting with it to make room in my closet! Super fun print that I've dressed up or down!" They are also clearly labeled: "Le Resale items are fulfilled by the community" (Clare V., n.d.).

Although Clare V. items are frequently resold on various third-party resale marketplaces, the launch of Le Resale allows the company to utilize its brand and create a sense of community through resale. In contrast to Patagonia's approach, brand-hosted peer-to-peer platforms enable companies to participate with minimal investment or participation in the process, making it a viable choice for companies with constrained resources or that are hesitant to invest heavily in this channel.

Partnership with Third-party Marketplace Case: Alexander McQueen

Alexander McQueen is a renowned luxury fashion brand founded by the late British designer of the same name. The designs are innovative and daring, often inspired by art, music, and culture. They boast a luxurious and edgy aesthetic, which has earned them numerous awards, including British Designer of the Year. Now owned by the French luxury fashion house Kering, Alexander McQueen remains a leader in the fashion industry. The brand was the first to partner with Vestiaire Collective, a third-party re-commerce site connecting luxury fashion fans with pre-owned designer items. In 2021, it launched its "Brand Approved" program, starting with Alexander McQueen as a partner, which allows its clients to receive store credit for secondhand items verified by the brand (Webb, 2022). Sales representatives selected clients to participate, evaluated their items, and assigned a buy-back price if eligible. This case exemplifies how high-end luxury brands can find ways to engage in resale by partnering with a third-party marketplace.

There are several advantages to the approach that Alexander McQueen took to engage in resale. First, Vestiaire Collective already has customers purchasing and selling secondhand products. Although the brand directly contacted its customers to invite sales of pre-owned products, the partnership opened the doors to new potential customers of high-end luxury apparel (Chen, 2021). This partnership allowed the brand to try resale with minimal investment and at a distance—the shopping experience was separated from its normal operations. Moreover, the temporary nature of the event helped the brand maintain its sense of exclusivity. Resale programs can reinforce the idea that luxury goods are a worthwhile investment, preserving their quality, tradition, and exclusiveness. In the resale market, customers can find vintage treasures, limited-edition pieces, and collector's items that maintain their original value, sometimes even selling for more than their original retail price. This highlights the enduring value of luxury items designed to withstand the test of time, and encourages consumers to adopt a "buy less, buy better" philosophy, extending the life cycle of these products. Finally, participating in the authentication process allowed new opportunities to engage with customers via digital IDs. The Alexander McQueen "Brand Approved" program included digital IDs with NFC tags on items. By tapping the digital tag with a smartphone, consumers accessed authentication information and viewed exclusive content about the item and the brand (Brand Approved: Alexander McQueen, n.d.). Beyond authenticating the item, Alexander McQueen could provide exclusive content to consumers that tells them more about the specific item and the brand. In return, the brand can collect real-time, first-party data on how and where these items were used. The brand could also use the experience to stay connected with the consumer—either in the experience directly or by collecting contact information to keep the conversation going on other channels—which can result in upselling related items through a long-term relationship.

Kering—the luxury conglomerate that owns Gucci, Balenciaga, and Alexander McQueen—acquired a 5 percent stake in Vestiaire Collective (Webb, 2022). This collaborative move signals the changing landscape of secondhand luxury goods. While information regarding the financial success of the Alexander McQueen resale program is limited, Kering's investment in Vestiaire Collective signals its belief in the resale potential of luxury brands. This case illustrates a model for high-end luxury brands that want to create curated experiences distinct from those offered to their mainstream customers. This model, a partnership with a third-party marketplace, offers the benefits of short duration, exclusivity, and the ability to customize the experience. It also has great potential to cut down on counterfeits.

FACTORS OF BRANDED RESALE APPAREL PROGRAMS

Our analysis identified three key approaches to branded resale apparel programs: centralized brand-owned program, brand-hosted peer-to-peer platform, and partnership with a third party. Based on this, we propose ten critical factors that warrant further exploration by researchers and careful consideration by brands aiming to launch a resale program. These factors encompass business relationship models, inventory management, RaaS technology visibility, pricing control, quality assurance, risk to brand image, trust facilitation, platform accessibility, consumer engagement, and sustainability considerations. We provide a summary of these elements in Table 10.1.

In exploring the intricacies of branded resale apparel programs, we uncover the unique relationships at their core. For instance, brand-owned models, exemplified by brands like Patagonia, prioritize brand–customer relationships, forming a dyad. In contrast, the brand-hosted model cultivates a triadic relationship where the brand enables peer-to-peer exchanges, while third-party models authenticate these peer-to-peer exchanges.

Shifting our focus to inventory management, we note the distinctive approaches taken by different models. Centralized brand-owned resale programs manage inventory with the assistance of RaaS providers, while brand-hosted peer-to-peer platforms delegate this task to individual sellers. In third-party partnership models, the third-party marketplace handles inventory management. RaaS's visibility to consumers differs between models. In the brand-owned model, its role is largely invisible, compared to the brand-hosted and third-party models, where RaaS's role is more apparent.

As brands contemplate entering the resale market, they must weigh various tactical factors that could potentially affect their strategic direction and, by extension, the brand's image. Centralized brand-owned platforms afford brands the authority to set pricing and implement strict quality control measures. However, this model poses the most significant risk to the brand image for several reasons. First, brands are fully responsible for quality control; any lapse allowing a faulty or counterfeit product to reach the customer can harm the brand's reputation. Second, the brand assumes complete ownership of the customer experience, spanning from the platform's user interface to customer service, order fulfillment, and returns. Any missteps here can lead to customer dissatisfaction and subsequent damage to the brand image. Third, the brand's

Table 10.1   *Critical factors for branded resale apparel programs*

Type	Centralized Brand-Owned Program	Brand-Hosted Peer-to-Peer Platform	Partnership with Third-Party Marketplace
Case	Patagonia	Clare V.	Alexander McQueen
Relationships in Business Model	Dyad: brand–customer relationships are central to the exchanges	Triad: brand enables peer-to-peer exchanges	Tetrad: brand authenticates peer-to-peer exchanges facilitated by the third party
Inventory Management & Logistics	Brand/RaaS	Sellers (peers)/RaaS	Third-party marketplace/ RaaS
RaaS Visibility to Consumer	Invisible	Visible	Depends on third party
Pricing Control	Brand controls pricing	Seller controls pricing	Can vary; could be dictated by the market on the third-party platform
Quality Assurance	Brand/RaaS determine quality control measures	Rely on seller honesty and buyer reviews	As an authenticator, the brand can determine quality control measures (e.g., "Brand Approved")
Risk to Brand Image/Control	Highest	Intermediate	Intermediate
Facilitating Trust Among Consumers	Brand-backed assurances like returns and guarantees	The resale platform must provide a mechanism to facilitate trust among peers	The brand authenticates product originality and value (e.g., digital IDs, NFC tags, etc.)
Access	Integrated into the brand's digital assets	Accessed from the brand's digital assets but hosted separately	Not accessed from the brand's digital assets; the resale platform is not affiliated with the main brand

Type	Centralized Brand-Owned Program	Brand-Hosted Peer-to-Peer Platform	Partnership with Third-Party Marketplace
Consumer Engagement and Community Building	Limited: interactions among consumers are mediated by brand	Higher: consumers act as service providers handling the listing, commenting on products, shipping, and so on	Varies depending on how the partnership is executed
Sustainability Considerations	Potential to promote circularity in fashion, reducing the environmental impact of production and waste disposal; offers the most flexibility to integrate with other sales channels, increasing adoption and scale	Lower carbon emissions by bypassing centralized handling of merchandise, but may have a smaller scale due to fewer choices and inconsistent quality	The impact may be limited if only deployed occasionally, and the environmental impact of shipping and logistics would depend on the third-party platform

control over pricing can be a double-edged sword; overpricing may drive customers away, while underpricing can undervalue the brand's new products. Lastly, inventory management and sustainability claims pose additional risks.

Conversely, brand-hosted peer-to-peer models and third-party partnerships limit the brand's control, presenting an intermediate level of risk to the brand image. These models incorporate unique strategies to cultivate consumer trust and engagement. For instance, brand-owned models like Patagonia offer brand-backed assurances, while brand-hosted models rely on platform mechanisms to foster trust. Third-party models leverage the brand's authenticity to engender trust.

Consumer access and engagement vary across models. Brand-owned models, while offering limited avenues for consumer interaction, seamlessly integrate with the brand's digital assets. Brand-hosted peer-to-peer models, though hosted separately, facilitate more consumer interaction. In contrast, third-party models provide a clear separation between retail and resale channels, with the level of consumer interaction contingent on the third-party platform's structure.

Sustainability implications also differ across models. Brand-owned models have more flexibility to foster a circular economy in fashion, extending the life cycle of apparel and providing the brand added opportunity to reduce its environmental impact. Because the platform is integrated seamlessly with other sales channels, it can reach new audiences that traditionally have not considered resale, increasing the scalability of its impact. However, logistics related to shipping items between consumers and the brand may increase carbon emissions. In contrast, brand-hosted peer-to-peer platforms offer lower carbon emissions potential, particularly for local transactions, as users directly handle reselling and shipping processes. Nevertheless, this model's limited control over resold items could result in product quality and sustainability variations. Partnering with third-party platforms allows brands to engage in the circular economy without significant investment in their own resale platforms. This model potentially reaches a broader consumer base and extends product life cycles but has the environmental impact of shipping and logistics, as well as the quality of resold items, contingent on the practices of the third-party platform.

To conclude, a branded resale apparel program's structure is adaptable to a brand's specific objectives. The brand can choose a high level of involvement and control, as seen in brand-owned models, or a lesser degree of involvement and distance from the main brand, as observed in third-party partnerships. Crucial considerations include consumer collaboration, additional technologies, and sustainability support. When implementing a branded resale apparel program, a brand should carefully evaluate these ten critical factors to align with its business goals.

OPPORTUNITIES AND CHALLENGES

The case studies illustrate that branded resale offers opportunities for apparel brands looking to penetrate the rapidly expanding collaborative consumption sector. These opportunities include the creation of new revenue streams, the strengthening of customer relationships, the preservation of brand reputation, and the demonstration of a commitment to sustainability. Furthermore, brand-owned resale platforms yield valuable consumer behavior data, facilitating informed business decisions.

Successful implementations of branded resale apparel programs can vary according to strategic goals. For instance, Reflaunt offers a modular and customizable RaaS system, enabling brand partners to develop their own resale offerings. Balenciaga and Net-a-Porter provide services for customers to have items collected from their homes listed and sold via multiple third-party external marketplaces. In contrast, H&M operates a peer-to-peer model through its brand-hosted online platform, allowing customers to buy and sell items, even from other brands. Ganni provides a blended model of resale, rental, and outlet sales (Webb, 2022), allowing customers to trade in pre-owned items for store credit, try rental products, and purchase older season stock, all while offering the option to buy and sell pre-owned Ganni products through the brand's Reflaunt-powered resale marketplace. Following a successful sale, sellers can either cash in the proceeds or receive an additional 20 percent credit for use on the brand's e-commerce site. As numerous brand-sponsored resale options are available, it is imperative for a brand to not only embrace resale but do so in alignment with its strategic goals.

While branded resale apparel programs offer many opportunities, they are not without challenges. Brands must grapple with the need to protect their reputation, competition with third-party resale platforms, and significant marketing and customer engagement investments. In addition, navigating the complexities of logistics and operations is a daunting task. To safeguard their reputation, brands must implement rigorous quality control measures and accurately represent their products. However, these strategies require a substantial infrastructure, logistics, and marketing investment, which may be prohibitive for smaller brands.

Consumer attitudes toward secondhand goods present another challenge. While some consumers eagerly participate in the circular economy, others have reservations about the quality and value of secondhand items. Therefore, brands are responsible for educating consumers and building trust in their resale programs. Marketing strategies, such as collaborations with influencers or loyalty programs, can effectively attract and retain customers. Despite the significant challenges, the potential benefits of branded resale apparel programs—increased customer loyalty, new revenue streams, and enhanced sustainability—make them an attractive proposition for fashion brands.

While it is crucial to acknowledge these challenges, it is equally important to discuss potential strategies to overcome them. To protect their reputation, brands must ensure stringent quality control measures and accurate product representation. Brands can also distinguish themselves from third-party platforms by offering superior customer service and leveraging their brand story to create a unique and personalized shopping experience. Effective marketing strategies, such as collaborations with influencers or loyalty programs, can attract and retain customers.

In conclusion, while the challenges associated with branded resale apparel programs may appear daunting, the potential benefits of increased brand loyalty, new revenue streams, and enhanced sustainability make it an attractive proposition for brands. As technology and consumer attitudes evolve, brands must remain attentive to the various ways to integrate resale into existing channels and adapt accordingly. The future of branded resale looks promising, and it holds significant potential to revolutionize the fashion industry and promote sustainability.

LIMITATIONS, FUTURE DIRECTIONS, AND CONCLUSION

Our study, while providing valuable insights, is not without limitations. We have focused on online branded resale apparel platforms and have drawn from a limited number of cases. The phenomenon continues to evolve as brands explore innovative ways to respond to collaborative consumption. Future research could expand on our findings by examining a larger sample and employing in-depth qualitative and quantitative analysis. Despite these limitations, our study underscores the potential of branded resale apparel programs to promote the circular economy and revolutionize the fashion industry. As technology and consumer attitudes evolve, branded resale apparel programs will likely become more prevalent, offering brands new avenues for revenue, increased customer loyalty, and a more sustainable business model.

Emerging technologies, such as computer vision, artificial intelligence (AI)-informed dynamic pricing, and blockchain, are set to revolutionize the future of branded resale in the apparel industry. Computer vision, for instance, can authenticate pre-owned products, evaluate their condition, and streamline inventory management (Dersarkissian, 2023). Similarly, RaaS providers are developing AI-powered dynamic pricing tools to adjust resale prices based on variables like inventory status and website traffic data (Dersarkissian, 2023). Blockchain and non-fungible tokens (NFTs) offer another innovative approach for brands to verify the authenticity of trade-in items, thereby streamlining processes and conserving resources (McKinsey and Business of Fashion, 2021). Leading retailers, such as Nike, are already leveraging NFTs to create value for their brands by offering consumers exclusive access to deals and pre-sale events thereby fostering brand loyalty offline and in the digital realm of the metaverse (Saunders, 2022). An example of this is Nike's venture into NFT sneakers known as CryptoKicks, which showcases the potential of NFTs to enhance brand loyalty within digital communities (Brooks, 2022). By efficiently combining these technologies with insights into customer behavior and preferences, brands can offer personalized recommendations and significantly enhance customer experiences and engagement in branded resale apparel programs.

In conclusion, examining branded resale programs highlights the potential for apparel brands to respond to the growing trend of collaborative consumption. By creating a resale program that is both trusted and community driven, brands are presented with opportunities to generate additional revenue streams, foster increased brand loyalty, and gather valuable insights into consumer behavior. Despite the challenges and investments required for successful implementation, the prospects for branded resale apparel programs appear promising as technology and consumer attitudes continue to evolve to support this sustainable business model. As such, this chapter provides a valuable contribution to the ongoing academic discourse surrounding the application of circular economy principles in the fashion industry.

REFERENCES

Albinsson, P. A., & Perera, B. Y. (2009). From trash to treasure and beyond: The meaning of voluntary disposition. *Journal of Consumer Behaviour: An International Research Review, 8*(6), 340353. https://doi.org/10.1002/cb.301

Arrigo, E. (2021). Collaborative consumption in the fashion industry: A systematic literature review and conceptual framework. *Journal of Cleaner Production, 325,* 129261. https://doi.org/10.1016/j.jclepro.2021.129261

Belk, R. W. (2014). You are what you can access: Sharing and collaborative consumption online. *Journal of Business Research, 67*(8), 1595–1600. https:// doi .org/ 10 .1016/j.jbusres.2013.10.001

Berns, J., Brinckman, R., Cronin, I., & Murphy, N. (2021, June 15). *How digital authentication could drive a resale revolution for fashion.* World Economic Forum. https:// www.weforum.org/agenda/2021/06/how-digital-authentication-could-drive -a-resale-revolution-for-fashion/

Brand Approved: Alexander McQueen. (n.d.). Help Center. Retrieved June 14, 2023, from https://faq.vestiairecollective.com/hc/en-us/articles/360017709477-Brand -Approved-Alexander-McQueen

Brooks, K. J. (2022, April 28). *Nike's new NFT sneakers selling for more than $100 000.* CBS News. https://www.cbsnews.com/news/nike-cryptokicks-nft-blockchain -metaverse-rtfkt/

Chen, C. (2021, November 19). *Vestiaire Collective announces resale partnership with Alexander McQueen.* The Business of Fashion. https://www.businessoffashion .com/news/retail/vestiaire-collective-announces-resale-partnership-with-alexander -mcqueen/

Clare V. (n.d.). Home. Retrieved June 14, 2023, from https://www.clarev.com/

Dersarkissian, S. (2023, January 11). *The solution to ecommerce's free returns problem.* Trove. https://trove.com/emerging-retail-technology-trends/

Dissanayake, D. G. K., & Weerasinghe, D. (2022). Towards circular economy in fashion: Review of strategies, barriers and enablers. *Circular Economy and Sustainability, 2,* 25–45. https://doi.org/10.1007/s43615-021-00090-5

Edelson, S. (2022, April 12). Resale as a service provider and thrift market-place ThredUP scales up with PacSun. *Forbes.* https:// www .forbes .com/ sites/ sharonedelson/ 2022/ 04/ 11/ resale -as -a -service -provider -and -thrift -marketplace -thredup-scales-with-pacsun/?sh=6d0770734f4c

Hancock, D. R., & Algozzine, R. (2017). *Doing case study research: A practical guide for beginning researchers.* Teachers College Press.

Henninger, C. E., Brydges, T., Iran, S., & Vladimirova, K. (2021). Collaborative fashion consumption: A synthesis and future research agenda. *Journal of Cleaner Production, 319,* 128648. https://doi.org/10.1016/j.jclepro.2021.128648

Kozinets, R. V. (2002). The field behind the screen: Using netnography for marketing research in online communities. *Journal of Marketing Research, 39*(1), 61–72. https://doi.org/10.1509/jmkr.39.1.61.18935

Le Zotte, J. (2017). *From goodwill to grunge: A history of secondhand styles and alternative economies.* University of North Carolina Press.

London, S. (2019). *When you pick that pre-worn jacket, the environment wins too.* McKinsey Sustainability. https://www.mckinsey.com/capabilities/sustainability/our -insights/when-you-pick-that-pre-worn-jacket-the-environment-wins-too

Lugosi, P., & Quinton, S. (2018). More-than-human netnography. *Journal of Marketing Management*, *34*(3–4), 287–313. https://doi.org/10.1080/0267257X.2018 .1431303

Martin, K. (2022). Take-back programs are gaining steam. Do they actually work? *Sourcing Journal*. https://sourcingjournal.com/sustainability/sustainability-news/ fashion-take-back-apparel-recommerce-resale-recycling-patagonia-eileen-fisher -382218/

McKinsey and Business of Fashion. (2021). *The state of fashion 2022*. https://www .mckinsey.com/~/media/mckinsey/industries/retail/our%20insights/state%20of %20fashion/2022/the-state-of-fashion-2022.pdf

McKinsey and Business of Fashion. (2022). *The state of fashion 2023*. https://www .mckinsey.com/~/media/mckinsey/industries/retail/our%20insights/state%20of %20fashion/2023/the-state-of-fashion-2023-holding-onto-growth-as-global-clouds -gathers-vf.pdf

Michel, G. M., Feori, M., Damhorst, M. L., Lee, Y. A., & Niehm, L. S. (2019). Stories we wear: Promoting sustainability practices with the case of Patagonia. *Family and Consumer Sciences Research Journal*, *48*(2), 165–180.

Nachbar, M. (2019, January 10). All eyes on Clare V. *Minneapolis St. Paul Magazine*. https://mspmag.com/shop-and-style/all-eyes-on-clare-v/

Owens, B. (2023, May 4). *Resale as a Service (RaaS): Is it time for brands to invest?* Whiplash. https://whiplash.com/blog/resale-as-a-service/

Park, H., & Armstrong, C. M. J. (2017). Collaborative apparel consumption in the digital sharing economy: An agenda for academic inquiry. *International Journal of Consumer Studies*, *41*(5), 465–474. https://doi.org/10.1111/ijcs.12354

Perren, R., & Kozinets, R. V. (2018). Lateral exchange markets: How social platforms operate in a networked economy. *Journal of Marketing*, *82*(1), 20–36. https://doi.org/10.1509/jm.14.0250

Recurate. (n.d.). *Circular fashion is now*. https://www.recurate.com/overview/ circular-fashion-is-now

Saunders, B. (2022, January 6). *Balmain X Barbie NFT and Apparel Collection is a hot pink ode to fashion*. Hypebeast. https://hypebeast.com/2022/1/balmain -barbie-nft-apparel-collection-info

Styvén, M. E., & Mariani, M. M. (2020). Understanding the intention to buy secondhand clothing on sharing economy platforms: The influence of sustainability, distance from the consumption system, and economic motivations. *Psychology and Marketing*, *37*(5), 724–739. https://doi.org/10.1002/mar.21334

Thomas, G. (2011). A typology for the case study in social science following a review of definition, discourse, and structure. *Qualitative Inquiry*, *17*(6), 511–521. https:// doi.org/10.1177/1077800411409884

ThredUP. (2022). *ThredUP resale report 2022*. https://www.thredup.com/resale/#whos -thrifting-and-why

ThredUP. (n.d.). *ThredUP the recommerce 100*. https://www.recommerce100.com/

Tortola, P. G., & Marcketti, S. B. (2021). *Survey of historic costume*. Fairchild Books. http://dx.doi.org/10.5040/9781501337345

Verdon, J. (2022, July 7). *Secondhand surge: Inflation, product scarcity, and new tech platforms fuel resale market*. US Chamber of Commerce. https://www .uschamber.com/co/good-company/launch-pad/small-businesses-enter-the-resale -market

Webb, B. (2022, March 31). *Where fashion resale is headed in the next two years.* Vogue Business. https:// www .voguebusiness .com/ sustainability/ where -fashion -resale-is-headed-in-the-next-two-years-vestiaire-kering-balenciaga

Worn Wear Patagonia. (2023). *Better than new gear: Used to be awesome... and still is.* https://wornwear.patagonia.com/

Yin, R. K. (2009). *Case study research: Design and methods* (4th ed.). SAGE.

11. Collaborative consumption providers: examining the roles, classifications, and earnings of gig workers

Mark R. Gleim and Alexander Davidson

INTRODUCTION

Have you ever been transported in an Uber or Lyft? Had food delivered through DoorDash or Grubhub? Stayed in an Airbnb or Vrbo? These are just a few of the collaborative consumption platforms that rely on independent contractors, also known as gig workers, to perform the essential services that affect customer satisfaction. Gig workers typically provide the only human interaction that a consumer has with a collaborative consumption platform. The service experience provided by the gig worker shapes consumer perceptions of service quality and satisfaction and, thus, customer loyalty (Cronin et al., 2000; Gleim et al., 2019; Sureshchandar et al., 2002). Despite the important role gig workers play as frontline service providers, marketing research is often interested in studying the consumers utilizing the services rather than the workers performing them (e.g., Hamari et al., 2016; Stevens et al., 2023; Wirtz et al., 2019). Therefore, in this chapter, we explore how gig workers are instrumental in the collaborative consumption triad (which also includes platforms and consumers) and examine their roles, classifications, and earnings.

It is estimated there were approximately 70 million gig workers in the US in 2021 (Bose, 2021), and that number is expected to continue to grow as new forms of gig work emerge. The phenomenon of gig work is not new, but the proliferation of collaborative consumption platforms has enabled an on-demand labor market for service providers in a wide range of industries (Stanford, 2017). This workforce of freelance labor contributes more than a trillion dollars to the US economy annually as people are able to work full-time to earn a living or part-time to supplement their income (Kurter, 2019). TaskRabbit alone offers more than a hundred on-demand services that can be performed by its diverse stable of gig workers (TaskRabbit, 2022a).

Gig workers are considered "a labor market of ad hoc, short-term, freelance, or otherwise non-permanent jobs" (Gleim et al., 2019, p. 142). Despite their status as independent contractors and non-traditional employees, gig workers play a vitally important role as the customer-facing service providers for collaborative consumption platforms. The following sections examine the collaborative consumption triad, outline the unique role gig workers have as service providers for platforms, discuss the classification of gig work and how it differs from traditional employment, and examine individual- and platform-level factors that affect the earnings of gig workers.

THE COLLABORATIVE CONSUMPTION TRIAD

Collaborative consumption can be defined as a technologically enabled marketplace facilitating resource circulation through a third-party platform (Ertz et al., 2016; Gleim et al., 2023). For example, Airbnb is an online platform that functions as a third-party mediator between hosts and guests, facilitating the exchange of accommodations, payments, and reviews. As a result, a triadic relationship forms between the consumer (i.e., guest), gig worker (i.e., host), and platform (i.e., Airbnb) whereby consumers can simultaneously function as gig workers (i.e., a guest can also be a host; Ertz et al., 2018; Gleim et al., 2023). This triadic relationship distinguishes collaborative consumption from other marketplace platforms that facilitate resource exchange strictly between the platform and the consumer, removing the necessity for a gig worker. Better known as access-based consumption, such marketplaces (i.e., ZipCar, Rent the Runway) offer users temporary access to resources (i.e., cars, clothes) through their own inventory and not from individual workers. Therefore, gig workers play a specific and important role for collaborative consumption platforms but not access-based consumption platforms.

Figure 11.1 depicts the collaborative consumption triad (adopted from Gleim et al., 2023). In the middle, the platform (e.g., Uber) enables a marketplace whereby the gig worker (e.g., Uber driver) can make their services available in exchange for payment. Consumers (e.g., Uber passengers) search the platform through an algorithm, and once the vehicle type is selected and the gig worker provides the service (i.e., transporting the passenger), a payment is collected from the consumer by the platform. By acting as a mediator, a fee is absorbed by the platform and the remaining amount is transferred to the gig worker. While the triadic relationship exists across collaborative consumption platforms, the interactions among all actors may vary according to the needs of the marketplace. For example, on Airbnb, the consumers (i.e., Airbnb guests) are more selective in choosing the gig worker (i.e., Airbnb host and their accommodation) since the service being provided has a longer duration than an Uber ride and may therefore warrant more careful attention. For instance, consumers are less likely to accept staying in a dirty accommodation for one week compared to riding in a dirty car for 10 minutes. Platforms recognize the needs of their marketplaces as reflected in their use of review and rating practices and reputation systems (Eckhardt et al., 2019; Perren & Kozinets, 2018). When the service is shorter and temporary (e.g., Uber), consumers are asked to provide a numerical rating (from one to five stars) that summarizes their service experience with the gig worker. When the service is longer and less temporary (e.g., Airbnb), consumers are asked to provide several numerical ratings (i.e., location, communication, cleanliness, etc.) and a written review that summarizes a more detailed experience with the gig worker.

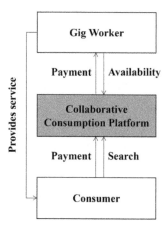

Figure 11.1   The collaboration consumption triad

The collaborative consumption triad represents the ongoing transformation and evolution of the firm–customer relationship (Benoit et al., 2017; Morrison & Robinson, 1997; Prahalad & Ramaswamy, 2000). While platforms create marketplaces, mediate payments, and facilitate service exchanges, they are largely absent from the process of creating transactional value for consumers, as this responsibility rests primarily with the gig worker. As such, conventional power dynamics between the firm and the customer shift as gig workers play an active role in the unconventional triadic relationship. Unlike the traditional service employee, the gig worker is largely autonomous in the deployment of their services and in the selection of which consumers to serve, which jobs to perform, and which platforms to work for. Similarly, this shift in power dynamics has also enabled consumers to be more selective in the types of services they receive, which gig workers they want to perform the service, and which platform they want to facilitate the service. As collaborative consumption and technologies continue to evolve, so will the power dynamics between platforms, consumers, and gig workers.

THE ROLES OF GIG WORKERS AS SERVICE PROVIDERS

As the face of collaborative consumption platforms, gig workers are the connection between the consumer and the platform and largely determine customer perceptions of quality and satisfaction (Singh et al., 2017). Consumers interact briefly with a collaborative consumption platform via a mobile app or website when seeking services; however, the bulk of the customer experience is based on the interaction with the gig worker. Given that customer satisfaction is an important driver of loyalty, repurchase intention, and customer commitment in a traditional service context (Abdul-Muhmin, 2005; Macintosh, 2007), gig workers play an important role as service providers (Dellaert, 2019; Wieland et al., 2017).

As independent service providers, gig workers are not restricted to working for a single collaborative consumption platform and often work for many of them. Several platforms have experienced an annual turnover rate of 500 percent (Kimberl, 2019), illustrating the lack of allegiance and commitment gig workers have to the platforms they work for. Combined with little interaction between gig workers, a strong organizational culture is likely limited among collaborative consumption platforms. This can be problematic in the long run as a strong organizational culture is considered essential to the consumer experience (Sundararajan, 2014, 2017).

Replacing the role of a strong organizational culture is the aforementioned review and rating practices which are designed to optimize consumer experiences. The use of a review- or rating-based reputation system helps to motivate gig workers to provide desirable and higher-quality service offerings (Newlands et al., 2019), as those with lower scores are less likely to be requested by consumers (Fagerstrøm et al., 2017; Pettersen, 2017). As such, the responsibility of providing service quality has shifted from traditional organizations emphasizing a strong culture to independent gig workers who are judged based on their review- and rating-based reputations (Davidson et al., 2023).

The growth of gig workers has consequently had an impact on service provision outside of collaborative consumption. As evidenced by the sentiment of Yelp reviews, consumers notice a drop off in service quality at restaurants as frontline workers leave to work for gig platforms (Shin et al., 2022). Thus, the ripple effect of gig workers' service provision is evident as they not only directly impact the consumers they interact with but have a more far-reaching impact on other marketplaces.

THE CLASSIFICATION OF GIG WORKERS

Despite being the face of collaborative consumption platforms, gig workers are not employees in a traditional sense but independent contractors. Gig workers are presented with distinct challenges and opportunities compared to traditional employment. While there is a mutuality of obligations found between traditional employees and the company they work for—wherein the employee has a set work schedule and pay rate provided by their employer (Davidov, 2005)—gig workers often do not have the financial consistency that comes from traditional employment, nor are they guaranteed insurance, social security benefits, overtime pay, or other benefits associated with traditional employment. As such, gig work has been described as "precarious work" due to the lack of stability compared to traditional employment (Quinlan, 2012).

There are five broad characteristics of gig work that are relevant not only to gig workers but to the platforms employing them (Stanford, 2017). First, the work is performed as needed or on demand, with no guarantee of continuous employment. Thus, an Uber driver only performs the service of driving a customer when it is requested in the mobile app. There is no guarantee that another ride will be requested. The lack of worker rights and protections has led several US states and the federal government to propose altering labor rules to better protect workers (Ivanova, 2022). However, an important benefit of not being a traditional employee is the amount of autonomy gig workers possess as they are able to determine their own hours and be employed by multiple collaborative consumption platforms at the same time, giving them the power to pick the one offering the highest pay at the time.

Second, gig workers "are paid for each discrete task or unit of output, not for their time" (Stanford, 2017, p. 384). For example, an Uber driver is only paid for driving a person to a specific location. The time it took to pick up the rider or make the trip is not compensated other than through the delivery fee. Providing a financial tip to gig workers is often encouraged, however, it is not required of consumers.

The third defining characteristic is that workers must supply their own assets (e.g., car, house, computer, tools) in addition to providing the service (Stanford, 2017). Airbnb hosts must have an available room or property to rent, Uber drivers must have a vehicle to transport passengers, and a TaskRabbit tasker must have the equipment needed to perform the tasks offered. This increases the investment and risk for the worker to provide the needed assets but reduces the financial burden on the platform. This business model has allowed Airbnb and Uber to expand much quicker than hotels or taxi companies.

The fourth characteristic of gig work is that the company facilitating the work is distinct from the consumer and worker (Stanford, 2017). All three parties are needed for an exchange to occur. Lastly, the platform acting as a digital intermediary is involved in the process of facilitating the transaction and payment between a gig worker and a consumer (Stanford, 2017). Prior to the digital revolution, intermediaries often helped facilitate work (e.g., newspaper, temporary employment agency, word-of-mouth recommendations). The inclusion of a digital intermediary has expanded the scale and scope of gig opportunities available. The Uber or Airbnb app or TaskRabbit website all enable the quick, convenient, and efficient matching of consumers with gig workers willing to provide a service for a fee. This enables a boundaryless matching of consumers seeking a service and workers with excess capacity available.

THE EARNINGS OF GIG WORKERS

Approximately one in six Americans have earned money from gig work as a means of generating extra income (Anderson et al., 2021). In this section, we first break down the individual-level factors followed by the platform-related factors that affect earnings among gig workers.

Individual-Level Factors

A majority of ride-share gig workers, both in the US and the UK, participate in collaborative consumption to supplement their household income. The flexibility of ridesharing enables many drivers to earn money on the side, with most working fewer than 10 hours per week and at the leisure of their own schedule. Ride-share earners are most likely to be in their 20s or 30s and from the bottom half of the income distribution (Anderson et al., 2021; Berger et al., 2019).

Earnings on home-sharing platforms, such as Airbnb, are typically higher than other types of gig work. For instance, hosts have the ability to leverage multiple assets as they can rent out an unlimited number of properties (Li et al., 2019; Schor et al., 2020). While the flexibility of home-sharing also enables hosts to earn money on the side and at the leisure of their own schedule, compared to ride-share earners, hosts are more likely to be older and from the middle class (Schor, 2017; Schor & Attwood-Charles, 2017).

Earnings have been shown to vary based on race, but this depends on the platform. For example, on Airbnb, ethnic minority versus majority hosts are more likely to rent out listings in less desirable locations and receive lower prices for their properties (Edelman & Luca, 2014; Jaeger & Sleegers, 2023). In contrast, there is no evidence to suggest that the race of a ride-share worker influences their earnings (Hall & Krueger, 2018).

Earnings differences have been observed between genders and across platforms. Female Uber drivers, for example, have been shown to earn 7 percent less than males, with research suggesting that males drive faster and are more flexible with times and locations, therefore they are able to serve more passengers and generate higher earnings (Cook et al., 2021). Similar differences have been found on Amazon's Mechanical Turk, Etsy, and Freelancer (Jourdain, 2021; Liang et al., 2018; Litman et al., 2020). On Airbnb, lower earnings among female hosts have been attributed to them setting lower prices, accepting fewer stays, and obtaining a fewer number of guests per stay (Davidson & Gleim, 2022).

While platforms may not be responsible for the earnings differences that have been observed between races or genders, they can help to rectify these disparities. By integrating research data that identify when and how these disparities emerge, platforms can provide insights to both gig workers and consumers that can help avoid reinforcing discriminatory practices in the future.

Platform-Level Factors

Across collaborative consumption platforms, workers can earn income through price-setting and non-price-setting platforms. Price-setting platforms, such as Airbnb, TaskRabbit, and Turo, allow workers to set their own prices for the services they offer. On Airbnb, for example, hosts determine a nightly price for their accommodation that can be customized based on particular days (e.g., weekends), dates (e.g., holidays), durations (e.g., long-term discount pricing), or rule-based incentives (e.g., early-bird booking discount; Airbnb, 2023a). On TaskRabbit, taskers also set their own prices for each task they are offering to complete. The platform provides pricing guidance based on client market data but does not determine rates itself (TaskRabbit, 2022b). Similarly, Turo's manual pricing option allows workers to set their own prices, but unlike TaskRabbit, it requires that prices remain within minimum and maximum limits based on the vehicle's value (Turo, 2021).

Non-price-setting platforms, such as Uber, Lyft, and DoorDash, do not allow workers to set their own prices and instead rely on a pricing algorithm determined by the platform. On Uber and Lyft, for example, the platforms determine a ride's fare based on the estimated length and duration of the trip (Uber, 2023a). Additionally, through surge pricing, a multiplier is applied to the rate when demand increases so that more drivers are incentivized to work (Uber, 2023b). Drivers can further increase their earnings through tips. On DoorDash, workers similarly earn a base pay for every delivery they make based on estimated time and distance and can likewise earn tips. Unlike Uber and Lyft, workers on DoorDash can also complete challenges for extra earnings, such as completing a certain number of deliveries in a specified amount of time (DoorDash, 2023).

Although price-setting platforms enable workers to set their own prices, they often provide options similar to non-price-setting platforms. On Airbnb, for example, hosts have the option to enable Smart Pricing, a price-generating algorithm that determines rates based on demand and supply. In these circumstances, hosts can provide a minimum and maximum amount so that they maintain a certain range without having to monitor the rates (Airbnb, 2023b). Despite this option, Airbnb hosts tend not to vary the price of their listings as much as hotels (Gibbs et al., 2018). Similarly, on Turo, automatic pricing dynamically adjusts a vehicle's price based on its make, location, and trip history, as well as demand and supply (Turo, 2021). Thus, even on platforms where gig workers have the power to set prices, platforms have the ability to determine the earnings of gig workers.

CONCLUSION

The market disruption caused by collaborative consumption platforms would not be possible without the gig workers performing the services. Uber and Lyft's growth have resulted in New York City regulators limiting the number of licenses granted to workers on ride-hailing platforms and, as a consequence, taxi drivers have started participating in these services (Marshall, 2022). Now, taxi drivers in New York City are able to be cross-listed such that they are still able to pick up traditional fares on the street, but they are also receiving ride requests through the Uber mobile app (Marshall, 2022). Another example: after less than a decade in existence, Airbnb's growth, fueled by hosts performing the services and making properties available, resulted in more properties being offered for rent than the five largest hotel brands combined (Hartmans, 2017).

As the frontline service providers for collaborative consumption platforms, gig workers are often the only human interaction a consumer has with the platform. As such, perceptions of service quality performed by the gig worker are important in determining a consumer's satisfaction with the platform. In this chapter, we explored how gig workers function as collaborative consumption providers and examined: (a) their roles as frontline service providers, (b) the classification of their unique type of employment, and (c) their earnings as affected by individual-level (e.g., income, age, race, gender) and platform-related factors (i.e., price setting versus non-price setting). Future research should continue to examine their roles, classifications, and earnings so that further insights can provide guidance to collaborative consumption platforms and the gig workers performing the services.

REFERENCES

Abdul-Muhmin, A. G. (2005). Instrumental and interpersonal determinants of relationship satisfaction and commitment in industrial markets. *Journal of Business Research, 58*(5), 619–628.

Airbnb. (2023a). *Set and customize nightly pricing.* Retrieved January 22, 2023, from https://www.airbnb.ca/help/article/474

Airbnb. (2023b). *Smart pricing.* Retrieved January 22, 2023, from https://www.airbnb.ca/help/article/1168/

Anderson, M., McClain, C., Faverio, M., & Gelles-Watnick, R. (2021). *The state of gig work in 2021.* Pew Research Center. https://www.pewresearch.org/internet/2021/12/08/the-state-of-gig-work-in-2021/

Benoit, S., Baker, T. L., Bolton, R. N., Gruber, T., & Kandampully, J. (2017). A triadic framework for collaborative consumption (CC): Motives, activities and resources & capabilities of actors. *Journal of Business Research, 79,* 219–227.

Berger, T., Frey, C. B., Levin, G., & Danda, S. R. (2019). Uber happy? Work and well-being in the "gig economy." *Economic Policy, 34*(99), 429–477.

Bose, N. (2021). *U.S. Labor Secretary supports classifying gig workers as employees.* Reuters. Retrieved November 13, 2023, from https://www.reuters.com/world/us/exclusive-us-labor-secretary-says-most-gig-workers-should-be-classified-2021-04-29/

Cook, C., Diamond, R., Hall, J. V., List, J. A., & Oyer, P. (2021). The gender earnings gap in the gig economy: Evidence from over a million rideshare drivers. *Review of Economic Studies, 88*(5), 2210–2238.

Cronin, J. J. Jr, Brady, M. K., & Hult, T. M. (2000). Assessing the effects of quality, value, customer satisfaction on consumer behavioral intentions in service environment. *Journal of Retailing, 76*(2), 193–216.

Davidov, G. (2005). Who is a worker? *Industrial Law Journal, 34*(1), 57–71.

Davidson, A., & Gleim, M. R. (2022). The gender earnings gap in sharing economy services: The role of price, number of stays, and guests accommodated on Airbnb. *Journal of Marketing Theory and Practice, 31*(4), 1–12.

Davidson, A., Gleim, M. R., Johnson, C. M., & Stevens, J. L. (2023). Gig worker typology and research agenda: Advancing research for frontline service providers. *Journal of Service Theory and Practice, 33*(5), 647–670.

Dellaert, B. G. (2019). The consumer production journey: Marketing to consumers as co-producers in the sharing economy. *Journal of the Academy of Marketing Science, 47*(2), 238–254.

DoorDash. (2023). *Dasher pay.* Retrieved January 24, 2023, from https://dasher.doordash.com/en-ca/about/pay

Eckhardt, G. M., Houston, M. B., Jiang, B., Lamberton, C., Rindfleisch, A., & Zervas, G. (2019). Marketing in the sharing economy. *Journal of Marketing, 83*(5), 5–27.

Edelman, B. G., & Luca, M. (2014). *Digital discrimination: The case of Airbnb.com.* Harvard Business School NOM Unit Working Paper (14–054).

Ertz, M., Durif, F., & Arcand, M. (2016). Collaborative consumption: Conceptual snapshot at a buzzword. *Journal of Entrepreneurship Education, 19*(2), 1–23.

Ertz, M., Durif, F., & Arcand, M. (2018). A conceptual perspective on collaborative consumption. *AMS Review, 9*(1), 27–41.

Fagerstrøm, A., Pawar, S., Sigurdsson, V., Foxall, G. R., & Yani-de-Soriano, M. (2017). That personal profile image might jeopardize your rental opportunity!

On the relative impact of the seller's facial expressions upon buying behavior on Airbnb. *Computers in Human Behavior, 72*, 123–131.

Gibbs, C., Guttentag, D., Gretzel, U., Yao, L., & Morton, J. (2018). Use of dynamic pricing strategies by Airbnb hosts. *International Journal of Contemporary Hospitality Management, 30*(1), 2–20.

Gleim, M. R., Johnson, C. M., & Lawson, S. J. (2019). Sharers and sellers: A multi-group examination of gig economy workers' perceptions, *Journal of Business Research, 98*, 142–152.

Gleim, M. R., Stevens, J. L., & Johnson, C. M. (2023). Platform marketplaces: Unifying our understanding of lateral exchange markets. *European Journal of Marketing, 57*(1), 1–28.

Hall, J. V., & Krueger, A. B. (2018). An analysis of the labor market for Uber's driver-partners in the United States. *Ilr Review, 71*(3), 705–732.

Hamari, J., Sjöklint, M., & Ukkonen, A. (2016). The sharing economy: Why people participate in collaborative consumption. *Journal of the Association for Information Science and Technology, 67*(9), 2047–2059.

Hartmans, A. (2017). *Airbnb now has more listings worldwide than the top five hotel brands combined.* Retrieved January 20, 2023, from https://www.businessinsider .com/airbnb-total-worldwide-listings-2017-8

Ivanova, I. (2022). Biden administration proposes new rule that could upend "gig" work. Retrieved November 2, 2022, from https://www.cbsnews.com/news/ biden-administration-proposes-new-rule-that-could-make-gig-workers-full-time -employees/

Jaeger, B., & Sleegers, W. W. (2023). Racial disparities in the sharing economy: Evidence from more than 100 000 Airbnb hosts across 14 countries. *Journal of the Association for Consumer Research, 8*(1), 33–46.

Jourdain, A. (2021). From commodification to free labour: The gendered effects of marketplace platforms on work. In C. Suter, J. Cuvi, P. Balsiger, & M. Nedelcu (Eds.), *The future of work* (pp. 119–145). Seismo Press.

Kimberl, M. (2019). *Has the gig economy jumped the shark?* Retrieved November 1, 2023, from https://www.td.org/insights/has-the-gig-economy-jumped-the-shark

Kurter, H. (2019). *California threatens $1 trillion gig economy with new law.* Retrieved November 1, 2023, from https://www.forbes.com/sites/heidilynnekurter/2019/10/ 31/california-destroys-1-trillion-gig-economy-with-new-law/#1f1553dd2f0d

Li, J., Moreno, A., & Zhang, D. J. (2019). Agent pricing in the sharing economy: Evidence from Airbnb. In *Sharing economy* (pp. 485–503). Springer.

Liang, C., Hong, Y., Gu, B., & Peng, J. (2018). Gender wage gap in online gig economy and gender differences in job preferences. https://papers.ssrn.com/sol3/ papers.cfm?abstract_id=3266249

Litman, L., Robinson, J., Rosen, Z., Rosenzweig, C., Waxman, J., & Bates, L. M. (2020). The persistence of pay inequality: The gender pay gap in an anonymous online labor market. *PloS One, 15*(2), e0229383.

Macintosh, G. (2007). Customer orientation, relationship quality and relational benefits to the firm. *Journal of Service Marketing, 21*(3), 50–159.

Marshall, A. (2022). *New York taxi drivers hated Uber. Now they're going to help it.* Retrieved January 20, 2023, from https://www.wired.com/story/uber-new-york -taxi/

Morrison, E. W., & Robinson, S. L. (1997). When employees feel betrayed: A model of how psychological contract violation develops. *Academy of Management Review, 22*(1), 226–256.

Newlands, G., Lutz, C., & Fieseler, C. (2019). The conditioning function of rating mechanisms for consumers in the sharing economy. *Internet Research, 29*(5), 1090–1108.

Perren, R., & Kozinets, R.V. (2018). Lateral exchange markets: How social platforms operate in a networked economy. *Journal of Marketing, 82*(1), 20–36.

Pettersen, L. G. B. (2017). Rating mechanisms among participants in sharing economy platforms. *First Monday, 22*(12). https:// doi .org/ 10 .5210/ fm .v22i12 .7908

Prahalad, C. K., & Ramaswamy, V. (2000). Co-opting customer competence. *Harvard Business Review, 78*(1), 79–90.

Quinlan, M. (2012). The "pre-invention" of precarious employment: The changing world of work in context. *Economic and Labour Relations Review, 23*(4), 3–24.

Schor, J. B. (2017). Does the sharing economy increase inequality within the eighty percent?: Findings from a qualitative study of platform providers. *Cambridge Journal of Regions, Economy and Society, 10*(2), 263–279.

Schor, J. B., & Attwood-Charles, W. (2017). The "sharing" economy: Labor, inequality, and social connection on for-profit platforms. *Sociology Compass, 11*(8), e12493.

Schor, J. B., Attwood-Charles, W., Cansoy, M., Ladegaard, I., & Wengronowitz, R. (2020). Dependence and precarity in the platform economy. *Theory and Society, 49*(5), 833–861.

Shin, M., Shin, J., Ghili, S., & Kim, J. (2022). The impact of the gig economy on product quality through the labor market: Evidence from ridesharing and restaurant quality. *Management Science, 69*(5), 2620–2638.

Singh, J., Brady, M., Arnold, T., & Brown, T. (2017). The emergent field of organizational frontlines. *Journal of Service Research, 20*(1), 3–11.

Stanford, J. (2017). The resurgence of gig work: Historical and theoretical perspectives. *The Economic and Labour Relations Review, 28*(3), 382–401.

Stevens, J. L., Johnson, C. M., & Gleim, M. R. (2023). Why own when you can access? Motivations for engaging in collaborative consumption. *Journal of Marketing Theory and Practice, 31*(1), 1–17.

Sundararajan, A. (2014). What Airbnb gets about culture that Uber doesn't. *Harvard Business Review, 11*.

Sundararajan, A. (2017). *The sharing economy: The end of employment and the rise of crowd-based capitalism.* MIT Press.

Sureshchandar, G. S., Rajendran, C., & Anantharaman, R. N. (2002). The relationship between service quality and customer satisfaction: A factor specific approach. *Journal of Services Marketing, 16*(4), 363–379.

TaskRabbit (2022a). *Your to-do list is on us.* Retrieved November 4, 2022, from https://www.taskrabbit.com/services

TaskRabbit (2022b). *How pricing guidance works on TaskRabbit.* Retrieved January 22, 2023, from https:// taskers.taskrabbit.com/2022/04/13/how-pricing-guidance -works-on-taskrabbit/

Turo (2021). *Pricing your vehicle.* Retrieved January 21, 2023, from https://help.turo .com/en_us/setting-your-vehicle-price-S12VrVlVc

Uber (2023a). *Uber's upfront pricing, explained.* Retrieved January 24, 2023, from https://www.uber.com/ca/en/ride/how-it-works/upfront-pricing/

Uber (2023b). *How surge pricing works.* Retrieved January 24, 2023, from https:// www.uber.com/ca/en/drive/driver-app/how-surge-works/

Wieland, H., Hartmann, N. M., & Vargo, S. L. (2017). Business models as service strategy. *Journal of the Academy of Marketing Science*, *45*(6), 925–943.
Wirtz, J., So, K. K. F., Mody, M. A., Liu, S. Q., & Chun, H. H. (2019). Platforms in the peer-to-peer sharing economy. *Journal of Service Management*, *30*(4), 452–483.

12. Canines and the chemistry of coworking

Will Low and Eileen Davenport

INTRODUCTION

This chapter explores how coworking, as a form of collaborative consumption that emphasizes community and community building over co-existence (Garrett et al., 2017; Spinuzzi et al., 2019), is growing and evolving as a means of organizing work. Knowledge and creative workers are increasingly choosing coworking options because of the communal and collaborative environment created by the staff and the members themselves (Spinuzzi, 2012; Surman, 2013; Garrett et al., 2017; Capdevila, 2014). But as the availability of coworking space expands, the sought-after community aspect of these spaces cannot be taken for granted. As Elam (2022) notes in a blog on coworking megatrends, "Anyone can offer a space; very few can build a community... [and] as corporations shut down more and more space we'll see a massive, yes massive, spike in the need for quality space run by humans that understand how to grow community."

Coworking is defined as "a diverse group of people who don't necessarily work for the same company or on the same project, working alongside each other, sharing the working space and resources" (DeGuzman & Tang, 2011, p. 22), or as people "working alone together" (Spinuzzi, 2012). The term coworking, which emerged in the early 2000s, traces its roots to digital media and technology communities in San Francisco and New York (Gandini, 2015). Oldenburg (1999) contrasts homes (first spaces) with traditional offices (second spaces) and libraries, cafes, and public squares (third spaces). Independent, self-employed, and contract workers have, for many years, used "third spaces" such as cafes as temporary desks/offices so as to not work alone at home (Sayers, 2009), but cafes lack privacy and can be very noisy (Hampton & Gupta, 2008). Coworking spaces evolved as a hybrid of second and third spaces in the mid-2000s to service demand for working alone together, offering desk space and "offices with doors" to people and companies seeking flexibility regarding the amount of time spent "in the office" while also avoiding the cost of office leases. However, this hybrid may replicate some of the third spaces' disadvantages, such as noise and interruptions from unwanted social interaction (Bouncken et al., 2020, p. 109).

In less than 20 years, the number of coworking spaces has grown to 22 000 locations globally, with 2.2 million coworking members, and membership is projected to reach 5 million by 2024 (Di Risio, 2020). A key driver of their speedy growth has been the emergence of a disruptive new generation of entrepreneurs and freelancers who are "breaking down corporate hierarchies, dismantling mentalities, redefining social norms and increasingly experimenting with new work practices and unconventional offices" (Berbegal-Mirabent, 2021, p. 1, referencing Applebaum, 2013).

This chapter contributes to the literature by examining the ways in which some collaborative consumption-based coworking spaces are using dog-friendly policies as part of community building. Though coworking spaces have become ubiquitous in many larger cities worldwide (Berbegal-Mirabent, 2021) and are increasingly emergent in smaller cities and suburban sites, very few studies examine the presence of dogs in this context (Servaty et al., 2018; Andersson & Gente, 2020; Merkel, 2019). This is despite the ever-expanding number of coworking spaces that have pet-friendly policies, mirroring the growth of pet-friendly policies in company-owned workspaces. Trends triggered by Covid-19 are combining – pandemic puppies (Waters, 2021) and increasing mobility of work arrangements (Hermann & Paris, 2020) – such that coworking spaces can capitalize on dog-friendly policies as a unique selling proposition.

The chapter is largely conceptual, but we anchor our analysis through exploratory qualitative research of four coworking spaces in Central London and Lisbon with dog-friendly policies chosen using convenience sampling. Our conceptual and empirical analyses of these coworking spaces suggest they represent distinctive examples of strong community building (e.g., Putman, 2000; Turkle, 2011) in the universe of collaborative consumption initiatives. First, coworking puts sharing into the "sharing economy" by promoting real-time, ongoing, face-to-face collaborative consumption among its members. Second, coworking spaces exhibit a greater degree of intentionality in community building than other forms of collaborative consumption by actively promoting "In Real Life" co-creation of the sharing experience. Third, this intentionality is reflected in the design of the buildings in which work takes place and the design of opportunities for interaction being created between members, with the introduction of dogs as coworking companions promoting more relaxed and playful, or "ludic," worksites.

COWORKING AS A FORM OF COLLABORATIVE CONSUMPTION

Collaborative consumption is broadly defined as "the set of resource circulation systems which enable consumers to both obtain, and provide, temporarily or permanently, valuable resources or services through direct interaction with other consumers or through the mediation of a third-party" (Ertz et al., 2016, p. 15). It intersects with the sharing economy, an economic model in which individuals share their resources, such as their homes, cars, and other assets, with others, most often for a fee. Schor (2014) argues there are four broad categories in the sharing economy: recirculation of goods, increased utilization of durable assets, exchange of services, and sharing of productive assets. The initiatives can be not-for-profit or for profit. Collaborative consumption spans a wide spectrum across these four categories, from the "access economy" conceptualized by Eckhardt and Bardhi (2015) in which technology-based platforms mediate transactions to create access points to shared resources (such as Zipcars), to "community hub" models (e.g., tool banks, toy libraries, and meal sharing) that foster social interactions in the process of service or product delivery (Albinsson et al., 2021). We conceive coworking as typically combining different elements of these categories by, for example, creating access points to shared resources within the working spaces while also intentionally acting as a "hub" for social interactions between coworking members.

Bouncken and Reuschl (2018) classified coworking into four types (corporate, open corporate, consultancy, and independent) and identified tensions regarding value creation and appropriation related to competition. Orel and Bennis (2021) developed a taxonomy of four coworking models: (a) the individual-purposed space in which freelancers and location-independent professionals work alongside each other; (b) the creation-purposed space, which focuses on jointly creating a makerspace; (c) a group-purposed space that includes teams, often of larger firms; and (d) a startup-purposed coworking space. Although there were a few small businesses wholly located in larger private offices and groups of corporate employees clustered in a private office away from their corporate offices, our four sites fit the category of independent coworking spaces in which freelancers and location-independent professionals work alongside each other.

Despite the very visible collapse and reconstitution of the WeWork coworking empire in 2019, coworking has increased substantially in terms of numbers of locations and members. The changing nature of work with more outsourced and precarious employment has resulted in a rising number of mobile multi-locational workers who are "looking for people, places, and connections" (Koroma et al., 2014, p. 139). According to a recent report by Coworking Resources (Di Risio, 2020), the global coworking market is expected to grow from an estimated 2.2 million coworking members in 2019 to nearly 5 million by 2024. This report also notes that the pandemic has created a surge in demand for coworking spaces. Even during the Covid-19 pandemic (roughly defined here as March 2020 to February 2023), coworking spaces did not completely close for long but adapted by instituting health and safety protocols. Surprisingly, perhaps, new locations even opened during the pandemic (as evidenced during our own research in London and Lisbon). Indeed, the Covid-19 pandemic that imposed a work-from-home model on office-based workers fueled a rising interest in coworking as some staff transformed into working digital nomads.

With goals ranging from mentoring emerging entrepreneurs to creating social enterprises through cross-sector networks, each coworking space has a distinct culture that reflects its membership (Bouncken & Reuschl, 2018; Gandini, 2015; Spinuzzi, 2012; Surman, 2013). Membership, in turn, provides: affordable, amenity-rich shared workspaces; access to services such as mentorship and business planning; and opportunities to collaborate with other users (Bouncken & Reuschl, 2018; Spinuzzi, 2012; Surman, 2013). Some for-profit spaces mainly offer workers an office outside of the home with desks, a wireless internet connection, and access to shared meeting spaces. A second category of coworking spaces, often overseen by a manager or concierge (or both), has an explicit mission to create animated, curated spaces (Merkel, 2019) to foster intentional interactions that may lead to a sense of community.

FOUR EXPLORATORY CASE STUDIES

Two dog-friendly coworking spaces in London, England (London #1 and London #2) and Lisbon, Portugal (Lisbon #1 and Lisbon #2) were selected as study sites using convenience sampling. Both cities are major hubs for coworking because their business and public policy environments encourage flexible work by digital nomads (Euronews Travel, 2023; Elton, 2023). Our data collection used short-form ethnography (Pink & Morgan, 2013) and semi-structured interview methodologies focusing on facility managers and coworking members. We interviewed two staff members at each site and three or four coworking members (both self-employed and employed by small companies) in September 2022. A follow-up visit was conducted in London in August 2023 in which we conducted a check-in and update with two client-facing staff and two coworking members at each site.

All four coworking spaces we visited were dog friendly from their inception; indeed, Lisbon #1 had waited for over a year to secure a location suitable for dogs. The Facilities Manager of each location indicated that most members were well aware of the dog-friendly policies prior to joining and in some cases sought out this aspect despite not having dogs. The manager of the Lisbon #2 site noted that the pandemic had sparked a rise in digital nomads who either had a dog or had acquired one subsequently and who were therefore looking for dog-friendly coworking space.

The four sites extended over two or more floors with a combination of private offices, hot desks (i.e., temporary use of unassigned space), and communal spaces. The ambience differed among the four: the architecturally striking Central London site with high-end art and plants (we refer to as London #1) contrasted with the more "functional" office feel of London #2 and Lisbon #1, and the very relaxed casual vibe at Lisbon #2. While the two London sites and the "functional" Lisbon #1 were parts of multi-location coworking organizations, the "casual" Lisbon #2 was an independent operation. Since 2022, London #1 has expanded physically to encompass new buildings adjacent to the original site.

Except for a minor restriction regarding some food service areas at the "functional" London #2 location, dogs were welcome throughout the buildings in all four coworking spaces. In addition, all provided specific dog-friendly amenities such as dog bowls in areas with dog beds or spaces for relaxing with your pet, and access to dog treats in common spaces. Lisbon #1 offered a dog play area on an outdoor deck where members would gather for social events. The manager stated that it was very popular among members as a space to watch the dogs play and to interact with them.

Perhaps unsurprisingly, the majority of dogs coming to these coworking spaces spend time in "private" offices (an office with a door). In a few cases, dogs were located at hot-desk facilities, especially those accompanying digital nomads who were visiting the city and using the facility on a short-term basis. Each location had between four and six dogs who came in on a daily basis in 2022 and roughly an equal number that visited more sporadically. From our follow-up visit to London, London #1 reported a significant rise in regular dog visits, with up to 10–12 dogs now present daily.

COWORKING AND COMMUNITY... AND DOGS AS SOCIAL GLUE

Community is defined as "networks of interpersonal ties that provide sociability, support, information, a sense of belonging, and social identity" (Huurne et al., 2020, p. 46; quoting Wellman, 2005). The idea that people join coworking spaces in search of community, or a "sense of community," is a key finding of research on this topic. Reviewing a number of papers, Rådman et al. (2023, p. 887) identify "being part of a community" as a prominent reason why people become members, and a study conducted in Chiang Mai, Thailand, by de Loyrn (2022, p. 161) found that approximately one-third of digital nomads interviewed specifically referred to the importance of community aspects of coworking. Several authors (e.g., Huurne et al., 2020, p. 46; Garrett et al., 2017, p. 827) refer to people feeling a "sense of community" if four dimensions identified by (Huurne et al., 2020, p. 46) are present:

> (1) membership – relating to the feeling that one is part of a group, (2) influence – whether one has some sort of influence in the group, (3) integration and fulfillment of needs – believing that one's needs will be met through the community, and lastly (4) shared emotional connection – concerning shared history and shared participation.

These dimensions are more broadly social than the functional expression of community adopted by Spinuzzi et al. (2019), who focus narrowly on work/ business collaboration among coworking members. Social factors such as shared values, interests, and a sense of purpose are important in building community in coworking spaces. Moreover, Garrett et al. (2017) report that, in addition to shared values, community emerges through meaningful relationships and a sense of belonging. This includes having a clear mission or vision for the space, promoting trust, and fostering democratic practices – all of which contribute to a sense of community and shared ownership of the space. Engagement occurs through involving members in decision-making, promoting transparency and accountability, and valuing diverse perspectives and contributions. In providing further evidence regarding the role of the social dimensions of community building in coworking, King (2017) found that 87 percent of respondents met other members for social reasons, 79 percent said that coworking had expanded their social networks, and 83 percent and 89 percent, respectively, reported that they were less lonely and happier since joining a coworking space.

As exemplified by Airbnb, Zipcar, Sniffspot, and TrustedHousesitters, the idea of community does arise in the expanding collaborative consumption universe. For example, Airbnb (2023) runs its Community Center, "a platform that allows Airbnb hosts to connect with each other and share their experiences." Zipcar's (2023) mission is to "build a community of trust by delivering excellence in convenience, dependability and service." TrustedHousesitters hosts an online community forum for pet sitters and hosts, and more recently an online newsletter called *Trusted Times*. However, in this chapter, we contrast the close quarters, enduring interactions, and collaboration occurring in real life that are broadly typical of coworking spaces with more arms-length mediated services where individuals virtually engage with their "peers" but only connect fleetingly in person, if at all. In these digitally mediated services, individuals create profiles and digitally post and review their experiences to create trust between users. In the case of TrustedHousesitters, once a sitter and host have connected via the online platform, it is up to the two parties to have conversations, typically over Zoom, phone, or another platform to decide if they are a good match. It is not inconceivable that users of Airbnb or Sniffspot or TrustedHousesitters could and do engender enduring relationships (between hosts and users), but it is more likely that the interpersonal experience is less important than the trust that a user develops in the service as a whole and the digital platform itself. Griffiths et al. (2022) argued that "sharing of goods... has the potential to build social ties and strengthen community bonds" (p. 2) and, as a result, they posited that community-based sharing initiatives, in particular, can emphasize social ties, trust, and reciprocity and thus also exhibit community-building characteristics less clearly exhibited in the examples cited above.

Coworking, as a form of collaborative consumption where the service being traded is the use of physical space, will almost inevitably lead to interpersonal interactions between most members as they use (share) the resources contemporaneously rather than sequentially. Over time, while occupying the same physical space, these interactions can lead to a sense of community and camaraderie as individuals develop strong interpersonal ties through curated or serendipitous scenarios (cf. Granovetter, 1973).

Dogs in the office can contribute to these strong interpersonal ties as they are often argued to "humanize the workplace" (Cunha et al., 2019; Hall & Mills, 2019). Besides providing a more intentionally friendly workplace, their presence results in less stress and greater physical and mental well-being among workers (e.g., Wagner & Cunha, 2021; Foreman et al., 2017). A canine companion-friendly workspace, we contend, contributes to the playful nature of the space and thus creates shared emotional connections that underpin the community-building potential of coworking. Interviewee #2 in Lisbon #2 stated, "I love seeing the dogs around and look out for them." The dogs are an integral part of these coworking communities. Interviewee #4 at London #2 (a manager) said: "I am regularly asked which dogs are in today."

Members interviewed would go out of their way to see the dogs who were present, and sometimes the reverse happened as dogs sought out favored people. Interviewee #2 at London #1 commented that, as she was located in a central place with a glass wall, people could see her dog and would make a point of stopping and introducing themselves to the dog. She said, "I probably didn't get to know all the names of the people who would stop, but they all left knowing the name of my dog." Interviewee #1 in London #1 remarked: "we have to keep the door closed or else he [the dog] will go out in search of people he knows." These opening interactions create the potential for ongoing and enduring relationships that characterize a community.

Our exploratory work in four coworking locations suggests that the presence of dogs not only creates serendipitous interactions and "humanizes" the workplace (Wilkin et al., 2016; Foreman et al., 2017), but also contributes directly to the sense of community and individual well-being. We argue that dogs in the coworking space can amplify the sense of community and individual well-being among members. Interviewee #2 in London #1 said: "I don't mind at all if the dogs come out of the office and pay a visit. It is a welcome little break from work."

Dogs can also have a positive impact on workspace morale and social dynamics, as they are often a source of fun and humor and their presence can help to break down social barriers and foster a sense of camaraderie among employees (Wagner & Cunha, 2021). Interviewee #1 in London #2 laughingly stated: "My dog knows more people than me. People stop by and always want to pet her, so we have a chat." Dogs are well-known to be points of contact between strangers and often act as a social lubricant and social glue (Colarelli et al., 2021). For example, people are more likely to speak to a homeless person with a dog than one without (Irvine, 2015). Thus, the propensity to interact with an individual accompanied by a dog increases the opportunity for serendipitous exchanges between coworkers from disparate backgrounds. We experienced this directly when introduced to members of Lisbon #1 as researchers examining how dogs impact coworking spaces. We were subsequently welcomed to join a group with a dog that was going out for lunch. Our interpretation of this experience is that our interest in dogs created an opening to engage with the members in a way that lay outside our "official" purpose, resulting in them welcoming us into their community.

THE "ARCHITECTURE OF PARTICIPATION"

The intentionality of community building is reflected in how space is organized within coworking facilities – often including cafes and areas for lounging and outdoor relaxation – as well as curated activities, such as social gatherings designed to encourage interaction. Lusch and Nambisan's (2015) work characterizes various mechanisms that facilitate structured and unstructured interactions among diverse stakeholders, including protocols governing interactions and modes of communication, as an ecosystem. By coordinating, guiding, and supporting exchanges among actors through physical design elements such as shared spaces, open-plan layouts, and amenities like communal kitchens, cafes, and lounges, coworking spaces represent an "architecture of participation" that helps to create a sense of community among members. Coworking spaces, described by Merkel (2015) as "urban sociomaterial infrastructure" (p. 133), provide members with the valued ability to socialize, share ideas, and establish new ventures with other members. Amenities and services, such as coffee machines, printing facilities, and fitness areas, contribute to members' well-being and comfort but also invite people to engage with others as they co-create their coworking experiences.

The physical space in which coworking takes place is therefore a "non-human actor" (e.g., Latour, 2007) within the context of human and non-human relationships that comprise the coworking ecosystem. To understand space as a central actor in the development of a coworking community, we use the lens of ludic spaces. The term "ludic" comes from the Latin word "ludus," which means "play" or "game." Stemming from Barthes (1975), who used the term ludic to refer to activities that are free of labor and have their own rules, logic, and motivation, ludic spaces are environments that are designed to encourage play, creativity, and exploration. While they can take many forms, ludic spaces are characterized by a sense of openness and flexibility and allow people to engage in activities "during which ordinary conventions may be suspended and participants allowed greater expressive, creative, and improvisational license" (Edensor, 2014, p. 3).

The concept has also been applied in educational theory as *ludic learning spaces* (Kolb & Kolb, 2010) where play occurs in ways that promote learning. Indeed, as play is not confined to childhood and is considered central to the human experience, Huizinga (1950) suggests that humans should be considered *Homo ludens* – literally the man (person) who plays – as much as *Homo sapiens*, the man (person) who knows (as cited in Kolb & Kolb, 2010, p. 26). Salen and Zimmerman (2004), in turn, posit "ludic space" as physical and social environments (that can include workplaces) that support and encourage play. Such spaces entail flexibility, permissiveness (risk taking), unpredictability, imagination, and immersive experiences (Salen & Zimmerman, 2004). In a workplace, ludic spaces might include explicit areas for play (e.g., table tennis or board games), lounging (e.g., couches), and creative activities (e.g., art projects, writing exercises).

In the context of coworking spaces, the presence of dogs enhances the sense of playfulness engendered by the physical space and the prevailing culture that invites interaction, particularly in areas that have been created or designed with humans and canines in mind. Thus, while coworking spaces are developed for work, the design of the space and the presence of dogs offer opportunities to break from the monotony of work and routine. Similarly, facilitating informal gatherings by providing eating areas, bar areas, or even (as in the future plans of a Lisbon coworking space we were told of) a pool and patio where dogs are welcome, encourages social interaction and community building.

One further interesting aspect of the architecture of participation was observed at all four coworking spaces. While clear guidelines existed regarding where dogs were and were not allowed as well as expectations of behavior, members actively negotiated many of the norms and community standards regarding the presence of dogs in the coworking space. This flexibility reflected the changing composition of dogs and coworking members present and shifting tolerances for dog and human interactions. As such, this reflects open, democratic processes that lead to norms and standards that govern a community. The fact that all the facilities demonstrated this degree of openness and participation could be accounted for by the contrast drawn by the manager of one of the London locations between the "suited and booted" culture of some coworking spaces (where dogs would not be permitted) and those more ludic "creative" spaces which welcomed dogs.

CONCLUSIONS ABOUT THE FUTURE OF DOGS IN (COWORKING) SPACE

Expectations for continued growth of membership in coworking spaces remain strong (Deskmag, 2023) and, in the last couple of years, a long-discussed march of coworking into the suburbs has gained momentum. Arguably, the impetus for such a move is a conflux of the pandemic changing the five-day, office-based work week and the increasing numbers of fully, or partially, remote and contracted workers. Additionally, the pandemic also encouraged new entrepreneurs and independent professionals to look for congenial working spaces, either as a result of losing their jobs or deciding that they want a different lifestyle.

Given that many companies now utilize a hybrid model, enabling employees to divide their work week between the office and home (or alternative work-space), a recent article in the *New York Times* suggested that, "In the New York City metropolitan area, home to the country's largest office districts, co-working spaces are increasingly targeting the hundreds of thousands of office workers who live in the suburbs" (Hong & Haag, 2021). Additionally, companies that are looking for smaller suburban offices to allow employees to work closer to home are finding that coworking spaces are a flexible and affordable option (Ali, 2020).

While the coworking sector has always been diverse, the increasing interest in this form of collaborative consumption by the corporate sector (in effect, the mainstreaming of coworking) poses interesting questions for the ongoing development of community within such spaces. We suggest that coworking will continue to grow as a form of workplace organization, and within that spectrum, all forms of coworking, from the "suited and booted" styles that exclude canines to the many versions where canines are welcome, will flour-ish. We would therefore suggest that the presence of dogs in coworking spaces as "actors" (they act on the environment and are acted upon; cf. Latour, 2007) adds what we term *ludicity* (elements of playfulness) that creates and maintains social glue. They act as coagulants in the chemistry of coworking by multiplying the opportunities for interactions that have nothing to do with work itself, but that build community and cohesion.

Moreover, they will increasingly come to work at suburban coworking spaces as their human companions migrate from downtown offices. Based on our research, we contend that the key factors of autonomy, flexibility, and open communication that Wagner and Cunha (2021) found to be so important to individual and collective well-being in pet-friendly workplaces equally apply to coworking spaces. Thus, further research into dog-friendly and non-dog-friendly coworking spaces is important to understand and elaborate the benefits and possible challenges posed by canines in such spaces.

REFERENCES

Airbnb. (2023). Community center. https://community.withairbnb.com/t5/Community -Center/ct-p/community-center

Albinsson, P. A., Perera, B. Y., & Griffiths, M. A. (2021). Overcoming scarcity through efficient consumption: Innovative sharing initiatives. In T. Sigler & J. Corcoran (Eds.), *A modern guide to the urban sharing economy* (pp. 55–70). Edward Elgar Publishing. https://doi.org/10.4337/9781789909562.00011

Ali, A. (2020, July 15). Suburban coworking spaces are the industry's future. *Daily Digest*. https://allwork.space/2020/07/suburban-coworking-spaces-are-the-industrys -future

Andersson, K., & Gente, G. (2020). *Coworking in an experiencescape – A case study on the consumption in a coworking space combined with a restaurant and café* [Unpublished master's thesis]. University of Gothenburg. https://gupea.ub.gu.se/ handle/2077/64790

Barthes, R. (1975). *The pleasure of the text* (R. Miller, Trans.). Hill and Wang.

Berbegal-Mirabent, J. (2021). What do we know about coworking spaces? Trends and challenges ahead. *Sustainability, 13*(3), 1416. https://doi.org/10.3390/su13031416

Bouncken, B., & Reuschl, J. (2018). Coworking-spaces: How a phenomenon of the sharing economy builds a novel trend for the workplace and for entrepreneurship. *Review of Management Science, 12*, 317–334. https://doi.org/10.1007/s11846-016 -0215-y

Bouncken, R., Ratzmann, M., Barwinski, R., & Kraus, S. (2020). Coworking spaces: Empowerment for entrepreneurship and innovation in the digital and sharing economy. *Journal of Business Research, 114*, 102–110. https://doi.org/10.1016/j .jbusres.2020.03.033

Capdevila, I. (2014). *Different entrepreneurial approaches in localized spaces of collaborative innovation.* ESG Management School. http://dx.doi.org/10.2139/ssrn .2533448

Colarelli, S. M., McDonald, A. M., Christensen, M. S., & Honts, C. (2021). A companion dog increases prosocial behavior in work groups. *Anthrozoös, 30*(1), 77–89. https://doi.org/10.1080/08927936.2017.1270595

Cunha, M. P., Rego, A., & Munro, I. (2019). Dogs in organizations. *Human Relations, 72*(4), 778–800. https://doi.org/10.1177/0018726718780210

DeGuzman, G. V., & Tang, A. I. (2011). *Working in the unoffice: A guide to coworking for indie workers, small businesses, and nonprofits.* Night Owls Press.

de Loyrn, B. (2022). Finding a balance between quiet work and being social: Exploring coworking space needs of digital nomads in terms of amenities and community. In T. Chaiechi & J. Wood (Eds.), *Community empowerment, sustainable cities, and transformative economies* (pp. 151–166). Springer.

Deskmag. (2023). *2023 coworking space business trends*. https://www.dropbox.com/s/kcscosjhlyj93ca/2023%20Coworking%20Space%20Business%20Trends%20Simplifed%20Results.pdf

Di Risio, A. (2020). *Global coworking growth study 2020*. https:// www .coworkingresources.org/blog/key-figures-coworking-growth

Eckhardt, G. M., & Bardhi, F. (2015). The sharing economy isn't about sharing at all. *Harvard Business Review.* https://hbr.org/2015/01/the-sharing-economy-isnt-about-sharing-at-all

Edensor, T. (2014). The potentialities of light festivals. *Insights, 7*(3). https:// www .iasdurham.org/wp-content/uploads/2021/03/Edensor_The-Potentialities-of-Light-Festivals.pdf

Elam, L. (2022). Coworking retrospective megatrends. *GCUC Blog.* https://gcuc.co/coworking-megatrends-2023/

Elton, C. (2023). Portugal welcomes hundreds of digital nomads under new visa scheme. Here's how it works. *EuroNews.* https://www.euronews.com/travel/2023/01/26/digital-nomads-will-be-able-to-live-and-work-in-portugal-full-time-with-this-new-visa

Ertz, M., Durif, F., & Arcand, M. (2016). Collaborative consumption: Conceptual snapshot at a buzzword. *Journal of Entrepreneurship Education, 19*(2), 1–23. http://dx.doi.org/10.2139/ssrn.2799884

Euronews Travel. (2023). *Want to meet other digital nomads? These are the most – and least – popular European countries*. https://www.euronews.com/travel/2023/05/26/want-to-meet-other-digital-nomads-these-are-the-most-and-least-popular-european-countries

Foreman, A. M., Glenn, M. K., Meade, B. J., & Wirth, O. (2017). Dogs in the workplace: A review of the benefits and potential challenges. *International Journal of Environmental Research and Public Health, 14*(5), 498. https:// www .doi .org/ 10 .3390/ijerph14050498

Gandini, A. (2015). The rise of coworking spaces: A literature review. *Ephemera, 15*(1), 193–205. https:// ephemerajournal .org/ contribution/ rise -coworking -spaces -literature-review

Garrett, L. E., Spreitzer, G. M., & Bacevice, P. A. (2017). Co-constructing a sense of community at work: The emergence of community in coworking spaces. *Organization Studies, 38*(6), 821–842. https://doi.org/10.1177/0170840616685354

Granovetter, M. (1973). The strength of weak ties. *American Journal of Sociology, 78*(6), 1360–1380. https://www.jstor.org/stable/2776392

Griffiths, M. A., Perera, B. Y., & Albinsson, P. A. (2022). Lives of the lonely: How collaborative consumption services can alleviate social isolation. *Frontiers in Psychology, 13*, 826533. https://www.doi.org/10.3389/fpsyg.2022.826533

Hall, S. S., & Mills, D. S. (2019). Taking dogs into the office: A novel strategy for promoting work engagement, commitment and quality of life. *Frontiers in Veterinary Science, 6*(138), 1–17. https://doi.org/10.3389/fvets.2019.00138

Hampton, K. N., & Gupta, N. (2008). Community & social interaction in the wireless city: Wi-fi use in public & semi-public spaces. *New Media & Society, 10*(6), 831–850. https://www.doi.org/10.1177/1461444808096247

Hermann, I., & Paris, C. M. (2020). Digital nomadism: The nexus of remote working and travel mobility. *Information Technology in Tourism*, *22*, 329–334. https://doi.org/10.1007/s40558-020-00188-w

Hong, N., & Haag, M. (2021, October 28). Why co-working spaces are betting on the suburbs. *New York Times*. https://www.nytimes.com/2021/10/28/nyregion/co-working-space-suburbs.html

Huizinga, J. (1950). *Homo ludens*. Beacon Press.

Huurne, M. T., Ronteltap, A., & Buskens, V. (2020). Sense of community and trust in the sharing economy. *Tourism Analysis*, *25*(1), 43–61. https://doi.org/10.3727/108354220X15758301241639

Irvine, L. (2015). *My dog always eats first: Homeless people and their animals*. Lynne Rienner.

King, S. (2017). Coworking is not about workspace – It's about feeling less lonely. *Harvard Business Review*. https://hbr.org/2017/12/coworking-is-not-about-workspace-its-about-feeling-less-lonely

Kolb, A. Y., & Kolb, D. A. (2010). Learning to play, playing to learn: A case study of a ludic learning space. *Journal of Organizational Change Management*, *23*(1), 26–50. https://doi.org/10.1108/09534811011017199

Koroma, J., Hyrkkänen, U., & Vartiainen, M. (2014). Looking for people, places and connections: Hindrances when working in multiple locations: A review. *New Technology, Work and Employment*, *29*(2), 139–159. https://doi.org/10.1111/ntwe.12030

Latour, B. (2007). *Reassembling the social: An introduction to actor-network theory*. Oxford University Press.

Lusch, R. L., & Nambisan, S. (2015). Service innovation: A service-dominant logic perspective. *MIS Quarterly*, *39*(1), 155–175. https://doi.org/10.25300/MISQ/2015/39.1.07

McMillan, D. W., & Chavis, D. M. (1986). Sense of community: A definition and theory. *Journal of Community Psychology*, *14*, 6–23.

Merkel, J. (2015). Coworking in the city. *Ephemera*, *15*(1), 121–139. https://ephemerajournal.org/contribution/coworking-city

Merkel, J. (2019). Curating strangers. In R. Gill, A. Pratt, & T. Virani (Eds.), *Creative hubs in question: Place, space and work in the creative economy* (pp. 51–68). Palgrave Macmillan. https://doi.org/10.1007/978-3-030-10653-9

Oldenburg, R. (1999). *The great good place: Cafes, coffee shops, bookstores, bars, hair salons and other hangouts at the heart of a community*. Da Capo Press.

Orel, M., & Bennis, W. M. (2021). Classifying changes. A taxonomy of contemporary coworking spaces. *Journal of Corporate Real Estate*, *234*, 278–296. https://doi.org/10.1108/JCRE-12-2020-0061

Pink, S., & Morgan, J. (2013). Short-term ethnography: Intense routes to knowing. *Symbolic Interaction*, *36*, 351–361. https://doi.org/10.1002/symb.66

Putnam, R. (2000). *Bowling alone: The collapse and revival of American community*. Simon & Schuster.

Rådman, E., Johansson, E., Bosch-Sijtsema, P., & Raharjo, H. (2023). In search of member needs in coworking spaces. *Review of Managerial Science*, *17*, 881–907. https://doi.org/10.1007/s11846-022-00546-4

Salen, K., & Zimmerman, E. (2004). Ludic space. In K. Tekinbaş & E. Zimmerman (Eds.), *The game design reader: A rules of play anthology* (pp. 445–466). MIT Press.

Sayers, J. (2009). Flat whites: How and why people work in cafés. *New Zealand Journal of Employment Relations, 34*(2), 77–86. https://www.nzjournal.org/NZJER34%282%29.pdf

Schor, J. (2014). Debating the sharing economy. *Great Transition Initiative.* http://www.greattransition.org/publication/debating-the-sharing-economy

Servaty, R., Perger, G., Harth, V., & Mache, S. (2018). Working in a cocoon: (Co)working conditions of office nomads – a health related qualitative study of shared working environments. *Working, 60*(4), 527–538. https:// doi .org/ 10 .3233/ WOR -182760

Spinuzzi, C. (2012). Working alone together: Coworking as emergent collaborative activity. *Journal of Business and Technical Communication, 26,* 399–441. https://doi.org/10.1177/1050651912444070

Spinuzzi, C., Bodrožić, Z., Scaratti, G., & Ivaldi, S. (2019). "Coworking is about community": But what is "community" in coworking? *Journal of Business and Technical Communication, 33*(2), 112–140. https://doi.org/10.1177/1050651918816357

Surman, T. (2013). Building social entrepreneurship through the power of coworking. *Innovations: Technology, Governance, Globalization, 8*(3/4), 189–195. https://direct.mit.edu/itgg/article/8/3-4/189/9769/Building-Social-Entrepreneurship -through-the-Power

Turkle, S. (2011). *Alone together: Why we expect more from technology and less from each other.* Basic Books.

Wagner, E., & Cunha, M. P. (2021). Dogs at the workplace: A multiple case study. *Animals, 11,* 89. https://doi: 10.3390/ani11010089

Waters, A. (2021). Pandemic puppy phenomenon is a reality. *Veterinary Record, 188*(5), 164. https://doi.org/10.1002/vetr.252

Wilkin, C. L., Fairlie, P., & Ezzedeen, S. R. (2016). Who let the dogs in? A look at pet-friendly workplaces. *International Journal of Workplace Health Management, 9*(1), 96–109. https://doi.org/10.1108/IJWHM-04-2015-0021

Zipcar. (2023). *About us.* https://www.zipcar.com/en-gb/about

13. From land to table: a sustainable chain towards collaborative consumption

Angelo Ranieri, Marco Tregua, and Irene Di Bernardo

INTRODUCTION

The United Nations' (UN) Sustainable Development Goals (SDGs) permeate a multiplicity of domains. Recently, due to the goals' implications with regard to fighting hunger, supranational institutions (e.g. the UN) have focused on food supply; responsible production and consumption, including better accountability in the use of water, energy, and other resources; and caring for natural ecosystems. This topic is garnering increased attention as new approaches emerge to reduce food waste, combining innovation and sustainability (e.g. Karki et al., 2021), and leveraging the transformative force of business (Schaltegger et al., 2018). Indeed, the Food and Agriculture Organization (FAO, 2018) has called for a more holistic approach to address the complexity of the food system, including the challenges stemming from food waste and losses.

The FAO proposed an alternative framework – the Food Wheel – that moves far beyond the traditional food chain, which entails a sequence of steps. The Food Wheel, which is centred on sustainable goals such as poverty reduction and food security, focuses on changing actors' behaviour at multiple levels. As such, it stresses the interplay among them beyond the basic business exchange. Similar to the UN (2018), such a view holds that multi-stakeholder collaboration is crucial to achieving concrete results.

Indeed, meetings focused on food-related issues (e.g. the 2018 National Model UN New York Conference, the UN Food Systems Summit in New York in 2021) allowed participants to share their experiences in the agri-food sector and compare food crises. While the main beneficiaries of such programs are nations fighting hunger (e.g. Uganda), the possibility of transforming the food system might be relevant for any country.

Scholars recently proposed an interplay between sustainable supply chains and SDGs (Balezentis et al., 2023) as a solution for shifting towards more sustainable processes and achieving better performance. Such propositions call for moving beyond a company's boundaries to leverage collaboration among multiple entities to attain sustainable solutions that support the natural ecosystem (e.g. Guimarães et al., 2022). Therefore, this chapter focuses on novel collaborative ways to achieve sustainable goals throughout the food supply chains (FSC). To do that, we review studies on collaborative consumption and on FSCs to set the foundation for our research. Then, we utilise evidence from the FSC to develop suggestions to further sustainable goals. Cases are discussed comparatively to illustrate the fact that efforts that extend beyond a given business can drive the industry towards the SDGs.

THEORETICAL BACKGROUND

New business processes can lead to more sustainable food systems. However, as stressed by supranational institutions, companies' efforts alone are insufficient due to the complexity of FSCs and the great challenge in shifting towards more sustainable solutions (Sarkis et al., 2019). Scholars highlight the role of focal firms (e.g. multinational companies such as Mondeléz and Unilever, as in Mc Loughlin et al., 2023) in furthering sustainable behaviours, both upstream and downstream. Such a view, which refers to a business's environmental and moral goals (Brandenburg et al., 2014), calls for the alignment among multiple actors to achieve sustainable solutions.

In terms of the marketplace, the variety of products and services consumers share – either with or without firms' mediation and ranging from homes and cars to farms, food, pets, and expertise – has increased significantly (Chasin et al., 2018). This phenomenon is based on the design, implementation, and dissemination of collaborative strategies. As such, we first analyse the general concept of collaborative consumption to better understand its meaning and its relationship with the food industry. Then, we discuss how collaborative consumption has been investigated at diverse levels of the FSC. This entails a multi-stakeholder view that expands the concept of consumption from eating to resource usage throughout the FSC. We conclude by proposing research directions to stimulate work that will provide concrete evidence on how to achieve sustainable solutions.

COLLABORATIVE CONSUMPTION

Commonly referred to as an alternative environmentally friendly and sustainable form of consumption (e.g. Belk, 2014) that is sometimes compared to the sharing economy (Armstrong & Park, 2017), collaborative consumption is the idea that people opt to share resources (e.g. goods, spaces, and skills) rather than own them individually (Botsman & Rogers, 2010). Indeed, psychological consumer behaviour studies (e.g. Lamberton, 2016) indicate that consumers engage in collaborative consumption to efficiently use available resources, thereby maximising utility, reducing waste, and promoting respect for the environment. Collaborative consumption, which at times assumes different forms and delivers different results but with the same underlying pattern, is currently of great interest throughout business studies. For instance, Altinay and Taheri (2019) note that, in the future, collaborative consumption will influence hospitality and tourism through value co-creation practices. Similarly, in analysing urban transportation systems, Cleophas et al. (2019) highlight the role of collaborative consumption in providing more sustainable and customer-friendly services. Within the context of the fashion industry, Arrigo (2021) discusses collaborative consumption in relation to sustainable manufacturing and conscious consumption in terms of the reuse or rental of items (Antanavičiūtė & Dobilaitė, 2015). As such, it is possible to see how the collaborative consumption of food may be of significant interest to address food waste (Parker et al., 2019).

To a great extent, collaborative consumption in the food industry pertains to food sharing, which can reduce food waste and pollutant emissions (Novel, 2014). However, the collaborative consumption of food also offers opportunities for local communities to share their food cultures and enjoy unique culinary experiences (Octavia et al., 2022) while stimulating green consumption (Khan et al., 2020). These opportunities raise awareness of food safety and sustainable production practices, thus helping to create a more sustainable future for societies (Fraanje & Spaargaren, 2019). Despite constraints due to limited trust among consumers (Popescu & Ciurlău, 2019), collaborative consumption is often facilitated by recent technologies (Albinsson & Perera, 2018) such as online platforms and the blockchain (Ashaduzzaman et al., 2022). As such, this model of consumption is more efficient and more accessible.

FOOD SUPPLY CHAINS

The development of transportation and communications has led to greater integration among companies, which have increasingly standardised their processes. The literature frames this phenomenon in the "supply chain", identified as a "manufacturing process wherein raw materials are converted into final products, then delivered to customers" (Beamon, 1998, p. 282). Essentially, the supply chain is widely regarded as a network of companies that collaborate by integrating and sharing their skills and activities to transform raw materials into finished goods or services and to finally deliver them to the end-consumer (Pienaar & Vogt, 2009). Therefore, it includes a "network of organisations that are involved, through upstream and downstream linkages, in the different processes and activities that produce value in the form of products and services in the hands of the ultimate consumer" (Christopher, 2005, p. 17). In practice, these entities include manufacturers of parts, semi-finished products, or finished goods, service providers, and the end-consumer.

As this chapter focuses on the food sector, an FSC has been described as "a group of interconnected businesses that collaborate closely to control the flow of goods and services throughout the value-added chain of agricultural and food products, in order to generate better consumer value at the lowest costs" (Folkerts & Koehorst, 1998, p. 385). Growing raw resources, processing them into food products, and distributing them to end customers are all part of the process (hereafter called farming, production, retail, and consumption, as in Saetta & Caldarelli, 2020).

However, along this broad path, many factors can influence the realisation of food, ranging from consumer preferences, production methods, and trade regulations to transportation challenges, as well as considerations regarding environmental and societal impacts of the FSC (e.g. Siddh et al., 2021). This is why FSC management has been theorised to depict and manage all the activities or operations that are necessary to preserve food safety and quality (Blandon et al., 2009).

As per the trajectories identified by supranational institutions (e.g. FAO, 2018; UN, 2018) and in line with scholars (e.g. Chauhan et al., 2022), we posit how FSCs can become sustainable through collaborative forms of resource use, including consumption. Such trajectories – with reference to farming, production, retail, and consumption – have considered collaboration as a means of pursuing the SDGs. Given that such work is fragmented, assuming a more holistic view – as per the directions of the FAO (2018) – would be beneficial.

Collaborative farming is theorised as an all-embedded approach, which entails much more than the sharing of tools and efforts among farmers in that it is seen as a common and shared business vision (e.g. Hardie Hale et al., 2022) that results from cross-industrial operations (e.g. Thow et al., 2018). The common view on food system entities that pursue sustainable goals is that they adopt collaborative approaches and experiment with new decision-making processes to leverage results and feedback to garner the most from the enacted changes (Hardie Hale et al., 2022). Indeed, change favours learning and improvement and inspires actors to cooperate with one another and with the communities to make farming sustainable. This posture towards cooperation not only describes the focal firm in FSCs, but also fits with both downwards and upwards partners (Thow et al., 2018). In this context, the public and private sectors are partners in improving farming-related matters, thus activating a virtuous process that inspires all levels of FSCs. Collaborative production is driven by economic goals as the food industry consists of several small and medium-sized enterprises (SMEs) that must take particular care of the cost structure in order to compete in crowded markets.

Collaborative production is regarded as the implementation of indus-trial collaboration to advance business opportunities, especially for SMEs (Matopoulos et al., 2007). It is interesting to note that the debate on collab-oration as a means of supporting sustainability in production comprises two contrasting approaches. The cross-industrial view considers collaboration aimed at protecting the environment and contrasting natural resource shortage (Cristiano, 2021), while the economic perspective (Michel-Villarreal et al., 2020) observes that the struggle for sustainability is driven by the search for economic efficiency. As such, collaborations might support the achievement of sustainability in multiple ways starting from either industrial partnerships or cross-sectoral cooperation. This chapter offers insights on how cooperation favours sustainable goals throughout the entire FSC.

While several initiatives around the world show the integration of multiple actors along FSCs to leverage collaborations, collaborative retail is less inves-tigated than farming, production, and consumption. Last-mile logistics, a key topic in recent years, affect environmental performance because the small quantities and multiple destinations of retailing systems make it difficult to achieve economies of scale. New options driven by technologies and social practices are foreseen as ways to counteract inefficiencies and environmental issues (Melkonyan et al., 2020). For instance, coordination of flows and users' involvement in new collection methods (e.g. click and collect) would support a decrease in environmental impacts and an increase in economic viability. The ongoing efforts must be properly assessed so that scholars (see Grosu, 2023, who reviewed indicators of green practices' impacts) and practitioners (see FAO, 2021, for the "presence of a development plan to strengthen resilience and efficiency of local food supply chains logistics") shape the establishment of new indicators. Overall, green measures mirror the intertwined environmen-tal and economic goals, as shown by the reduction in resource usage and the deriving decrease in costs. In both views, retailers' efforts can better express their potential through a farm-to-fork strategy, thus suggesting the integration of the views of all actors – including consumers – along the FSC.

In line with the aforementioned considerations on retail, collaborative consumption shows the key role that consumers might play. The efforts of farmers, producers, and retailers might be lost if consumers do not act prop-erly, as referred to in the above-mentioned social practices. When business vision and philosophy are paralleled with human values, the overlap between economic-driven motivations (i.e. savings and environmentally friendly reasons) might emerge as a surprise (Roos & Hahn, 2019). Therefore, the well-established normative motives (Albinsson & Perera, 2012), partnered with other reasons, lead the actors responsible for collaborative consumption initiatives to adopt proper engagement techniques. Additionally, the recent debates on collaborative consumption have led to the acknowledgement of negative externalities (Griffiths et al., 2019; Griffiths et al., Chapter 14, this book). Likewise, Parker et al. (2019) investigated how cognitive errors can result in overconsumption and waste, which are contrary to the aims of collaborative initiatives.

In summary, new interactions have disrupted business routines, and highlighted potential economic and social changes that focus on different objectives and cross diverse levels and industries to develop sustainable solutions. On the one hand, strong digitisation has led to new ways of delivering goods to companies and end-consumers (Gharehgozli et al., 2017). On the other hand, increases in waste and pollution and the greater attention paid to environmental sustainability have introduced new methods of collaboration within the supply chain. From this dual perspective, each company is both a seller and a consumer, thereby linking the FSC and collaborative consumption. Moreover, the focus shifts from only consumption to resource usage and process performance, meaning that the entire food system participates in the collaborative efforts towards change.

METHOD

Similar to Blanka and Traunmüller (2020), we use a qualitative research case study approach, which is appropriate to understand new phenomena such as collaborative consumption (Barnham, 2015) in a well-established business (as the food industry). We present multiple case studies representing diverse levels of the FSC. To ensure objectivity, we collect data from multiple archival sources such as firms' official websites, social media pages, and online news. All the cases represent practice-leading organisations with robust sustainable and collaborative models. Besides the four Italian cases, three cases from other countries and one global case were selected to reduce bias and provide a comparative perspective on the data (Kaipainen et al., 2022). Each section includes one Italian and one international case, strategically chosen to showcase diverse viewpoints on collaborative consumption within the FSC. These cases provide valuable insights into successful sustainable practices and collaborative strategies employed by organisations. Table 13.1 summarises the cases and data sources.

By adopting this approach, we aim to gain alternative viewpoints on the subject (e.g. Stavros & Westberg, 2009), showing how collaborative forms of operating can support the achievement of sustainable goals for multiple actors. To further enhance objectivity, the data analysis was conducted both individually and as a team, which facilitated comparison.

Table 13.1   Summary of cases

Name	Location	Stage of supply chain	Data sources
Scagnammece 'A Semmenta!	Naples, Italy	Farming	Co-founder, official social media page
WeFarm	UK	Farming	Official website, newspaper articles
Vin.Co	Ortona, Italy	Production	Official website, official social media page
Banco de Maquinaria Compartida	Andalusia, Spain	Production	Official website, newspaper articles, online videos
OltreFood Corp	Parma, Italy	Retailing	Official website, official social media page
ButcherCrowd	Australia	Retailing	Official website, official social media page
'O Vascio	Naples, Italy	Consumption	Official website, official social media page, online customer reviews, site visit
EatWith	*Global*	Consumption	Official website, online customer reviews

Source: Authors' elaboration.

FINDINGS

This chapter examined exemplary FSC-based collaborative consumption initiatives that bring food from the land to the table, thus allowing for collaborative consumption. As this supply chain entails farming, production, retail, and consumption, the widened view allows for the examination of the variety of contributions to sustainability that might be achieved via collaboration (Blandon et al., 2009; Chauhan et al., 2022). In this sense, guidelines and suggestions stemming from the data are provided as a basis for the achievement of sustainable goals. The examples are described together with a collaboration-based definition of food-related activity.

Farming

Farming involves the use of natural resources, as well as knowledge and human resources. Collaborative farming is theorised as the process aimed at increasing agricultural firms' profitability by relying on shared capital among farmers and protecting local natural ecosystems for future generations (Omer, 2022). This goes beyond the sharing of technical tools, confirming that a common vision is fertile ground for sustainability-driven goals achieved through collaboration (Hardie Hale et al., 2022). Exhibits 13.1 and 13.2 describe two contexts furthering such goals. The first, set in Naples, is aimed at achieving common goals for agricultural entities through the sharing of seeds for both preserving plant species and creating new ones. The second describes the creation of an online platform to share tools and other resources that farmers might need.

EXHIBIT 13.1　　SCAGNAMMECE 'A SEMMENTA!

Scagnammece 'A Semmenta! is a peer-to-peer non-profit association whose name in the Neapolitan dialect means "Let's switch seeds". It began in 2018 as a means for farmers to exchange seeds and preserve traditional vegetables and plants. Beyond being a simple market, farmers come together periodically to share ideas, experiment with plant species, and discuss old traditions during public meetings. The association collaborates with other local farmers' groups and uses social media to interact and spread awareness about their activities.

While the Scagnammece 'A Semmenta! involves dozens of farmers and a thousand online followers, the next UK-based example is one of the largest farmers' networks in the world. Small-scale farmers join WeFarm to share information or market solutions, thus recalling the needs of SMEs and the advantages of cross-industrial collaboration (Thow et al., 2018). Both forms of collaboration support farming by sharing knowledge and natural resources. This favours the viability of businesses commonly jeopardised by several challenges, including the market power of big competitors and the ongoing changes in natural ecosystems.

EXHIBIT 13.2　　WEFARM

WeFarm, designed in the UK and founded as a Silicon Valley startup in 2015, raised about US$32M from venture capitalists. This company establishes a network of farmers who connect via SMS or social media to exchange innovative ideas, troubleshoot farming challenges, and explore collaboration opportunities. Farmers can join for free, and WeFarm organises international debates and meetings on the integration of digital technologies in agriculture.

Production

Collaborative production in the agri-food business moves well beyond traditional FSC relations. It aims to achieve a mutual advantage by making viable activities (i.e. cultivating, collecting, transforming) that represent significant investments for SMEs, shortening the FSC, and improving economic conditions. De Lima et al. (2019) describe such collaborations as a set of relationships among farmers and other entities partnering to "share risks and benefits that result in higher commercial performance than individual organisations"

(p. 123). Such collaborations can improve the efficiency of transformation, as agri-food is normally a fragmented sector lacking cooperation and, in parallel, food production often involves SMEs that mainly face challenges of economic viability (Matopoulos et al., 2007). Exhibit 13.3 describes an innovative project of Italian wineries that joined forces to establish shared facilities, which reduced the need for investment. Exhibit 13.4 explains a similar initiative among small olive farmers in Spain.

EXHIBIT 13.3   VIN.CO

Vin.Co is a cooperative of sparkling wine producers located in Ortona, Italy. It involves ten wineries that aim to restore the value of their territory through the production of sparkling wines. The initiative has three main goals: improving the competitiveness of producers by better integrating them into the wine supply chain; characterising the product to make it recognisable and territorial; and increasing the added value of sparkling wine. Currently, sparkling wines sold in the marketplace are mostly unbranded without any ties to local features, which results in low profitability.

The cooperation at Vin.Co reveals the producers' willingness to share knowledge and techniques to strengthen the business viability and the image of the local area as a traditional wine-making region. Social sustainability and SMEs' viability are ensured because of the cooperation among multiple actors, which benefits local communities. Thus, while economic sustainability can be framed as a starting point (as in Michel-Villarreal et al., 2020), it extends to the other domains of sustainability. Similarly, the next case describes a machinery-sharing initiative that aims to increase business viability by, once again, lowering the need for investments.

EXHIBIT 13.4   BANCO DE MAQUINARIA
COMPARTIDA

The name of this initiative translates to "Bank of Shared Machinery". It entails a group of farmers using shared facilities and machinery to restore the soil for farming purposes and to decrease their environmental footprint. By sharing machinery over three areas in Andalusia, Spain, the farmers primarily benefit by reducing the need to invest in machinery that they would only use a few times a year.

Retail

Apart from the retailers' cooperatives, collaborative retail in the food industry is not frequently discussed. Scholars have identified collaborative ways of sharing data, and predictions for storage and sales are ways to improve efficiency (Cachon & Fisher, 2000). Recent advances were achieved through the interplay among policymakers, the industry as a whole, and retailers to get the best from the multichannel sales (i.e. online and on-site shops; Kumar & Bakshi, 2021), and to counteract the shortcomings of the existence of both channels, namely, the need for a unique presentation of the products and the cannibalism from internal competition. Such collaborations have multiple goals, starting – as in the case of production – from the economic perspective, and then embedding environmental issues (Melkonyan et al., 2020; Teufer & Grabner-Kräuter, 2023). The two following cases (Exhibits 13.5 and 13.6) describe a participatory approach to establishing a food store in Parma, and a shortened FSC in Australia, with families buying meat and fish directly from the producers through an online marketplace.

EXHIBIT 13.5 OLTREFOOD CORP

OltreFood Corp has launched an innovative and collaborative store in Parma, Italy, aimed at offering to its members environmentally sustainable, ethical, and high-quality products at affordable prices. The store directly sources goods from local small-scale producers, bridging the gap between producers and consumers. By involving members as trade intermediaries, the store reduces markup on product costs and ensures a better quality–price ratio. This participatory approach challenges conventional distribution methods used by large retailers that may prioritise profits over product quality, working conditions, and environmental and social values.

This case describes a novel approach to collaboration in food retail that goes beyond the well-known model of cooperatives. The members play multiple roles, thus reducing costs and favouring more competitive prices without abandoning quality. Moreover, while some well-established cooperatives incorporated additional goals only years after their founding, this collaboration leverages environmental and social goals that are innate. The common root of such goals is the reduction in resource usage and the scale effect, as in Grosu (2023), but with the opportunity to also consider communitarian goals. The shortening of the FSC, health issues, and the infusion of local values is showcased in Exhibit 13.6 from Australia.

EXHIBIT 13.6   BUTCHERCROWD

ButcherCrowd is an Australian marketplace that supports commercial performance of small farmers and fisherpeople. Products are aligned to sustainable conditions both in farming and in selling food directly to families, as well as with sustainable packaging and free delivery. This company encourages sustainable sourcing and farming and allows families to buy better food through the support of nutritionists who offer their advice. Customers are selected according to their alignment with the values of this company and their willingness to help local farmers and fisherpeople.

Consumption

The transition from self-interested actions to a more citizen-oriented approach increasingly reveals a connection between food consumption and broader societal concerns (Ray Chaudhury & Albinsson, 2015). This encourages the adoption of collaborative models in food consumption. However, most of the collaborative actions reported in the literature deal with reducing food loss and waste by sharing food in communities, recirculating food surpluses, and donating unsold products, besides eating on one's own (Falcone & Imbert, 2017). Less attention has been paid to collaborative consumption in the form of sharing meals. Limited work has considered consumers' motivations for eating together, apart from celebrations or sharing co-working spaces (Schanes & Stagl, 2019). There are normative and economic reasons for shopping for food and having a meal together (Albinsson & Perera, 2012; Roos & Hahn, 2019), but new goals emerge, such as the willingness to experience something novel. Though aiming at different goals – that is, preserving tradition (as in the first case) and strictly counteracting waste (as in the second case) – Exhibits 13.7 and 13.8 show on-site and online contexts for eating together. 'O Vascio is an excellent example of how collaborative consumption can promote sustainability and social inclusion by reducing waste and making nutritious food more accessible to the broader community.

EXHIBIT 13.7   'O VASCIO

'O Vascio adopts a collaborative approach to reduce waste and promote sustainable consumption. It collects surplus food from restaurants and supermarkets, transforming it into affordable ready-to-eat meals. By repurposing food waste, it ensures access to fresh and healthy food for those in need. 'O

Vascio also conducts educational activities, such as workshops and cooking classes, to raise awareness about food waste and sustainability. Members actively manage operations, making it a participatory initiative.

'O Vascio integrates collaborative initiatives at multiple levels (Ray Chaudhury & Albinsson, 2015). While sourcing is sustainable because it prevents food waste and loss, offering meals with educational activities preserves tradition and promotes biodiversity more widely. Knowledge sharing is crucial in counteracting the cognitive errors of food-sharing initiatives: indeed, consumers buy more than needed when shopping in social groups, leading to waste.

Exhibit 13.8 focuses on experience and tradition as knowledge that is to be transferred (Parker et al., 2019). EatWith, an online platform connecting travellers and locals for shared meals and cultural experiences, is an example of how digital transformation changes economic practices, enabling the formation of networks that foster meal sharing with strangers (Veen & Dagevos, 2019). Locals can indulge in their hobby of cooking while visitors can enjoy unique, healthy, and sustainable experiences. By facilitating engagement through an online platform, common food experiences are created by individuals sharing stories and knowledge about food.

EXHIBIT 13.8   EATWITH

EatWith adopts a collaborative approach to connect people in food consumption. Hosts offer their homes or private spaces as venues, and guests can choose from a variety of experiences based on their interests. The offerings range from home-cooked meals to wine tastings and cooking classes and provide an authentic and immersive experience. EatWith operates in over 130 countries, with diverse hosts providing opportunities to learn about local culture and cuisine.

CONCLUSIONS

Developing an FSC oriented towards sustainable goals is challenging but achievable. Indeed, the examples above describe the sharing of natural resources and machinery, shortened FSCs, and developing new forms of meal consumption to achieve results for different entities, including keeping culinary and industrial traditions alive, improving the viability of food SMEs, providing better conditions for both firms and territories, and reducing food waste.

The integration of the activities along the FSC is doable but it might be difficult to connect a multitude of entities, from producers to retailers to customers, with similar goals (Brandenburg et al., 2014). The cases considered indicate that a reduced number of actors join such efforts, as sometimes participation is geographically limited or related to just one stage of the FSC. This mirrors the need to further understand the performance of collaborative actions (Chauhan et al., 2022). Therefore, increasing awareness of the expected results is a necessary step and can support communication for all entities.

The cases also indicate that various actors are willing to share resources and knowledge as well as generate novelties through interactions at multiple levels. The goal of sharing is not just to save money but also to preserve species and tradition, thus leading to collaborations as levers for social and environmental sustainability. Most of the advantages might be observed for microenterprises and SMEs as reducing costs; by extension, increasing investments would make the business viable. This is aligned with the disruptiveness of collaborative forms, as in Gharehgozli et al. (2017).

This research aligns with some previous studies on collaborative consumption and collaborative farming (Falcone & Imbert, 2017; Omer, 2022), while advances are achieved with reference to collaborative forms of production and retail. This study offers a novel view on such activities that stresses the potentialities of the collaborative form of production and retail, in addition to cooperative organisations. In addition, this chapter offers the opportunity to observe collaboration in activities related to food prior to its consumption. Farming, production, and retailing are key activities involved in bringing food to the table, thus creating the prerequisites to achieve sustainable goals.

Moreover, goals are intertwined and solutions can embed multiple goals. Indeed, this chapter suggests that saving resources can lead to advantages from both the economic and environmental perspectives. Similarly, considering local conditions is useful for preserving traditions and supporting local activities, thus creating opportunities for local communities to survive. Also, taking care of traditions is an additional form of sustainability, thus sustainability also embeds cultural sustainability.

Finally, technologies favour collaborations in terms of establishing relationships and sharing insights with multiple actors, in line with the need for increased awareness. In any event, technology should be seen as a tool for promoting sustainable conditions and for creating interactions among multiple actors. This is especially so because on-site activities are still significant, and people consider online interactions as an add-on to, and not a substitute for, human interactions.

Future research might observe whether there are dark sides in collaborative forms and seek to highlight additional factors stimulating such initiatives, including local culture and the frequent occurrence of collaborations in some areas.

REFERENCES

Albinsson, P. A., & Perera, B. Y. (2012). Alternative marketplaces in the 21st century: Building community through sharing events. *Journal of Consumer Behavior, 11,* 303–315.

Albinsson, P. A., & Perera, B. Y. (Eds.). (2018). *The rise of the sharing economy: Exploring the challenges and opportunities of collaborative consumption.* Praeger.

Altinay, L., & Taheri, B. (2019). Emerging themes and theories in the sharing economy: A critical note for hospitality and tourism. *International Journal of Contemporary Hospitality Management, 31*(1), 180–193.

Antanavičiūtė, A., & Dobilaitė, V. (2015). Principles of slow fashion application in clothing collection creation. *Environmental Research, Engineering and Management, 71*(2), 54–59.

Armstrong, C. M., & Park, H. (2017). Sustainability and collaborative apparel consumption: Putting the digital "sharing" economy under the microscope. *International Journal of Fashion Design, Technology and Education, 10*(3), 276–286.

Arrigo, E. (2021). Collaborative consumption in the fashion industry: A systematic literature review and conceptual framework. *Journal of Cleaner Production, 325,* 129261.

Ashaduzzaman, M., Jebarajakirthy, C., Weaven, S. K., Maseeh, H. I., Das, M., & Pentecost, R. (2022). Predicting collaborative consumption behaviour: A meta-analytic path analysis on the theory of planned behaviour. *European Journal of Marketing, 56*(4), 968–1013.

Balezentis, T., Zickiene, A., Volkov, A., Streimikiene, D., Morkunas, M., Dabkiene, V., & Ribasauskiene, E. (2023). Measures for the viable agri-food supply chains: A multi-criteria approach. *Journal of Business Research, 155,* 113417.

Barnham, C. (2015). Quantitative and qualitative research: Perceptual foundations. *International Journal of Market Research, 57*(6), 837–854.

Beamon, B. M. (1998). Supply chain design and analysis: Models and methods. *International Journal of Production Economics, 55*(3), 281–294.

Belk, R. (2014). You are what you can access: Sharing and collaborative consumption online. *Journal of Business Research, 67*(8), 1595–1600.

Blandon, J., Henson, S., & Cranfield, J. (2009). Small-scale farmer participation in new agri-food supply chains: Case of the supermarket supply chain for fruit and vegetables in Honduras. *Journal of International Development, 21*(7), 971–984.

Blanka, C., & Traunmüller, V. (2020). Blind date? Intermediaries as matchmakers on the way to start-up: Industry coopetition. *Industrial Marketing Management, 90,* 1–13.

Botsman, R., & Rogers, R. (2010). Beyond Zipcar: Collaborative consumption. *Harvard Business Review, 88*(10), 30.

Brandenburg, M., Govindan, K., Sarkis, J., & Seuring, S. (2014). Quantitative models for sustainable supply chain management: Developments and directions. *European Journal of Operational Research, 233*(2), 299–312.

Cachon, G. P., & Fisher, M. (2000). Supply chain inventory management and the value of shared information. *Management Science, 46*(8), 1032–1048.

Chasin, F., von Hoffen, M., Cramer, M., & Matzner, M. (2018). Peer-to-peer sharing and collaborative consumption platforms: A taxonomy and a reproducible analysis. *Information Systems and e-Business Management, 16*, 293–325.

Chauhan, C., Kaur, P., Arrawatia, R., Ractham, P., & Dhir, A. (2022). Supply chain collaboration and sustainable development goals (SDGs): Teamwork makes achieving SDGs dream work. *Journal of Business Research, 147*, 290–307.

Christopher, M. (2005). *Logistics and supply chain management, creating value-adding networks* (3rd ed.). Financial Times Prentice Hall.

Cleophas, C., Cottrill, C., Ehmke, J. F., & Tierney, K. (2019). Collaborative urban transportation: Recent advances in theory and practice. *European Journal of Operational Research, 273*(3), 801–816.

Cristiano, S. (2021). Organic vegetables from community-supported agriculture in Italy: Energy assessment and potential for sustainable, just, and resilient urban–rural local food production. *Journal of Cleaner Production, 292*, 126015.

De Lima, Y. C. C., de Morais, S. P. R., de M. Araujo, L. A. M., da SA Castelo Branco, D., & de A. Nääs, I. (2019). Collaborative production chains: A case-study of two agri-food companies in Brazil. In Ameri, F., Stecke, K., von Cieminski, G., Kiritsis, D. (Eds.), *Advances in production management systems. Production management for the factory of the future APMS 2019. IFIP Advances in Information and Communication Technology, 566.* (pp. 123–129).

Falcone, P. M., & Imbert, E. (2017). Bringing a sharing economy approach into the food sector: The potential of food sharing for reducing food waste. In Morone, P., Papendiek, F., Tartiu, V. (Eds.), *Food waste reduction and valorisation: Sustainability assessment and policy analysis* (pp. 197–214). Springer.

Food and Agriculture Organization (FAO). (2018). *Sustainable food system: Concept and framework.* https://www.fao.org/3/ca2079en/CA2079EN.pdf

Food and Agriculture Organization (FAO). (2021). *Milan urban food policy pact monitoring framework.* https://www.fao.org/3/cb4034en/cb4034en.pdf

Folkerts, H., & Koehorst, H. (1998). Challenges in international food supply chains: Vertical co-ordination in the European agribusiness and food industries. *British Food Journal, 100*(8), 385–388.

Fraanje, W., & Spaargaren, G. (2019). What future for collaborative consumption? A practice theoretical account. *Journal of Cleaner Production, 208*, 499–508.

Gharehgozli, A., Iakovou, E., Chang, Y., & Swaney, R. (2017). Trends in global e-food supply chain and implications for transport: Literature review and research directions. *Research in Transportation Business & Management, 25*, 2–14.

Griffiths, M. A., Perera, B. Y., & Albinsson, P. A. (2019). Contrived surplus and negative externalities in the sharing economy. *Journal of Marketing Theory and Practice, 27*(4), 445–463.

Grosu, R. M. (2023). "Green" practices in the food retail sector: Evidence from the Romanian market. *British Food Journal, 126*(1), 173–190. https://doi.org/10.1108/BFJ-12-2022-1119

Guimarães, Y. M., Eustachio, J. H. P. P., Leal Filho, W., Martinez, L. F., do Valle, M. R., & Caldana, A. C. F. (2022). Drivers and barriers in sustainable supply chains: The case of the Brazilian coffee industry. *Sustainable Production and Consumption, 34*, 42–54.

Hardie Hale, E., Jadallah, C. C., & Ballard, H. L. (2022). Collaborative research as boundary work: Learning between rice growers and conservation professionals to support habitat conservation on private lands. *Agriculture and Human Values*, *39*(2), 715–731.

Kaipainen, J., Urbinati, A., Chiaroni, D., & Aarikka-Stenroos, L. (2022). How companies innovate business models and supply chains for a circular economy: A multiple-case study and framework. *International Journal of Innovation Management*, *26*(9), 1–24.

Karki, S. T., Bennett, A. C., & Mishra, J. L. (2021). Reducing food waste and food insecurity in the UK: The architecture of surplus food distribution supply chain in addressing the Sustainable Development Goals (Goal 2 and Goal 12.3) at a city level. *Industrial Marketing Management*, *93*, 563–577.

Khan, R., Awan, T. M., Fatima, T., & Javed, M. (2020). Driving forces of green consumption in sharing economy. *Management of Environmental Quality: An International Journal*, *32*(1), 41–63.

Kumar, S., & Bakshi, S. (2021). Reform, perform and transform of Indian retail market. *Advance and Innovative Research*, *8*(2), 284–289.

Lamberton, C. (2016). Collaborative consumption: A goal-based framework. *Current Opinion in Psychology*, *10*, 55–59.

Matopoulos, A., Vlachopoulou, M., Manthou, V., & Manos, B. (2007). A conceptual framework for supply chain collaboration: Empirical evidence from the agri-food industry. *Supply Chain Management: An International Journal*, *12*(3), 177–186.

Mc Loughlin, K., Lewis, K., Lascelles, D., & Nudurupati, S. (2023). Sustainability in supply chains: Reappraising business process management. *Production Planning & Control*, *34*(1), 19–52.

Melkonyan, A., Gruchmann, T., Lohmar, F., Kamath, V., & Spinler, S. (2020). Sustainability assessment of last-mile logistics and distribution strategies: The case of local food networks. *International Journal of Production Economics*, *228*, 107746.

Michel-Villarreal, R., Vilalta-Perdomo, E. L., & Hingley, M. (2020). Exploring producers' motivations and challenges within a farmers' market. *British Food Journal*, *122*(7), 2089–2103.

Novel, A. S. (2014). Is sharing more sustainable? The environmental promises of the sharing economy. *Innovation for Sustainable Development*, *139*, 144.

Octavia, D., Nasution, R. A., & Yudoko, G. (2022). A conceptual framework for food sharing as collaborative consumption. *Foods*, *11*(10), 1422.

Omer, A. (2022). A club model of nature-smart agriculture for biodiversity, climate, and productivity enhancements. *Integrated Environmental Assessment and Management*, *9*(2), 214–230.

Parker, J. R., Umashankar, N., & Schleicher, M. G. (2019). How and why the collaborative consumption of food leads to overpurchasing, overconsumption, and waste. *Journal of Public Policy & Marketing*, *38*(2), 154–171.

Pienaar, W. J., & Vogt, J. J. (2009). *Business logistics management: A supply chain perspective*. Oxford University Press Southern Africa.

Popescu, G. H., & Ciurlău, F. C. (2019). Making decisions in collaborative consumption: Digital trust and reputation systems in the sharing economy. *Journal of Self-Governance and Management Economics*, *7*(1), 7–12.

Ray Chaudhury, S., & Albinsson, P. A. (2015). Citizen-consumer oriented practices in naturalistic foodways: The case of the slow food movement. *Journal of Macromarketing*, *35*(1), 36–52.

Roos, D., & Hahn, R. (2019). Understanding collaborative consumption: An extension of the theory of planned behavior with value-based personal norms. *Journal of Business Ethics, 158,* 679–697.

Saetta, S., & Caldarelli, V. (2020). How to increase the sustainability of the agri-food supply chain through innovations in 4.0 perspective: A first case study analysis. *Procedia Manufacturing, 42,* 333–336.

Sarkis, J., Gonzalez, E. D. S., & Koh, S. L. (2019). Effective multi-tier supply chain management for sustainability. *International Journal of Production Economics, 217,* 1–10.

Schaltegger, S., Beckmann, M., & Hockerts, K. (2018). Collaborative entrepreneurship for sustainability. Creating solutions in light of the UN sustainable development goals. *International Journal of Entrepreneurial Venturing, 10*(2), 131–152.

Schanes, K., & Stagl, S. (2019). Food waste fighters: What motivates people to engage in food sharing? *Journal of Cleaner Production, 211,* 1491–1501.

Siddh, M. M., Kumar, S., Soni, G., Jain, V., Chandra, C., Jain, R., Chandra, C., Jain, R., Kumar Sharma, M., & Kazancoglu, Y. (2021). Impact of agri-fresh food supply chain quality practices on organizational sustainability. *Operations Management Research, 15,* 146–165.

Stavros, C., & Westberg, K. (2009). Using triangulation and multiple case studies to advance relationship marketing theory. *Qualitative Market Research: An International Journal, 12*(3), 307–320.

Teufer, B., & Grabner-Kräuter, S. (2023). How consumer networks contribute to sustainable mindful consumption and well-being. *Journal of Consumer Affairs, 57*(2), 757–784.

Thow, A. M., Verma, G., Soni, D., Soni, D., Beri, D. K., Kumar, P., Siegel, K. R, Shaikh, N., & Khandelwal, S. (2018). How can health, agriculture and economic policy actors work together to enhance the external food environment for fruit and vegetables? A qualitative policy analysis in India. *Food Policy, 77,* 143–151.

United Nations. (2018). *Promoting sustainable food systems by improving multi-stakeholder collaboration.* https://sdgs.un.org/partnerships/promoting-sustainable -food-systems-improving-multi-stakeholder-collaboration

Veen, E. J., & Dagevos, M. (2019). Diversifying economic practices in meal sharing and community gardening. *Urban Agriculture & Regional Food Systems, 4*(1), 1–10.

PART V

Negative externalities and emerging trends

14. Negative externalities of collaborative consumption: the cost of exploitation

Merlyn A. Griffiths, Chantell LaPan, and Channelle D. James

INTRODUCTION

Collaborative consumption (CC) entails the sharing of idle assets. It nurtures peer-to-peer creativity and engagement by facilitating sharing (e.g., properties, supplies, and other possessions) rather than buying with the intent to own. CC has many names, including sharing economy, on-demand economy, platform economy, and access economy. Platforms upon which CC functions, and the players who operate within it, form a ubiquitous ecosystem facilitated by technology. In this chapter, we focus on CC and several aspects of the sharing economy, utilizing both terms where appropriate throughout the chapter.

Griffiths et al. (2019) acknowledge that the modern-day sharing economy affords a multiplicity of benefits to global users and providers. The CC model features access over ownership, typically relying on ratings-based marketplaces and in-app payment systems. CC may be an antidote to materialism and overconsumption – especially in the sharing of idle or unused assets (Belk, 2014), with beneficial outcomes for the participants. However, there are unplanned outcomes, some of which include exploitation, that may challenge the execution and efficacy of CC. These are negative externalities in that they are untoward consequences of CC that impact those outside of the CC relationship. Negative externalities are secondary effects that produce inefficiencies in resource allocation (Lazăr, 2018).

In the CC transactional space, some negative externalities manifest in the form of exploitation of unsuspecting consumers and other stakeholders. While data are limited, there is emerging evidence of additional vulnerabilities in the CC model relative to traditional business models. For example, Geissinger et al. (2022) argue that exploitation of labor is more likely in CC because independent contractors rely more on "gigs" that are temporary and unpredictable, whereas in the traditional space, employment contracts, labor laws, and regulations are more likely to minimize such exploitation. Platform exploitation also occurs where "a matched agent and customer may knowingly break platform rules and engage in subsequent transactions off the platform to avoid platform fees" (Zhou et al., 2022, p. 106). Bypassing the sharing of revenues on the platform is possible because the agent can exploit information asymmetry (Anand et al., 2023) without penalty, unlike in the traditional exchange where underreporting revenue can be met with penalties from governmental agencies (e.g., Internal Revenue Service). While there are growing categories of exploitations emerging from CC, this chapter focuses on two types: (1) assaultive exploitation (e.g., sex and labor trafficking exacerbated through transportation and accommodation sharing) and (2) digital surveillance exploitation (e.g., collecting and selling personal and behavioral information of platform users) as negative externalities that have significant costs to consumers and society. In doing so, we posit that the allure of profits is a lucrative attraction that fuels exploitation.

LUCRATIVE ATTRACTION

The CC space has transformed traditional sharing among people. Business entities and entrepreneurs recognize opportunities embedded within the various models, capitalizing on them to create streams of profit. Projections are that the sharing economy will grow from $15 billion in 2013 to $335 billion by 2025 (Radjou, 2021). Consumer acceptance of collaborative sharing services like Airbnb, Lyft, and Uber, has become globally normalized. For example, in 2021, Uber, which had services in 10 500 cities across 69 countries, provided 6.4 billion trips, equivalent to nearly 21 million trips per day (Wall Street Zen, n.d.). Airbnb has over 4 million hosts with 6 million listings in over 100 000 cities, with over 150 million worldwide users booking more than 1 billion stays in 2022 (iPropertyManagement, 2022). The extensive growth of these businesses along with changing technological dynamics make regulation and oversight a significant challenge for governmental bodies and policy advocates. This, coupled with the ease of entry for peer-to-peer sharers and service providers, magnifies the potential for exploitative negative externalities affecting consumers, businesses, and societal well-being.

The vast adoption of CC practices, platforms, and peer-to-peer exchanges adds complexities on a global level. Traditional economic models are also subject to negative externalities, but the sheer volume of these CC establishments is cause for concern. It represents a significant change in industry scale, business models, and economic efficiencies. Klenow and Rodríguez-Clare (2005) argue that externalities can result from "accumulation of knowledge possessed by firms (organizational capital) or by workers (human capital), [or] from the introduction of new goods, in the form of surplus to consumers and/ or firms" (p. 819). Economists have urged governments and policy advocates to "adopt policies that internalize an externality, so that costs and benefits will affect mainly parties who choose to incur them" (Boudreaux & Meiners, 2019, p. 1). As such, appreciating the true effect of negative externalities requires greater examination.

EXTERNALITIES

Externality, introduced by Pigou (2002), has its origins in economic theory in which "the action of one economic agent influences the utility or production function of another, and no mechanism for compensation exits… essentially unintended byproducts of activities undertaken primarily with a view to generating private benefits" (Cornes & Sandler, 1996, pp. 5–6). Economists explain that externalities can be positive or negative. "Positive externalities are benefits that are infeasible to charge to provide; negative externalities are costs that are infeasible to charge to not provide" (Boudreaux & Meiners, 2019, p. 1). Externalities may include "pollution activities (e.g., air pollution, water pollution, noise pollution, etc.), malevolence and benevolence, positive interaction of production activities" (Laffont, 2008, p. 192). From a cost–benefit standpoint, positive externalities are those that produce benefits for others, while negative externalities create costs for individuals, community, and society.

As side effects generated from overproduction of supply beyond the capabilities of societal demands, some externalities come from consumption (e.g., waste), while others stem from production (e.g., carbon emissions). They occur frequently when resource property rights are uncertain or non-existent so negative externalities producers are not responsible for the external costs generated (Lazăr, 2018). For example, a positive externality of ridesharing is less traffic in cities and reduced carbon emissions. For home sharing, it is increased efficiency in lodging, requiring fewer new buildings and decreased use of resources. In CC, positive externalities are "reflected in the reduction of transaction costs and improvement of transaction efficiency" (Jing & Sun, 2018, p. 152), whereas negative externalities "occur when the product and/ or consumption of a good or service exerts a negative effect on a third-party independent of the transaction" (CFI Team, 2023, para 1). For example, over-saturation of bicycle-sharing companies in a city with no infrastructure to collect and repair bicycles that are abandoned on sidewalks results in accidents and other hazards for residents and the community. Consequently, externalities play a prominent role in theories and practices related to economic growth.

Extant research has explored the contrived surplus of negative externalities (Griffiths et al., 2019) in tourism (Nieuwland & Van Melik, 2020), housing (Suzuki et al., 2022), and politics (Peksen, 2019). Building on this research, we explore the exploitative cost of negative externalities emerging in CC, the magnitude of which is evident in transportation (e.g., ridesharing) and lodging (e.g., home sharing). Hatzis (2015) explains that immoral behavior creates negative externalities when immoral activities spill over onto moral people. Sometimes "their acts or transactions have negative external effects of such magnitude that they can have detrimental effects to social order itself" (p. 233). Some participants in CC engage in immoral behaviors like assault and digital surveillance based on self-interest, with the intent to exploit others through CC platforms.

ASSAULTIVE EXPLOITATION

CC has created opportunities for emerging entrepreneurs by allowing them to utilize their existing and idle resources (e.g., automobiles, housing) in new ways. However, it also creates opportunities for assaultive exploitation (e.g., sexual assault, human trafficking, violence against workers) in unanticipated ways. In the CC context, we define assaultive exploitation as the act of using sharing platforms to gain personal benefit while forcing, compelling, or exerting undue influence over users in ways that cause them physical harm. Women have reported being sexually assaulted, fearful of kidnapping, or otherwise being held against their will in ridesharing (Alterisio, 2022; Rohrlich, 2021). In 2019, more than 30 customers sued Lyft, alleging the company did not do enough to keep them safe from assault, kidnapping, or rape (Homes, 2019). In 2022, more than 500 women filed a class-action lawsuit against Uber alleging sexual assault by drivers (Dent, 2022). A California Uber driver was sentenced to 46 years to life in prison for repeated sex crimes (CBS San Francisco, 2021), and Uber agreed to pay $9 million for underreporting sexual assaults (Hussain, 2021). Despite a significant decline in ridesharing during the COVID-19 pandemic, Uber reported 998 sexual assault incidents in 2020 including 141 rapes (O'Brien, 2022). The non-profit Polaris found that 82 percent of sex-trafficked survivors who encountered the transportation sector during their exploitation reported that rideshare platforms like Uber and Lyft were the key transportation sources used (Anthony, 2018). The unrestrained digital platform spaces that facilitate CC transactions are less regulated, making it easier to exploit assaultive opportunities like human trafficking and driver violence.

Allegations have also emerged that Uber sacrificed drivers' safety in locations that were hostile toward Uber's expansion in the area (Freedberg et al., 2022). Uber's former CEO said, "I think it's worth it. Violence guarantee[s] success" (para 35). According to Kerr (2022), a St. Louis Uber driver was carjacked at gunpoint by two passengers wearing COVID-19 face masks in 2021. Uber was non-responsive to police requests for information on the riders until three weeks later when a Lyft driver was murdered in the same location. Within hours of receiving the information, the suspect was also tied to the death of the Lyft driver. A quick response from Uber may have prevented the death (Kerr, 2022).

Some reports have indicated that Uber has attempted to avoid responsibility for driver behavior by claiming they are independent contractors rather than employees (Mulvaney, 2020). This stance minimizes the likelihood of adopting security measures that could increase customer safety. Until 2018, the company required mandatory arbitration for assault victims, limiting the transparency of these exploitations (Noguchi, 2018). To minimize fallout, Uber intentionally handles complaints in-house, forming their own justice system outside of established legal protections (Hulse, 2022). Dara Khosrowshahi has been CEO of Uber since 2017. Under his leadership, the company has virtually reinvented itself, with at least 90 percent of its current employees having joined since the changeover (Reed, 2022). However, it is unclear if this reinvented version of the company comes with new protocols against exploitations, but research suggests it has not (Sherer & Poydock, 2023)

Assaultive exploitations are not limited to ridesharing. The home-sharing platform Airbnb has been said to unknowingly facilitate what are being called "pop-up brothels" (Ardis, 2019) or increases in human trafficking incidents in some cities (Marchildon, 2018). The company has been criticized for not doing enough to prevent human trafficking while profiting from the exploitation (Goudreau, 2019). Anthony (2018) suggests that traffickers are turning to vacation rentals more often than hotels and motels, as the former are not policed as frequently. There is also growing concern that women who rent an Airbnb for vacations may be walking into situations where they are abducted and trafficked from their paid accommodation (Walker, 2022). Airbnb has been strategic about limiting public knowledge of safety issues including assembling a secretive critical safety team to handle accusations quietly (Carville, 2021) and requiring non-disclosure agreements to keep safety violations out of the news (Sonnemaker, 2021). The lack of policing and legal regulations, coupled with the transient nature of use, has increased the potential for sex and labor trafficking. Moreover, while these digitally enabled app-based platform environments can create physical vulnerabilities, they also allow other exploitative activities, such as digital surveillance, to flourish.

DIGITAL SURVEILLANCE EXPLOITATION

The expansion of digital technologies is accompanied by the widespread collection of user data, which is ripe for exploitation. This includes personal information (e.g., addresses and credit card, banking, and social security numbers), consumer data (e.g., purchasing behavior and preferences), and social data (e.g., connections and friends). Zuboff (2019) calls this "surveillance capitalism" or "a new economic order that claims human experience as free raw

material for hidden commercial practices of extraction, prediction, and sales"
(p. 10). For example, while Uber discloses selling data to third parties and uses
the information to manage surge pricing (Bajpai, 2021), privacy rights groups
have nonetheless sounded the alarm regarding its data collection practices and
have accused the company of abusing location data and causing direct harm to
consumers (Singer & Isaac, 2015). Airbnb has amassed an incredible wealth
of user information that they manipulate to maximize profit (Pereira, 2022).
This includes image recognition and analysis and natural language processing
(Project Pro, 2023). Stockpiling these data through surveillance capitalism
creates a negative externality of unrestrained power that can threaten democracy (Zuboff, 2019). While the company claims they do not sell the data, the
circumstances raise questions as to what purpose the collection of such big
data serves and what value it holds for the company (Pereira, 2022).

Kim (2021) suggests that Web 2.0 companies in the sharing economy
started out operating in partnership with their users. However, through
surveillance exploitation they now follow an "extraction imperative" or a
"growth-at-all-costs" approach to go public and please shareholders. Rather
than engaging in CC, Kim argues that these platforms are "intermediaries who
siphon the value away from the value creators and into the hands of wealthy
shareholders" (para 7). This power differential has left those that provide the
assets (i.e., cars, homes) vulnerable to a "feudal state," where companies like
Airbnb benefit disproportionately from the labor of the hosts (Kim, 2021).
What makes digital surveillance a negative externality of CC is the fact that
users are not fully aware of the types of information being collected, methods
used, and utilization intent.

The consumer advocacy group CHOICE explains that Airbnb's patented
algorithm is collecting information to assess people's personalities (e.g.,
narcissism, conscientiousness) and behavioral traits (e.g., drug, alcohol, crim-
inal record) to determine a trustworthiness score (Blakkarly, 2022). Data are
gathered through third parties (e.g., Facebook, LinkedIn) and aggregated with
public records (e.g., marriage certificates, property records, arrest reports) to
determine the score (Pereira, 2022). Bergemann et al. (2022) suggest that social
data create a data externality, producing a surplus extraction where individual
consumption data might also convey the shopping preferences of people with
similar purchase histories. Data intermediaries (e.g., Uber, Airbnb) are not
part of the initial transaction between the producer and consumer but instead
intrude in the relationship, controlling access, collecting, and redistributing
the data. Bergemann et al. (2022) suggest they auction off access to the user,
thereby providing other service providers with critical information that they
can use to shape their interactions with consumers.

Digital exploitation has led to a significant loss of consumer privacy
(Manwaring, 2018), with consumer data becoming a currency that is bought,

sold, and traded for a variety of benefits. Like the extraction imperative, Zuboff (2019) calls this the "prediction imperative" (p. 201), driven by the competition toward "higher degrees of certainty" (p. 203) in predicting consumer behavior. Scholars suggest that intensive profiling, which can undermine personal sovereignty and individual self-determination, harbors serious threats (Clarke, 2019), such as digital discrimination (Snow, 2022). For example, Black Airbnb users have faced various forms of online discrimination (Olson, 2022), including being denied bookings until they changed their name, used generic profile pictures, or even used photos of white individuals. A Harvard Business School study confirmed these claims by showing that users with distinctively sounding Black names were 16 percent less likely to be accepted for a booking than those with distinctively white-sounding names (Edelman et al., 2017). Hashtags such as #AirbnbWhileBlack and #UberWhileBlack on social media platforms highlight the pervasiveness of such discrimination (Olson, 2022). While consumer privacy is being violated, exploiters can maintain a certain level of anonymity using vague profiles and sharing minimal information on platforms. The lack of regulations and contactless space was exacerbated during the COVID-19 pandemic, thereby creating fertile ground for exploiters to test weaknesses in platforms that allow for manipulation (Russell, 2021). As CC platforms continue to evolve, more points of access that allow for exploitation will undoubtedly emerge.

In summary, assaultive exploitations and digital surveillance are advancing as common negative externalities and growing at an exaggerated pace without proper checks and balances. The pace at which regulators, law enforcement, and policy advocates react is at a snail's pace compared to the development and ubiquitousness of the technology fueling these platforms. Consequently, the costs imposed on individuals and society are not additive but exponential.

COST OF NEGATIVE EXTERNALITIES IN CC

Assaultive exploitations and digital surveillance create costs for those outside the initial exchange. The costs may not be present in monetary terms but in personal, psychological, and physical terms. For example, victims of human trafficking and sexual assault suffer deep and long-lasting consequences from these incidents. Research shows that victims battle chronic post-traumatic stress disorder (PTSD) and depression (Logan et al., 2009). Caring for these victims often falls to underfunded non-profits and non-governmental organizations, thus creating an additional negative externality as society must bear the costs to care for the growing pool of victims (Graham et al., 2019). Moreover, some victims experience significant impacts from having had a false sense of trust in the platforms and those who provide the service.

In terms of data surveillance or "dataveillance," there are a variety of costs to individuals, including self-censorship (i.e., limiting freedom of expression, speech, and thought) and discrimination (i.e., denied equal access and opportunity (Büchi et al., 2022). Marwick (2022) argues that marginalized communities have been disproportionate victims of surveillance. Privacy, or the lack thereof, creates additional costs when the use of personal data and proprietary algorithms bring racist and sexist judgments to scale (Crooks, 2022). Exploitations of digital platforms also create costs for companies as additional negative externalities emerge that produce liabilities for outside entities (e.g., governments, businesses, non-profits, non-governmental organizations, society at large). Whereas the host platform has the power to mediate unwanted behavior through sanctions and rewards (Hofmann et al., 2017), outside groups often pay for the consequences of this undesirable behavior. Society also incurs emotional and financial damages from the traumatic injuries and after-effects that victims experience (Lave, 1987). People close to the victims and in the community can be affected negatively by the trauma (Zhou & Wang, 2021), and trust among peers is eroded as hosts and service providers may be seen as dishonest.

RESPONSIVENESS TO ACCOUNTABILITY

In the CC model, trust is the foundation for successful interactions and the key driver of cooperative behavior, whereas power is most effective in managing this relationship in the business-to-consumer model (Hofmann et al., 2017). When trust or power is abused, exploitations can occur and generate negative externalities. The bevy of exploitations surrounding CC in transportation and lodging is indicative of a breakdown in trust (users distrust entities and believe they are self-serving) and an abuse of power (business entities exert power to suppress victims' voices). Although the incidents may be a very small number in relation to all the rides and stays provided, they nonetheless have detrimental impacts and must be addressed, and the platforms have a responsibility to be transparent and address issues, as it reflects good business ethics and social responsibility. The business model for CC transportation and lodging rests on the idea that strangers can trust one another. Were this premise undermined, the outcome would be fewer users, increased legal actions, and tighter regulations (Carville, 2021). What, then, are the tactics adopted to curtail these exploits? What actions has Airbnb taken considering the exploitations perpetuated through its platform? What steps have transportation companies like Uber and Lyft taken to add layers of safety for drivers and riders?

To be accountable means accepting the responsibility of customers – both buyers (guests, riders) and sellers (hosts, drivers). To instill trust, there must be transparency in conveying the risks of patronage. Airbnb has several approaches aimed at minimizing or eliminating the unsanctioned use of its platforms and housing accommodations for exploitative means. For example, the company has partnered with anti-human trafficking organizations, including "It's a Penalty" (itsapenalty.org), Polaris, the National Center for Missing and Exploited Children (NCMEC), the World Travel and Tourism Council (WTTC) global task force, and INTERPOL (Airbnb, 2021). Moreover "Airbnb screens all hosts and guests globally against regulatory, terrorist, and sanctions watch lists. For US residents, we also run background checks looking for prior felony convictions, sex offender registrations, and significant misdemeanors" (Airbnb, 2021, para 9). The range of efforts includes educating hosts and guests to recognize signs of human trafficking, raise awareness, and report suspected activities.

Uber now offers anonymization of customer information and a safety toolkit as in-app features (Payne, 2022), including notifications if GPS tracking goes off course and the ability to call 911 from within the app (Uber, n.d.-c). Uber has also partnered with PACT (formerly ECPAT-USA), which provides online anti-child trafficking training; Polaris, to mobilize communities, raise awareness, and advocate for policy legislation (Uber, n.d.-b); and the security company ADT, allowing riders to contact an agent during a trip (Forristal, 2022). The company's website provides tips to prevent sexual assault, including watching for social cues, enlisting allies to notify authorities, friends sticking together rather than leaving a bar or club alone, and checking the driver's photo and the car make, model, and license plate (Uber, n.d.-d.). The company has pledged $5 million to women's safety organizations through 2022 and has partnered with RAIIN, the National Sexual Assault Hotline, and the Department of Defense Safe Helpline; A Call to Men, which is a violence-prevention organization; and Futures Without Violence, which advocates for an end to family and gender-based violence (Uber, n.d.-d). Drivers now undergo a multi-step safety screening for violent offenses and impaired driving, with rescreening occurring every year (Uber, n.d.-c.).

Lyft has partnered with Businesses Ending Slavery and Trafficking (BEST) and the Dressember Foundation to provide education for drivers around human trafficking prevention (Lyft, 2020). Lyft has also partnered with Polaris to provide free rides for victims and survivors of human trafficking (Lyft, 2019). The company's website advocates a safety check for riders and drivers, like Uber, but adds that riders must ask drivers "who they're here for?" before getting in the car (Lyft, n.d.). Safety advisory council members are listed as advisors on products, features, and safety processes, including RAIIN, the National Association of Women Law Enforcement Executives, It's on US, National Sheriff's Association, National Organization of Black Law Enforcement Executives, Human Rights Campaign, Black Women's Roundtable, and the United State of Women (Lyft, n.d.).

Advocacy partnerships, safety councils, and information are commendable steps in the right direction and are similar to what other public transportation, lodging, and accommodation services may already have in place. Regardless, whatever steps that are taken, they should include what riders and drivers can or should do if embroiled in the middle of an attack to protect themselves. For example, what defensive responses or actions should be taken? What self-defense training or posturing might be recommended? While Uber, Lyft, and Airbnb have partnered with Polaris and others, the tangible results from these partnerships are less clear. Recently, US senators have questioned Uber, for example, about the training and resources available to drivers to help them recognize and respond to human trafficking (Alcorn, 2023).

SUSTAINABILITY IN THE CC ECONOMY PAST THE IMPACT OF NEGATIVE EXTERNALITIES

In the examples outlined in this chapter, platform-based CC companies have expanded rapidly with little consideration of negative externalities. Founders focused on growth and global expansion in terms of providing basic services; however, as issues began to arise, the companies were forced to respond by further refining their offerings to account for stakeholder well-being. They began by taking small steps (e.g., written policies) to address unanticipated costs levied on society. In some instances, they created programs (e.g., training) and formed alliances (e.g., partnerships) to curtail the negative externalities produced. The efforts of these multinational companies should be commended; however, are these actions enough to stem the rising social and economic costs? While some companies have made efforts to address these challenges, the lack of robust outcomes calls into question the extent of their commitment. For example, while Airbnb has policies against "child sexual exploitation and human trafficking," they are not highlighted on their website. Such lack of prominence may cause the public to question the company's commitment to address trafficking. Likewise, while Uber has made some progress, we posit that they still need to have a higher level of scrutiny over their rideshare process, such that they are more likely to detect human trafficking. A hands-off approach will most likely exacerbate the situation and overshadow customer experience. This aligns with the service recovery literature, which suggests that companies should take a more proactive stance on customer care. These efforts include providing compensation to redress the grievances of customers, showing them respect, and establishing procedures that will make it easier to address their concerns (Gelbrich & Roschk, 2011). Once a company starts to address customer complaints at any level, consumers recognize and believe that justice plays a part in the customer–company interaction.

In terms of digital surveillance, due to profit motives, large companies have little incentive to change. From a legal standpoint, many instances of digital surveillance are legitimate. However, when intermediaries use digital surveillance to evade government officials and jeopardize the right to privacy of consumers, the legality of these practices comes into question. It was reported that, as late as 2017, Uber used fake apps and digital surveillance to circumvent regulators and help unlicensed drivers evade the law. They also used these dummy apps to show riders either phantom cars (give the illusion of available drivers) or no cars at all (imply that there are no drivers in a particular region), a practice called "Greyball" (Davies & Bhuiyan, 2022; Mills, 2017). This was a fraudulent way to avoid fines and penalties against drivers. With Uber's new leadership and being a publicly traded company, the practice of "Greyball" is said to have been discontinued (Garrett, 2022).

Given the negative externalities and their impact, is there sustainability for ridesharing and lodging in the collaborative economy which, at a broad level, was founded with prosocial intent? Changes across law enforcement, governmental bodies, and advocacy groups must occur to ensure that the value of CC (i.e., trust, convenience, mobility, and sustainability) to individuals, firms, and society is not diminished by these exploitations. Critical action, such as imposing public policies that encourage transparency through regulations, is needed so that companies are held responsible for the externalities created and the remediation costs. Sustainability beyond the negative externalities also calls for greater transparency in that companies be required to report occurrences of human trafficking. Doing so will raise public awareness and allow customers to make informed choices regarding accommodation and transportation. Further, CC companies that are not taking reasonable proactive measures to enhance the safety of their services should be compelled to fund rescue and rehabilitation programs and services for victims. Simultaneously, local and federal laws must intersect to impose heavy fines when the platforms are found to be engaged in exploitative activities or lack the stringency and security protocols to minimize and even prevent this. Finally, investment in education, awareness, and training for the hosts, drivers, and other service providers is of immediate necessity. It should include self-defense training and actions that participants can take during an attack. Other protective measures may include advancing self-defense shields (e.g., mace). The content and actions must be specific, giving participants the tools needed to bring immediate attention to trafficking, illegal data capture, and other such exploitative behaviors.

REFERENCES

Airbnb. (2021, January 20). *Airbnb and it's a penalty partner to combat human traffick-ing* [Press release]. *Hospitality Net.* https://www.hospitalitynet.org/news/4102573.html

Alcorn, C. (2023, June 14). *Senators push for rideshares to take more action to crack down on human trafficking.* https://www.11alive.com/article/news/local/senators -push -rideshares -stop -human -trafficking/ 85 -7de2763a -75d4 -4ab2 -b835 -3d67f027dcfa

Alterisio, H. (2022, April 20). *Uber driver faces kidnapping charge after allegedly refusing to stop at teen passenger's destination.* Boston.com. https://www.boston.com/news/local-news/2022/04/20/uber-driver-faces-kidnapping-charge-bourne/

Anand, A., Dutta, S., & Mukherjee, P. (2023). Platform exploitation in the sharing economy. *Operations Research Letters, 51*(1), 47–53.

Anthony, B. (2018, July). *On-ramps, intersections, and exit routes: A roadmap for systems and industries to prevent and disrupt human trafficking.* Polaris. https://polarisproject.org/wp-content/uploads/2018/08/A-Roadmap-for-Systems-and -Industries-to-Prevent-and-Disrupt-Human-Trafficking.pdf

Ardis, M. (2019, November 20). *Pop-up brothels and Airbnb: A disturbing human trafficking trend.* Anti-Trafficking International. https://preventht.org/editorial/pop -up-brothels-and-airbnb-a-disturbing-human-trafficking-trend/

Bajpai, P. (2021, September 20). *How Uber uses your ride data.* Investopia. https://www.investopedia.com/articles/investing/030916/how-uber-uses-its-data-bank.asp

Belk, R. (2014). You are what you can access: Sharing and collaborative consumption online. *Journal of Business Research, 67*(8), 1595–1600.

Bergemann, D., Bonatti, A., & Gan, T. (2022). The economics of social data. *The Rand Journal of Economics, 53*(2), 263–296.

Blakkarly, J. (2022, March 21). *Is Airbnb using an algorithm to ban users from the plat-form?* CHOICE. https://www.choice.com.au/consumers-and-data/data-collection -and-use/how-your-data-is-used/articles/airbnb-banning-users

Boudreaux, D. J., & Meiners, R. (2019). Externality: Origins and classifications. *Natural Resources Journal, 59*(1), 1–34.

Büchi, M., Festic, N., & Latzer, M. (2022). The chilling effects of digital dataveillance: A theoretical model and an empirical research agenda. *Big Data & Society, 9*(1), 1–14.

Carville, O. (2021, June 15). *Airbnb is spending millions of dollars to make night-mares go away.* Bloomberg. https://www.bloomberg.com/news/features/2021-06 -15/airbnb-spends-millions-making-nightmares-at-live-anywhere-rentals-go-away

CBS San Francisco. (2021, April 28). *Former uber driver gets 46 years to life for raping, stealing from passengers in central California.* CBS Bay Area. https://www.cbsnews.com/sanfrancisco/news/former-uber-driver-gets-46-years-to-life-for -raping-stealing-from-passengers/

CFI Team. (2023, May 29). *Negative externalities.* Corporate Finance Institute. https:// corpo ratefinanc einstitute .com/ resources/ knowledge/ economics/ negative -externalities/

Clarke, R. (2019). Risks inherent in the digital surveillance economy: A research agenda. *Journal of Information Technology, 34*(1), 59–80.

Cornes, R., & Sandler, T. (1996). *The theory of externalities, public goods, and club goods.* Cambridge University Press.

Crooks, R. (2022). Seeking liberation: Surveillance, datafication, and race. *Surveillance & Society*, *20*(4), 413–419.

Davies, R., & Bhuiyan, J. (2022, July 12). Uber used Greyball fake app to evade police across Europe, leak reveals. *Guardian News and Media*. https://www.theguardian.com/news/2022/jul/12/uber-used-greyball-fake-app-to-evade-police-across-europe-leak-reveals

Dent, S. (2022, July 14). Uber sued by more than 500 women over sexual assault and kidnapping claims. *Engadget*. https://www.engadget.com/uber-sued-by-more-than-500-women-over-rapes-kidnappings-assaults-092733782.html

Edelman, B., Luca, M., & Svirsky, D. (2017). Racial discrimination in the sharing economy: Evidence from a field experiment. *American Economic Journal. Applied Economics*, *9*(2), 1–22. https://doi.org/10.1257/app.20160213

Forristal, L. (2022, August 30). Uber partners with ADT to let riders get in touch with a live safety agent. *Tech Crunch*. https://techcrunch.com/2022/08/30/uber-partners-with-adt-to-let-riders-get-in-touch-with-a-life-safety-agent/#:~:text=Now%2C%20Uber%20has%20partnered%20with,easier%20access%20to%20the%20tools

Freedberg, S., Sadek, N., Medina, B., Armendariz, A., & Kehoe, K. (2022, July 10). *How Uber won access to world leaders, deceived investigators and exploited violence against its drivers in battle for global dominance*. International Consortium of Investigative Journalists. https://www.icij.org/investigations/uber-files/uber-global-rise-lobbying-violence-technology/

Garrett, A. (2022, March 7). *Uber's Greyball program was real – how the app identified and sabotaged law enforcement*. Market Realist. https://marketrealist.com/p/uber-greyball-explained/

Geissinger, A., Laurell, C., Öberg, C., Sandström, C. and Suseno, Y. (2022). The sharing economy and the transformation of work: Evidence from Foodora. *Personnel Review*, *51*(2), 584–602.

Gelbrich, K., & Roschk, H. (2011). A meta-analysis of organizational complaint handling and customer responses. *Journal of Service Research*, *14*(1), 24–43.

Goudreau, G. (2019, October 9). *Airbnb continues to profit from the global sex trafficking trade*. Illicit Trade News Network. https://www.illicit-trade.com/2019/10/airbnb-continues-to-profit-from-the-global-sex-trafficking-trade/

Graham, L. M., Macy, R. J., Eckhardt, A., Rizo, C. F., & Jordan, B. L. (2019). Measures for evaluating sex trafficking aftercare and support services: A systematic review and resource compilation. *Aggression and Violent Behavior*, *47*, 117–136. https://doi.org/10.1016/j.avb.2019.04.001

Griffiths, M. A., Perera, B. Y., & Albinsson, P. A. (2019). Contrived surplus and negative externalities in the sharing economy. *Journal of Marketing Theory and Practice*, *27*(4), 445–463.

Hatzis, A. N. (2015). Moral externalities: An economic approach to the legal enforcement of morality. In A. N. Hatzis & N. Mercuro (Eds.), *Law and economics: Philosophical issues and fundamental questions* (pp. 226–244). Routledge.

Hofmann, E., Hartl, B., & Penz, E. (2017). Power versus trust: What matters more in collaborative consumption? *Journal of Services Marketing*, *31*(6), 589–603.

Homes, A. (2019, October 25). *More than 30 women are suing Lyft, saying the company didn't do enough to protect them from sexual assault and kidnapping*. Business Insider. https://www.businessinsider.com/lyft-lawsuit-women-claiming-lack-of-sexual-assault-kidnapping-protection-2019-10

Hulse, S. (2022, October 6). What is Uber keeping quiet about? Sexual assaults and a data breach for starters. *Grit Daily.* https://gritdaily.com/uber-sexual-assaults-and -data-breach/

Hussain, S. (2021, December 2). Uber agrees to pay $9-million California settlement on sexual assault reporting failure. *Los Angeles Times.* https://www.latimes.com/ business/technology/story/2021-12-02/uber-9-million-california-settlement-regulators -sexual-assault-data

iPropertyManagement. (2022, August 3). *Airbnb statistics.* https://ipropertymanagement .com/research/airbnb-statistics

Jing, W., & Sun, B. (2018). Negative externalities in the sharing economy: Sources, paths and recommendations. *International Journal of Crowd Science, 2*(2), 149–163. https://doi.org/10.1108/IJCS-08-2018-0016

Kerr, D. (2022, December 9). *When drivers are attacked, Uber leaves police waiting for help.* The Verge. https://www.theverge.com/2022/12/9/23500458/uber-driver -attacks-police-cooperation

Kim, L. (2021, July 8). Airbnb is exploiting its users, but decentralized alternatives are possible. *Cointelegraph.* https://cointelegraph.com/news/airbnb-is-exploiting-its -users-but-decentralized-alternatives-are-possible

Klenow, P. J., & Rodríguez-Clare, A. (2005). Externalities and growth. In P. Aghion & S. N. Durlauf (Eds.), *Handbook of economic growth* (pp. 817–861). Elsevier B.V. https://doi.org/10.1016/S1574-0684(05)01011-7

Laffont, J. J. (2008). Externalities. In S. N. Durlauf & L. E. Blume (Eds.), *The new Palgrave dictionary of economics* (pp. 192–195). Palgrave Macmillan.

Lave, L. B. (1987). Injury as externality: An economic perspective of trauma. *Accident; Analysis and Prevention, 19*(1), 29–37.

Lazăr, A. I. (2018). Economic efficiency vs. positive and negative externalities. *Review of General Management, 27*(1), 112–118.

Logan, T. K., Walker, R., & Hunt, G. (2009). Understanding human trafficking in the United States. *Trauma, Violence, and Abuse, 10*(1), 3–30. https://doi.org/10.1177/ 1524838008327262

Lyft. (2019, July 30). *Lyft & Polaris partner to provide free rides for victims of human trafficking.* https://www.lyft.com/blog/posts/lyft-amp-polaris-partner-to-provide -free-rides-for-victims-of-human-trafficking

Lyft. (2020, June 7). *Lyft partners with anti-trafficking organizations to educate drivers on human trafficking prevention.* https://www.lyft.com/blog/posts/best-and -lyft-partner-to-educate-drivers-on-human-trafficking-prevention

Lyft. (n.d.) *Lyft Safety Advisory Council. Lyft safety.* https://www.lyft.com/safety #looking-out

Manwaring, K. (2018). Will emerging technologies outpace consumer protection law? The case of digital consumer manipulation. *Competition and Consumer Law Journal, 26*(2), 141–181.

Marchildon, J. (2018, February 23). *Airbnb rentals are increasingly being used for human trafficking, Police say.* Global Citizen. https://www.globalcitizen.org/fr/ content/airbnb-human-trafficking/

Marwick, A. (2022). Privacy without power: What privacy research can learn from surveillance studies. *Surveillance & Society, 20*(4), 397–405.

Mills, C. (2017, March 3). *Uber uses a fake app and digital surveillance to evade government officials in some cities.* Yahoo! Finance. https://finance.yahoo.com/news/ uber-uses-fake-app-digital-surveillance-evade-government-205102221.html

Mulvaney, E. (2020, March 2). *Uber, Lyft talk responsibility on assaults but deny in court*. Bloomberg Law. https://news.bloomberglaw.com/daily-labor-report/uber-lyft -talk-responsibility-on-assaults-but-deny-in-court

Nieuwland, S., & Van Melik, R. (2020). Regulating Airbnb: How cities deal with perceived negative externalities of short-term rentals. *Current Issues in Tourism, 23*(7), 811–825.

Noguchi, Y. (2018, May 15). *Under pressure, Uber drops arbitration requirement for sexual assault victims*. NPR. https://www.npr.org/2018/05/15/611230115/under -pressure-uber-drops-arbitration-requirement-for-sexual-assault-victims

O'Brien, S. A. (2022, June 30). *Uber releases safety data: 998 sexual assault incidents including 141 rape reports in 2020*. CNN Business. https://www.cnn.com/2022/06/ 30/tech/uber-safety-report/index.html

Olson, C. (2022, January 24). Airbnb blocks Oregon hosts from seeing guests' names in push against racial bias. *The Guardian*. https://www.theguardian.com/technology/ 2022/jan/03/airbnb-race-oregon-names-discrimination

Payne, R. (2022, August 30). *Uber's new safety toolkit featuring live help from a safety agent*. Uber Newsroom. https://www.uber.com/newsroom/ubers-new-safety-toolkit/

Peksen, D. (2019). Political effectiveness, negative externalities, and the ethics of economic sanctions. *Ethics & International Affairs, 33*(3), 279–289.

Pereira, A. (2022, May 23). *Op-ed: Just how much does Airbnb need to know?* CHOICE. https://www.choice.com.au/consumers-and-data/data-collection-and-use/ how-your-data-is-used/articles/airbnb-data-misuse-op-ed

Pigou, A. (2002). *The economics of welfare* (1st ed.). Routledge. https://doi.org/10 .4324/9781351304368

Project Pro. (2023, July 15). *How data science increased AirBnB's valuation to $25.5 bn?* https://www.projectpro.io/article/how-data-science-increased-airbnbs-valuation -to-25-5-bn/199

Radjou, N. (2021, April 14). *The sharing economy's next target: Business-to-business*. Fast Company. https://www.fastcompany.com/90624859/the-sharing-economys -next-target-business-to-business

Reed, B. (2022, July 10). "We will not make excuses": Uber responds to Uber files leak. *The Guardian*. https://www.theguardian.com/news/2022/jul/10/uber-response -uber-files-leak

Rohrlich, J. (2021, March 21). *Mass. uber driver accused of kidnapping passenger*. Daily Beast. https://www.thedailybeast.com/massachusetts-uber-driver-kamal -essalak-accused-of-kidnapping-passenger

Russell, M. (2021, September 10). *The dark side of contactless check-in*. Professional Convention Management Association. https://www.pcma.org/human-trafficking -contactless-check-in/

Sherer, J., & Poydock, M. (2023, February 23). *Flexible work without exploitation*. Economic Policy Institute. https://www.epi.org/publication/state-misclassification-of -workers/

Singer, N., & Isaac, M. (2015, June 22). Uber data collection changes should be barred, privacy group urges. *New York Times*. https://www.nytimes.com/2015/06/ 23/technology/uber-data-collection-changes-should-be-barred-privacy-group-urges .html

Snow, O. (2022, December 26). Sex workers have been banned from Airbnb for years. will you be next? *The Nation*. https://www.thenation.com/article/society/airbnb -banning-sex-workers/

Sonnemaker, T. (2021, June 16). *Airbnb deals with thousands of sexual-assault allegations every year, but manages to keep many out of the public eye, report says.* Business Insider. https://www.businessinsider.com/airbnb-faces-thousands-sexual-assault-claims-yearly-report-2021-6

Suzuki, M., Hino, K., & Muto, S. (2022). Negative externalities of long-term vacant homes: Evidence from Japan. *Journal of Housing Economics, 57*, 101856.

Uber. (n.d.-b). *Help stop human trafficking.* https://www.uber.com/us/en/community/safety/fighting-human-trafficking/

Uber. (n.d.-c). *Our commitment to safety.* https://www.uber.com/us/en/safety/

Uber. (n.d.-d) *Tips to help you stay safe and prevent sexual assault.* https://www.uber.com/us/en/safety/womens-safety/safety-tips/

Walker, N. (2022, July 24). *Black women report frightening experiences with an Airbnb host as a warning to others.* The Grio. https://thegrio.com/2022/07/24/black-women-allege-frightening-experiences-with-tulum-airbnb-host/

Wall Street Zen. (n.d.). *Uber technologies Inc statistics & facts.* https://www.wallstreetzen.com/stocks/us/nyse/uber/statistics

Zhou, Q., Allen, B. J., Gretz, R. T., & Houston, M. B. (2022). Platform exploitation: When service agents defect with customers from online service platforms. *Journal of Marketing, 86*(2), 105–125.

Zhou, W., & Wang, S. (2021). The externality of negative emotion. *Research Square.* https://doi.org/10.21203/rs.3.rs-743332/v1

Zuboff, S. (2019). *The age of surveillance capitalism: The fight for a human future at the new frontier of power.* Public Affairs.

15. Cryptocurrency communities: an overview of collaborative currency systems

Lagnajita Chatterjee, Pia A. Albinsson, Dan R. Bradbury, and Adrienne F. Muldrow

INTRODUCTION

For much of human history, people relied on bartering goods and services that were mutually agreed to be of equal value (Beattie, 2022). For instance, one might have decided whether the effort required to provide food for a week was a worthy trade to another's efforts to build and maintain basic shelter. This is the truest meaning of "peer-to-peer" (P2P) exchange. Subsequently, this bartering system progressed to using various mediums of exchange that could "store value," such as animal hides, coins made of precious metals, or even precious stones (Beattie, 2022), which also served as a means of accounting for various exchanges. These mediums of exchange eventually became referred to as "money," which in its simplest definition is an "instrument" that represents, in part, "a claim on the future" (Haberly & Wójcik, 2022, p. 5). Importantly, this "claim on the future" eventually developed into the financial system that most are familiar with today: a "layered" system that provides varying degrees of liquidity, immutability, and transferability to individuals, governments, and institutions (Bhatia, 2021). Over the years, "money" and exchanges have appeared in different forms.

Today, aside from alternative marketplaces such as Freecycle, Really Really Free Markets, free stores, and neighborhood swaps where no cash or other payment systems are used (e.g., Albinsson & Perera, 2012; Arsel & Dobscha, 2011; Nelson & Rademacher, 2009), the simplest layer of financial systems, or what is referred to as "layer 0," is cash and is typically transacted very much in a P2P manner (Bhatia, 2021). For instance, a consumer interested in acquiring a used blender from a colleague or stranger might hand them the mutually agreed-upon $20. In this case, money, instead of a similarly valued item, is exchanged for a good, and both parties immediately receive what they are seeking. As opposed to bartering, where a good is exchanged for another, or where money is exchanged for a good, ensuring both parties receive "their end of the bargain," transactions can be more challenging in digital settings. However, collaboration nonetheless exists within digital payment systems.

The collaborative digital economy is continuously transforming how consumers engage in the marketplace in their various roles as producers, consumers, borrowers, financiers, and learners through networks of peers and their specific communities (Ertz & Boily, 2019). In terms of financial practices, the traditional global financial system relies heavily on intermediaries, such as banks, lending companies, clearing services, and centralized authorities, such as governments and central banks, to facilitate, enforce, and secure transactions (Haberly & Wójcik, 2022). Even payments on early P2P exchange platforms such as eBay were facilitated by centralized intermediaries (Denegri-Knott & Molesworth, 2010). Recent developments in blockchain technology, however, have provided an opportunity for decentralization, which reduces the established central controls of financial transactions (Nakamoto, 2008). Blockchain technology is referred to as a "peer-to-peer network that sits on top of the internet" (Iansiti & Lakhani, 2017, p. 5; see Gleim & Stevens, 2021, and Ertz & Boily, 2019, for information on blockchain use in marketing and the collaborative economy, respectively).

Blockchain technology has also facilitated the growth of cryptocurrencies. Cryptocurrency is broadly defined as a "decentralized" digital system that uses cryptography on a (typically) public blockchain to secure and verify transactions and ownership of individual "tokens" (Antonopoulos, 2019). Along with the P2P (i.e., consumer-to-consumer) aspect, one of the underlying principles of cryptocurrency is to enable individuals and organizations to freely and securely transact with reduced costs, no limitations, and rapid settlement (Narayanan et al., 2016). Cryptocurrencies are unique because value is efficiently and securely transferred through P2P transactions without the interference of intermediaries. Essentially, instead of centralized institutions as third-party intermediaries, efficiencies are driven through enabling and incentivizing individuals (i.e., miners) to collectively validate transactions over a distributed network that they each contribute to maintaining (Nofer et al., 2017). Instead of requiring banks, clearing houses, and settlement agencies to validate and agree upon transactions, cryptocurrency networks rely on individuals to collectively validate a transparent ledger of every transaction that occurs with a given currency. Through various incentive mechanisms, such as proof of work, proof of stake, proof of capacity, and numerous others, these individuals are rewarded with a native token (such as Bitcoin, Ethereum, or Solana) for maintaining a public ledger, sometimes through a fixed inflationary rate, percentage of transaction fees on the network, or a mix of these (Aggarwal & Kumar, 2021). At a user level, anyone with any given cryptocurrency can send the token to another individual or organization over this network. As this is done, the network ledger will (nearly) automatically record and post this transaction so the recipient receives the currency instantaneously. To this end, cryptocurrency and other decentralized (DeFi) platforms allow individuals to freely conduct financial transactions (e.g., borrowing, lending, exchanging currencies, insuring certain products) at any time, from any location, with nearly instantaneous approval and settlement (Schueffel, 2021).

Relative to traditional financial institutions, cryptocurrency and other DeFi platforms offer noteworthy benefits to users. For instance, one key advantage is the potential reduction of subjective biases, which have led to discriminatory practices in various sectors of the financial industry including banks (Brandt & Li, 2003), stock brokerages (Madden, 2012), and automobile insurance (Cather, 2020). Further, as with FTX's (a digital currency exchange) recent collapse, the centralized structure of financial organizations has been blamed for headline-making collapses and losses of user funds (Ramaswamy & Lurie, 2022). In contrast, DeFi utilizes blockchain technology to provide full transparency, lower transaction costs, and rapid settlement, while providing inclusive, around-the-clock access to traditionally disadvantaged individuals (Chen & Bellavitis, 2020). Overall, the adoption of blockchain technology, cryptocurrencies, and DeFi represents a significant paradigm shift that may transform and perhaps improve how value is transacted online (Goldstein, 2020).

Cryptocurrency, blockchain technology, and DeFi technology have also led to a shift in the sharing economy realm. For instance, marketplaces such as ShareRing, which is built on the "Tendermint" blockchain, have begun to utilize blockchain technology to eliminate the need for third-party platforms (Amoils, 2020). Other decentralized examples include OpenBazaar, a marketplace similar to eBay and Amazon but without intermediaries, and La'Zooz, a community-owned transportation platform that serves as an alternative to Uber (De Filippi, 2017; Schneider, 2015). These platforms allow for sharing, pseudo-sharing, and collaborative consumption among peers. Cryptocurrencies are suitable for micropayments, mobile payments, and P2P lending communities in the sharing economy (Möhlmann et al., 2021).

Given the shifts in financial systems as a result of cryptocurrency and associated communities, and its impact on collaborative consumption, reviewing and analyzing research on cryptocurrency communities is timely. In the following sections, we develop the concept of internal and external crypto communities by first reviewing P2P lending as an early form of a decentralized financial community system, and then discussing nascent research on cryptocurrency communities.

EARLY DECENTRALIZED FINANCIAL COMMUNITIES

P2P lending platforms are two-sided platforms involving lenders, borrowers, and P2P communities (Bachmann et al., 2011). More recently, these platforms have been referred to as *multi-sided platforms*, which are services that bring together two or more groups of customers and businesses (Trabucchi & Buganza, 2020). While P2P lending was launched in 2005, the P2P platforms rose in popularity during the financial crisis of the late 2000s, when trust in financial institutions was at an all-time low (Bednorz, 2020). Since then, erosion of trust in traditional financial institutions (Basha et al., 2021; Bachmann et al., 2011) and advancements in digital financial technologies (Bollaert et al., 2021), among others, have contributed to their diversification.

Since the initial P2P lending communities were launched, multiple factors have contributed to their diversification, such as the advancement in digital financial technologies (Bollaert et al., 2021). Beyond macro-societal factors, adoption of P2P lending communities has other psychological determinants that enhance its success. For instance, research shows that strong narratives that include identity traits such as trustworthiness or being successful increase the potential for acquiring loans and lower interest rates (Duarte et al., 2012; Herzenstein et al., 2011). Community memberships (Berger & Gleisner, 2009; Everett, 2015) and interpersonal relationships (Wang et al., 2020) also impact loan decisions. Along with these soft factors, hard factors, such as the borrower's financial status, also shape P2P loan decisions (Bachmann et al., 2011; Basha et al., 2021). Even though there have been a few instances in which P2P financial system users have expressed instances of discrimination based on gender and socio-economic status (Chen et al., 2017; Wu et al., 2023), in general, P2P platforms have enhanced inclusivity, such as increasing lending and fund accessibility within different socio-economic groups. Following these mostly positive and inclusive aspects of P2P lending communities, we have recently seen developments of cryptocurrency-based communities.

CRYPTO COMMUNITIES

Cryptocurrencies vary widely in terms of their purpose and utility (Rossolillo, 2022). While they can be used for purchases, repayment, or for lending directly to individuals (i.e., Venmo), other uses include creating, trading, and purchasing NFTs (non-fungible tokens) to provide access to games (Yoo et al., 2023). Cryptocurrencies developed after the 2008 global financial crisis amid increasing levels of distrust in governments and global financial instability (Saiedi et al., 2021). One of the first cryptocurrencies, Bitcoin, was developed in 2008 to challenge mainstream financial markets (Breidbach & Tana, 2021). In 2021, less than 13 years from its inception, Bitcoin became so popular that it reached a peak global market cap of nearly \$1.2T in 2021 (Statista, 2023). Cohen (2017) suggests that the rise in cryptocurrency was "driven by the grassroots, and technologically empowered, movement to confront the ills perceived to be powered and exacerbated by market-based capitalism, such as climate change and income inequality" (p. 739). Simos and Tan (2019) echo the perspective that bottom-up grassroots innovation is the driving force behind the cryptocurrency market's sudden growth.

Subsequently, grassroots "cryptocurrency communities with a shared interest in cryptocurrencies, blockchain, or Web3 have developed over time" (Binance Academy, 2023; Casey, 2023). Although it is quickly gaining ground, the extant research on collaborative consumption in cryptocurrency communities is still limited (e.g., Breidbach & Tana, 2021; Caliskan, 2022a, 2022b; Ertz & Boily, 2019; Möhlmann et al., 2021). Much of the research focuses on financial or technical aspects of how blockchain works or how cryptocurrencies are used as commodities or assets in terms of assetization and pricing, derivation, pricing volatility, and trading movements. For example, literature on financial products in the collaborative realm has discussed crowdfunding (e.g., Indiegogo, Kickstarter), ethical and alternative banking (e.g., Charity Banks), and P2P lending, also referred to as social lending (e.g., LendingClub, Zopa Bank; see Kamalaris & Prenafeta-Boldu, 2018). Perspectives on how non-institutional individual actors unite to form consumer collectives (i.e., communities) that shape or reshape markets are rare (Breidbach & Tana, 2021; Martin & Schouten, 2014). Such research is necessary to better understand shifts in market offerings and acceptance (Slimane et al., 2019).

Internal and External Crypto Communities

Simply being an investor does not necessarily make one a part of either an internal or external crypto community. Some of these communities are structured to allow consumers to share ideas and opinions, ask questions, and network (CoinDCX, 2022). Other communities such as Impact Market, that operate in developing countries with the aim of empowering local community members provide a "protocol designed for communities to develop financial inclusion and social-impact projects" (Casey, 2023). The members of such collectives act as a family and assume the responsibility to educate others on how to trade, invest, and act within the community (Breidbach & Tana, 2021; CoinDCX, 2022). For example, DCX Learn, a subsidiary of India's largest cryptocurrency exchange, CoinDCX, considers it a "moral responsibility to educate and bring a learning revolution in the world's cryptocurrency ecosystem" (dcxlearn.com, 2022). According to its website, DCX Learn strives to educate, enrich, enlighten, and empower their consumers. In our estimation, this is an external community, as not all consumers engage in the internal work, such as mining and staking (see below) with the currency. Other examples of external communities include interest groups on social media, public forums, and so on.

In contrast, within internal crypto communities, certain consumers take on the roles of miners and stakers. Though they may not necessarily be an "active" part of groups that form around the given currency, they are nonetheless crucial for enabling the overall network. Since the decentralization of a given crypto network is contingent on individuals actively maintaining it on their own personal computers and servers, miners and stakers act as "network validators" (Antonopoulos, 2019). While these individuals may not directly participate in a crypto community by joining a specific community's messaging group or participating in conversations with other members, miners and stakers are a critical part of the digital asset ecosystem because they passively facilitate transactions on the network through processes known as proof of work (PoW) and proof of stake (PoS), respectively (Binance Academy, 2018). Within technologies that use blockchain, users follow rules to protect the overall integrity of the technology chain, meaning that users can only change their own blocks.

The motivation for maintaining such networks is relatively straightforward: both miners and stakers are rewarded for their contributions. Miners, who engage in the PoW consensus mechanism, compete to solve complex mathematical puzzles, and the successful miner is rewarded with newly minted cryptocurrency tokens and transaction fees (Whittaker & Adams, 2023). On the other hand, stakers, who participate in PoS-based networks, lock up a certain amount of cryptocurrency tokens as a stake and, in return, have the opportunity to validate transactions and create new blocks, thereby earning staking rewards (Napoletano & Curry, 2023). While the specifics of the mining or staking process and the rewards vary depending on the cryptocurrency and consensus mechanism employed, the design of the underlying cryptocurrency protocols typically involves a system that scales with the number of miners or stakers (Sergeenkov, 2023). This ensures that the network remains secure, and transactions can be processed in a decentralized manner (Antonopoulos, 2019). Without these individuals actively maintaining the network's transactions and activity (i.e., the blockchain), the network would presumably not exist. Next, we illustrate some additional roles assumed by internal community members.

In an investigation of an Australian cryptocurrency collective, also referred to as a collaborative space, Breidbach and Tana (2021) posited a typology of roles performed by its members. The authors suggested that retirees or individuals without prior cryptocurrency knowledge who perform the *Freshman* role are motivated to learn more about cryptocurrency and expand their network. The more sophisticated *Fortune Hunters*, who are more experienced with trading, initial coin offerings, or mining, are motivated by monetary benefits. They also strive to expand the impact of their community and change tax regulations to further benefit cryptocurrency investors. *Idealists*, often composed of academics, students, and developers (information technology professionals), are motivated by developing, extending, and sharing knowledge and skills of cryptocurrency with others through research and learning about the technical aspects that are beneficial to society. The *Trail-Blazers*, or so-called communal entrepreneurs, which is the smallest group, attempt more commercial cryptocurrency activities. They have expert knowledge, and though they too strive to benefit society through community activities, they also want to earn money. Interestingly, the Electra Protocol community's core team display similar characteristics, as they have published three white papers illustrating how research (i.e., knowledge creation) and money-making go hand in hand in some cryptocurrency communities (Caliskan, 2022a; Breidbach & Tana, 2021).

Similar to what Breidbach and Tana (2021) found with *Idealists* and *Trail-Blazers*, while Electra core team members belong to a cryptocurrency platform, their interactions and topics of discussion extend beyond the value of XEP and other currencies to focus on "making economic things possible in a new way" (Caliskan, 2022b, p. 184). Oftentimes, cryptocurrency community members aim to disrupt centralized banking systems with their community-generated technology (Maddox & Heemsbergen, 2021). The motivation of "constructing" (i.e., creating and being part of a cryptocurrency community) aligns with "architectures of collaboration, cooperation, and coordination developed by technically savvy populations" (Maddox & Heemsbergen, 2021, p. 4).

CONCLUSION, FUTURE RESEARCH, AND LIMITATIONS

In conclusion, cryptocurrencies, P2P lending, and DeFi provide a unique setting in which collaborative consumption unites with finance digitization (Figure 15.1 presents a comparative analysis of the two systems). Cryptocurrency-driven lending and DeFi communities help democratize financing options and enhance collaborative consumption in this realm. According to Ertz and Boily (2019), blockchain technology appears to play an important role in the development of innovative collaborative practices through the implementation "of more egalitarian principles of production and distribution by facilitating P2P interventions that advance community interests" (p. 88) by individual consumers.

The collaborative nature of the mechanisms and platforms underpinning cryptocurrency and P2P lending, the latter of which is firmly situated within

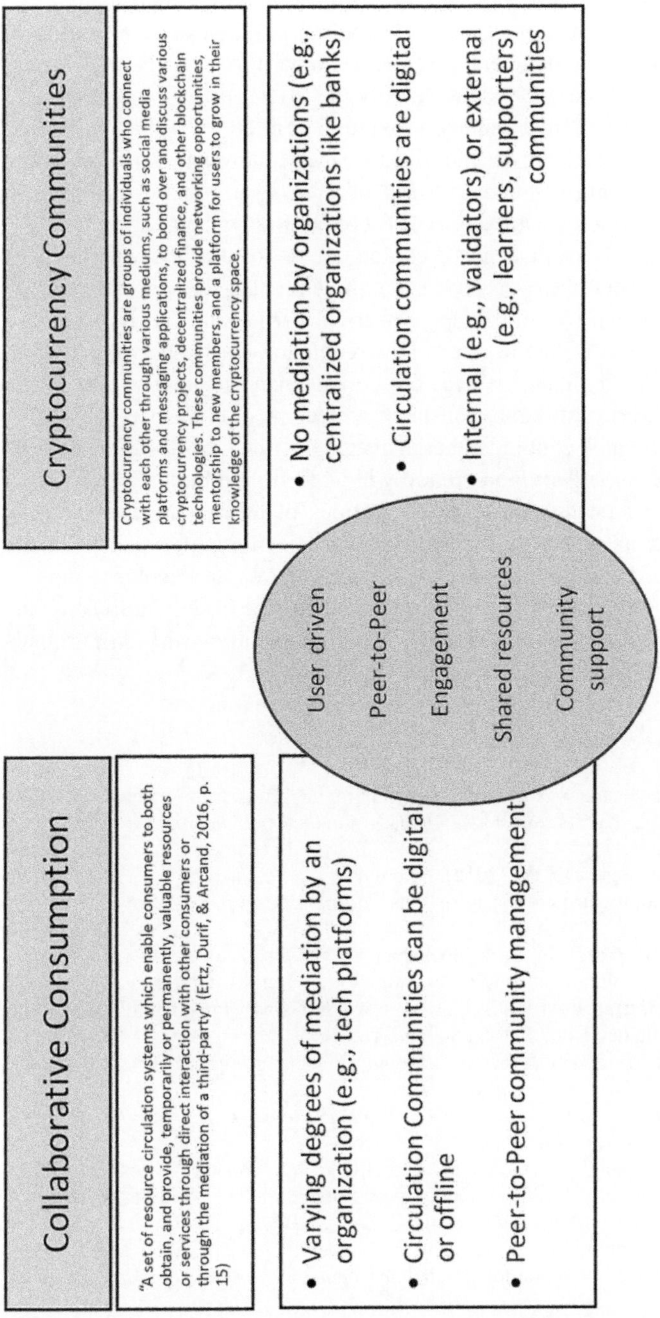

Collaborative Consumption

"A set of resource circulation systems which enable consumers to both obtain, and provide, temporarily or permanently, valuable resources or services through direct interaction with other consumers or through the mediation of a third-party" (Ertz, Durif, & Arcand, 2016, p. 15)

- Varying degrees of mediation by an organization (e.g., tech platforms)
- Circulation Communities can be digital or offline
- Peer-to-Peer community management

Cryptocurrency Communities

Cryptocurrency communities are groups of individuals who connect with each other through various mediums, such as social media platforms and messaging applications, to bond over and discuss various cryptocurrency projects, decentralized finance, and other blockchain technologies. These communities provide networking opportunities, mentorship to new members, and a platform for users to grow in their knowledge of the cryptocurrency space.

- No mediation by organizations (e.g., centralized organizations like banks)
- Circulation communities are digital
- Internal (e.g., validators) or external (e.g., learners, supporters) communities

(Circle) User driven, Peer-to-Peer, Engagement, Shared resources, Community support

Figure 15.1   Cryptocurrency communities as a form of collaborative consumption

the sharing economy (Eckhardt et al., 2019), raise important considerations. One such concern is whether these collaborations' financial groupings are equally accessible to all members of society who wish to participate. Another concern is the truthfulness or accountability of various "learning resources," such as "DCX Learn," that mainly provide simplified and often unvetted educational resources about decentralized financial currencies to those with limited experience and resources instead of offering a comprehensive discussion on how they may equitably access both centralized and decentralized systems. Another aspect in need of exploration is to examine whether the current financial incentives (e.g., reward for solving puzzles) will continue to be motivating enough for miners and stakers to participate. Lastly, research agendas must be established to assess how regulation may impact the appeal of cryptocurrency, facilitate the need for digital financial literacy as well as lead to effective forms of digital consumer protection. With respect to collaboration, future research should further analyze the structures of P2P currency systems and the use of cryptocurrency within them. Additionally, research is required to understand consumer perceptions of these networks and the multitude of factors that have led to them being increasingly mainstreamed and attractive to consumers. As this field rapidly grows and evolves, a more thorough cross-examination is needed regarding the role of decentralization in global financial structures and the many ways communities will form around decentralized and digitized finance options.

REFERENCES

Aggarwal, S., & Kumar, N. (2021). Cryptographic consensus mechanisms. In S. Aggarwal, N. Kumar, & P. Raj (Eds.), *Advances in computers* (Vol. 121, pp. 211–226). Elsevier.

Albinsson, P. A., & Perera, B. Y. (2012). Alternative marketplaces in the 21st century: Building community through sharing events. *Journal of Consumer Behaviour, 11*(4), 303–315.

Amoils, N. (2020). ShareRing uses blockchain to solve self sovereign identity and proof of health simultaneously. *Forbes.* https://www.forbes.com/sites/nisaamoils/2020/08/02/sharering-uses-blockchain-to-solve-self-sovereign-identity-and-proof-of-health-simultaneously/?sh=1cab8c083e61

Antonopoulos, A. M. (2019). *Mastering Bitcoin: Unlocking digital cryptocurrencies.* O'Reilly Media.

Arsel, Z., & Dobscha, S. (2011). *Hybrid pro-social exchange systems: The case of Freecycle.* ACR North American Advances.

Bachmann, A., Becker, A., Buerckner, D., Hilker, M., Kock, F., Lehmann, M., Tiburtius, P., & Funk, B. (2011). Online peer-to-peer lending: A literature review. *Journal of Internet Banking and Commerce, 16*(2), 1–18.

Basha, S. A., Elgammal, M. M., & Abuzayed, B. M. (2021). Online peer-to-peer lending: A review of the literature. *Electronic Commerce Research and Applications, 48,* 101069.

Beattie, A. (2022, September). *The history of money.* Investopedia. https://www.investopedia
.com/articles/07/roots_of_money.asp

Bednorz, J. (2020, August). *The history of peer-to-peer lending.* P2PMarketData.
https://p2pmarketdata.com/articles/p2p-lending-history/

Berger, S. C., & Gleisner, F. (2009). Emergence of financial intermediaries in electronic markets: The case of online P2P lending. *Business Research, 2*(1), 39–65.

Bhatia, N. (2021). *Layered money: From gold and dollars to Bitcoin and central bank
digital currencies.* Nik Bhatia.

Binance Academy. (2018). *Proof of work (PoW) vs. proof of stake (PoS).* https://www
.fool.com/investing/stock-market/market-sectors/information-technology/metaverse
-stocks/metaverse-crypto/

Binance Academy. (2023). *What are Crypto communities and how to join one?* https://
academy.binance.com/en/articles/what-are-crypto-communities-and-how-to-join
-one#What-Is-a-Crypto-Community?

Bollaert, H., Lopez-de-Silanes, F., & Schwienbacher, A. (2021). Fintech and access to
finance. *Journal of Corporate Finance, 68*, 101941.

Brandt, L., & Li, H. (2003). Bank discrimination in transition economies: Ideology,
information, or incentives? *Journal of Comparative Economics, 31*(3), 387–413.

Breidbach, C. F., & Tana, S. (2021). Betting on Bitcoin: How social collectives shape
cryptocurrency markets. *Journal of Business Research, 122*, 311–320.

Caliskan, K. (2022a). The rise and fall of Electra: Emergence and transformation of
a global cryptocurrency community. *Review of Social Economy.* https://doi.org/10
.1080/00346764.2022.2039404

Caliskan, K. (2022b). Data money makers: An ethnographic analysis of a global cryptocurrency community. *British Journal of Sociology, 73*(1), 168–187.

Casey, M. J. (2023). *Worldwide grassroots projects can lead crypto recovery.* Coindesk.
https://www.coindesk.com/layer2/2023/01/13/worldwide-grassroots-projects-can-lead
-crypto-recovery/

Cather, D. A. (2020). Reconsidering insurance discrimination and adverse selection
in an era of data analytics. *The Geneva Papers on Risk and Insurance: Issues and
Practice, 45*(3), 426–456.

Chen, D., Li, X., & Lai, F. (2017). Gender discrimination in online peer-to-peer
credit lending: Evidence from a lending platform in China. *Electronic Commerce
Research, 17*, 553–583.

Chen, Y., & Bellavitis, C. (2020). Blockchain disruption and decentralized finance:
The rise of decentralized business models. *Journal of Business Venturing Insights,
13*, e00151.

Cohen, B. (2017). The rise of alternative currencies in post-capitalism. *Journal of
Management Studies, 54*(5), 739–746.

CoinDCX. (2022). *Top 30 crypto communities you shouldn't miss out on.* https://
coindcx.com/blog/cryptocurrency/top-crypto-communities/

DCX Learn. (2022). https://dcxlearn.com/about-us/. Retrieved February 15, 2024.

De Filippi, P. (2017). What blockchain means for the sharing economy. *Harvard
Business Review, 15*(3).

Denegri-Knott, J., & Molesworth, M. (2010). "Love it. Buy it. Sell it." Consumer desire
and the social drama of eBay. *Journal of Consumer Culture, 10*(1), 56–79.

Duarte, J., Siegel, S., & Young, L. (2012). Trust and credit: The role of appearance in
peer-to-peer lending. *The Review of Financial Studies, 25*(8), 2455–2484.

Eckhardt, G. M., Houston, M. B., Jiang, B., Lamberton, C., Rindfleisch, A., & Zervas,
G. (2019). Marketing in the sharing economy. *Journal of Marketing, 83*(5), 5–27.

Ertz, M., & Boily, É. (2019). The rise of the digital economy: Thoughts on blockchain technology and cryptocurrencies for the collaborative economy. *International Journal of Innovation Studies, 3*(4), 84–93.

Ertz, M., Durif, F., & Arcand, M. (2016). Collaborative consumption: Conceptual snapshot at a buzzword. *Journal of Entrepreneurship Education, 19*(2), 1-23.

Everett, C. R. (2015). Group membership, relationship banking and loan default risk: The case of online social lending. *Banking and Finance Review, 7*(2). http://dx.doi.org/10.2139/ssrn.1114428

Gleim, M. R., & Stevens, J. L. (2021). Blockchain: A game changer for marketers? *Marketing Letters, 32*, 123–128.

Goldstein, J. (2020). *Money: The true story of a made-up thing.* Atlantic Books.

Haberly, D., & Wójcik, D. (2022). *Sticky power: Global financial networks in the world economy.* Oxford University Press.

Herzenstein, M., Sonenshein, S., & Dholakia, U. M. (2011). Tell me a good story and I may lend you money: The role of narratives in peer-to-peer lending decisions. *Journal of Marketing Research, 48*, S138–S149.

Iansiti, M., & Lakhani, K. R. (2017). The truth about blockchain. *Harvard Business Review, 95*(1), 1–11.

Kamalaris, A., & Prenafeta-Boldu, F. X. (2018). Mapping the collaborative economy landscape and its relationship with information and communication technologies. In P. A. Albinsson & B. Y. Perera (Eds.), *The rise of the sharing economy: Exploring the challenges and opportunities of collaborative consumption* (pp. 97–128). Praeger.

Madden, J. F. (2012). Performance-support bias and the gender pay gap among stockbrokers. *Gender & Society, 26*(3), 488–518.

Maddox, A., & Heemsbergen, L. J. (2021). Diggin in crypto-communities' future-making: From dark to doge. *M/C Journal, 24*(2). https://doi.org/10.5204/mcj.2755

Martin, D. M., & Schouten, J. W. (2014). The answer is sustainable marketing, when the question is: What can we do? *Recherche et applications en marketing, 29*(3), 107–109.

Möhlmann, M., Teubner, T., & Graul, A. (2021). Levering trust on sharing economy platforms: Reputation system, blockchain technology and cryptocurrencies. In R. W. Belk, G. M. Eckhardt, & F. Bardhi (Eds.), *Handbook of the sharing economy* (pp. 290–302). Edward Elgar Publishing.

Nakamoto, S. (2008). *Bitcoin: A peer-to-peer electronic cash system.* Bitcoin. https://bitcoin.org/bitcoin.pdf

Napoletano, E., & Curry, B. (2023). Proof of stake explained. *Forbes.* https://www.forbes.com/advisor/investing/cryptocurrency/proof-of-stake/

Narayanan, A., Bonneau, J., Felten, E., Miller, A., & Goldfeder, S. (2016). *Bitcoin and cryptocurrency technologies: A comprehensive introduction.* Princeton University Press.

Nelson, M. R., & Rademacher, M. A. (2009). *From trash to treasure: Freecycle.org as a case of generalized reciprocity.* ACR North American Advances.

Nofer, M., Gomber, P., Hinz, O., & Schiereck, D. (2017). Blockchain. *Business & Information Systems Engineering, 59*(3), 183–187.

Ramaswamy, V., & Lurie, M. (2022). Centralization caused the FTX fiasco. *Wall Street Journal.* https://www.wsj.com/articles/centralization-caused-the-ftx-fiasco-sam-bankman-fried-regulation-lobbying-assets-funds-cryptocurrency-exchange-11669566906

Rossolillo, N. (2022). *The metaverse and crypto: Learn how crypto interacts with the metaverse and why they are so intertwined.* https://www.fool.com/investing/stock-market/market-sectors/information-technology/metaverse-stocks/metaverse-crypto/

Saiedi, E., Broström, A., & Ruiz, F. (2021). Global drivers of cryptocurrency infrastructure adoption. *Small Business Economics, 57*(1), 353–406.

Schneider, N. (2015). La'Zooz: The decentralized, crypto-alternative to Uber. https://www.shareable.net/lazooz-the-decentralized-crypto-alternative-to-uber/

Schueffel, P. (2021). DeFi: Decentralized finance: An introduction and overview. *Journal of Innovation Management, 9*(3), i–xi.

Sergeenkov, A. (2023). *Bitcoin mining difficulty: Everything you need to know.* Coindesk. https://www.coindesk.com/learn/bitcoin-mining-difficulty-everything-you-need-to-know/

Simos, E., & Tan, T. (2019). *State of adoption.* State of Crypto. https://www.stateofcrypto.report/

Slimane, K. B., Chaney, D., Humphreys, A., & Leca, B. (2019). Bringing institutional theory to marketing: Taking stock and future research directions. *Journal of Business Research, 105*, 389–394.

Statista. (2023). *Bitcoin (BTC) price per day from Apr 2013–Jul 30, 2023.* https://www.statista.com/statistics/326707/bitcoin-price-index/

Trabucchi, D., & Buganza, T. (2020). Fostering digital platform innovation: From two to multi-sided platforms. *Creativity and Innovation Management, 29*(2), 345–358.

Wang, Z., Jiang, C., Zhao, H., & Ding, Y. (2020). Mining semantic soft factors for credit risk evaluation in peer-to-peer lending. *Journal of Management Information Systems, 37*(1), 282–308.

Whittaker, M., & Adams, M. (2023). How does Bitcoin mining work? *Forbes*, https://www.forbes.com/advisor/investing/cryptocurrency/bitcoin-mining/

Wu, B., Liu, Z., Gu, Q., & Tsai, F. S. (2023). Underdog mentality, identity discrimination and access to peer-to-peer lending market: Exploring effects of digital authentication. *Journal of International Financial Markets, Institutions and Money, 83*, 101714.

Yoo, K., Welden, R., Hewett, K., & Haenlein, M. (2023). The merchants of meta: A research agenda to understand the future of retailing in the metaverse. *Journal of Retailing, 99*(2), 173–192.

16. Modern social trends that facilitate collaborative consumption adoption: an exploration of new opportunities

Yang (Jenny) Guo, Xiaodong Nie, and Debi P. Mishra

INTRODUCTION

Collaborative consumption (CC), or the so-called "sharing economy," has been gaining popularity in the last decade (Bardhi & Eckhardt, 2017). CC refers to a technology-mediated exchange mode in which the transaction does not involve the transfer of legal ownership but allows consumers to gain temporary legal access to goods or services by paying a usage fee (Eckhardt et al., 2019; Fritze et al., 2021). Nowadays, CC offerings are available across a wide range of product categories, including transportation (e.g., Zipcar, Uber), lodging (e.g., Airbnb), clothing (e.g., Rent the Runway), financial services (e.g., Kiva), and tools (e.g., NextDoor), among others. With the growth of CC, it is imperative to understand what drives consumers to substitute the traditional ownership-based consumption with CC.

Prior research has identified several fundamental motives for consumers to engage in CC, such as saving money (Bardhi & Eckhardt, 2012; Davidson et al., 2018; Guo & Lamberton, 2021), seeking convenience (Moeller & Wittkowski, 2010) and variety (Guo & Lamberton, 2021; Lawson et al., 2016), and alleviating loneliness (Griffiths et al., 2022). Additionally, research indicates that consumers may prefer CC in certain situations, such as when the perceived scarcity of shared resources is low (Lamberton & Rose, 2012), when consumers have more knowledge about CC (Lamberton & Rose, 2012), and when information about prior users of the shared goods is unknown (Stough & Carter, 2023). Lastly, individual differences, such as intelligence (Aspara & Wittkowski, 2019), materialism (Davidson et al., 2018), sense of power (Liu & Mattila, 2017), the global–local identity (Nie et al., 2022), and economic justification beliefs (Cakanlar & Ordabayeva, 2023), also predict CC adoption. However, given that CC is rooted in social structure changes (Bardhi &

Eckhardt, 2017; Eckhardt & Bardhi, 2020b), scant research has considered how modern social trends might impact consumers' adoption of CC.

Since consumer preferences are often shaped by social influences via social identity verification and signaling (Bellezza, 2022; Berger & Heath, 2007), two types of social trends may facilitate consumers' adoption of CC: (1) those that can give consumers positive social identities, and (2) those that can increase consumers' perceived social desirability (White et al., 2019). Indeed, identity verification, defined as a process in which "individuals monitor their own behaviors to manage and reinforce their identities" (Reed et al., 2012, p. 310), and status signaling, defined as an act that facilitates signaling an ideal social status (Anderson et al., 2015; Morhart et al., 2020), are two universal social motives that consumers seek through their CC consumption (Belk, 2014; Eckhardt & Bardhi, 2020a; Morhart et al., 2020). However, it is unclear how these social motives might interact with certain social trends in driving CC adoption.

To gain a fuller understanding of CC, we conduct a thorough literature analysis and propose that sustainability, minimalism, and digitalization are the three modern social trends that not only naturally co-exist with CC but also have the potential to interact with the above universal social motives. In upcoming sections, we provide definitions, evidence, and explanations according to the following structure. We first discuss each social trend and its synergy with CC. Next, based on prior findings, we derive propositions on how consumers might satisfy each social motive through CC in relation to each social trend. Overall, this chapter provides scholars and practitioners with a theoretical framework to explore various ways of extracting value from modern social trends when promoting CC.

SUSTAINABILITY

Sustainability is one of the biggest social trends that raise consumers' aware-ness of the environmental harm caused by their daily consumption (White et al., 2019). Prior research suggests that sustainability and CC naturally co-exist. Specifically, sustainable consumption styles are proposed to mitigate the environmental impact of consumer behavior, such as recycling, repairing, and buying second-hand goods (see White et al., 2019). Within this context, CC has emerged as one of these alternatives, further underscoring its role as a new phenomenon to stimulate sustainable practices (Davies et al., 2020; Morewedge et al., 2020; Shrivastava et al., 2021). The positive impact of CC on the environment is in line with the notion of sustainability. Essentially, if we consume less and share more, fewer resources will be used to produce new products, and less waste will be generated through extracting the full value of resources in the CC landscape – the outcome is a "greener" environment. As such, forgoing ownership to engage in CC is more eco-friendly (Davies et al., 2020). Companies that provide CC opportunities, such as Feature, a furniture rental company that "Keeps Furniture in Homes and Out of Landfills," also highlight the sustainable value in their business model (Feather, n.d.).

While prior work has explored the role of sustainability in driving CC adoption, the results are inconsistent. For instance, Bardhi and Eckhardt (2012) showed that sustainability was not a salient motivation for consumers to use Zipcar, a car-sharing company. However, Hartl et al. (2020) found that, while car owners were motivated to share their cars with others in a peer-to-peer CC context due to sustainability concerns, car users were not. Therefore, it is still unclear if and how sustainability can motivate consumers to use CC. We argue that existing work does not account for consumers' social motives, potentially making sustainability less appealing given that its value is typically revealed in social environments (Griskevicius et al., 2010). Thus, we re-examine the literature to better understand how CC might be marketed when the aforementioned social motives (i.e., identity verification and status signaling) are made salient in relation to the trend of sustainability.

Identity Verification

Given the increased awareness of climate change worldwide, in general, most people are aware of sustainability in their daily lives (Frey et al., 2023; Gibbs et al., 2023). With recurrent exposure, it is reasonable to expect that more and more consumers will begin to behave like an environmentalist in terms of proactively seeking ways to benefit the environment through sustainable consumption. If the sustainability trend makes being an environmentalist a salient "green" identity, it can therefore be an opportunity to promote CC framed in terms of sustainability. However, how can market communications facilitate consumers' environmentalist identity-verification process in CC?

First, marketers may activate consumers' environmentalist identity to increase their adoption of CC. The social identity literature has shown that, while consumers can simultaneously hold multiple identities, one identity may be more salient and thus more influential in guiding behavior based on the situational factors (Brewer, 1991). Prior research has used priming tasks to situationally activate one's specific identity temporarily. For example, Nie et al. (2022) used advertising brochures to situationally activate an individual's local/global identity. A CC brand can borrow this strategy to activate consumers' environmentalist identity to increase the adoption of CC. Hence, we propose:

P1: Activating an individual's environmentalist identity may boost CC adoption among environmentalists.

Second, marketers may motivate consumers by focusing on group identity. Environmentally friendly behaviors are perceived as feminine (Brough et al., 2016). Since females care more about the environment than males do (Brough et al., 2016), a male's non-eco-friendliness may motivate his female partner's environmentalist identity. Such compensatory behavior is documented by Cakanlar et al. (2023). Therefore, CC may be marketed to compensate for non-eco-friendly family members' non-sustainable behaviors. Hence, we propose:

P2: Framing CC as an environmentalist's choice to compensate for non-eco-friendly family members or significant others may boost CC adoption among females.

Status Signaling

Research has shown that many consumers engage in sustainable consumption due to status-signaling motives (Griskevicius et al., 2010) rather than pure environmental beliefs because sustainable consumption typically enjoys a price premium (Berger, 2019) and is perceived as being prosocial (White et al., 2019). As a result, sustainable consumption allows consumers to signal their financial status (Bagwell & Bernheim, 1996; Nelissen & Meijers, 2011) and pro-sociality (Mick, 1996), therefore making it appealing in a public decision-making context (Griskevicius et al., 2010).

Given the characteristics of CC, signaling status by expenditure may not be feasible (Guo et al., 2023), making the well-known "going green to be seen" strategy not applicable for CC. Alternatively, prior research suggests virtue signaling as another way to satisfy one's status motives (Bai et al., 2019) through elevating the self's need for status (Griskevicius et al., 2010; Puska et al., 2018) or prioritizing others' needs (Nault & Yap, 2022). We therefore propose two corresponding propositions, as noted below.

First, marketers can utilize existing superior status symbols to elevate consumers' need for status when communicating the environmental values of CC. The need for status describes a tendency to consume products that can confer status or social prestige value on their owners (Eastman et al., 1999; Han et al., 2010). Research has shown that brand prominence can activate such needs (Han et al., 2010) and has been used in real-life situations. For instance, Turo, a car-sharing company, advertises itself as allowing people to access luxury sports cars. Also, a CC brand can simultaneously advertise its environmental sustainability to make its offering more prosocial (i.e., "Consume luxury products in the most sustainable way").

Another symbol can come from the superior social status of the primary users of a CC brand, as research shows that others' superior status may increase the self's need for status (Gao et al., 2016). Indeed, Rent the Runway, a designer clothing rental company for women, emphasizes its Wall Street clientele in its brand story (Boniface, 2019). To make its offerings more prosocial, a CC brand may advertise itself as a service for superior customers who care about the environment (i.e., "Achieving professionalism with green-conscious behaviors").

Therefore, we propose:

P3: Marketing communications that can sequentially elevate consumers' need for status and then offer a virtue-signaling symbol via environmental sustainability may attract consumers to adopt CC.

Second, marketers can highlight that a person's adoption of CC may positively impact others' well-being through a variety of ways to attract consumers in different segments. For instance, CC brands may emphasize how using their products will benefit other community members by collectively achieving an environmental goal (e.g., healthy air quality for the elderly, more greens for toddlers and pets). In a community with more elderly members, a CC car company may promote itself by communicating the benefits for others (e.g., "share more, care more; through car-sharing, you're improving your elderly neighbors' well-being with better air quality"). For the same business, the other beneficiaries can be children and pets if car-sharing reduces the need for land to be utilized as parking lots and extended roads, which may increase the number of greenspaces and playgrounds, especially in cities. Therefore, we suggest that such framing (i.e., the environmental benefits as an outcome of one's CC adoption that will benefit others) may facilitate virtue signaling, potentially increasing CC's adoption. Hence, we propose:

P4: Marketing communications that emphasize how others' well-being can be improved by CC may encourage consumers to adopt CC.

MINIMALISM

Minimalistic consumption is a modern trend derived from the broad anti-consumption social movement (Lee & Ahn, 2016). It deviates from mainstream consumerism and advocates for a consumption mindset that focuses on simplicity (Lee & Ahn, 2016; Pangarkar et al., 2021). Recent research shows that minimalism is a three-fold concept that includes: (1) buying less and storing fewer physical possessions, (2) preferring a minimalist aesthetic design, and (3) carefully considering one's needs before making a purchase (Wilson & Bellezza, 2022).

The increasing popularity of minimalism forms a new group of consumers: minimalists. To pursue minimalistic consumption, these consumers may voluntarily choose to sacrifice enjoyment and a sense of control from owning products (Belk, 1988; Lamberton & Goldsmith, 2020). Alternatively, minimalists may enjoy having fewer possessions and may gain their sense of control by consuming less. In both cases, minimalists may experience the "burden of ownership" in the traditional ownership-based consumption (Schaefers et al., 2016) that requires them to permanently keep and store what they consume. However, engaging in CC to achieve a minimalist lifestyle may allow one to optimize their possession portfolio (Haws & Reczek, 2022) without generating excessive physical possessions and liabilities (Wilson & Bellezza, 2022). In recent years, society has witnessed a growing trend of minimalism, increasing the potential market size of minimalists. Before the pandemic, about 40 percent of Americans described themselves as minimalists or indicated that they would like to be a minimalist (Ballard, 2019). During and after the pandemic, with the increased frequency of remote work and time spent at home with family, many may voluntarily develop a minimalist lifestyle to achieve visual simplicity in the home space (Woods, 2021).

CC maximizes the variety of choices one can enjoy, which has been shown to increase happiness (Guo & Lamberton, 2021). Specifically, through renting or borrowing items needed for the short term and routinely replacing older possessions with new items, consumers can keep their living space tidy, clean, and fun – this echoes the visual simplicity rule for a minimalist lifestyle. The marketplace has also observed such offerings. For instance, accessing rather than purchasing household items and tools (e.g., KitchenAid, camping tools) through community-based sharing platforms, such as NextDoor and Buy Nothing, enables people to meet their temporary needs without storing physical goods (Dolly, 2018). For families with children, accessing toys via a toy library enables them to have fun while keeping their living space organized (Ozanne & Ballantine, 2010).

The above-mentioned synergies between minimalism and CC shed light on new opportunities to promote the latter. We discuss and propose several unique strategies related to minimalism that may facilitate the adoption of CC.

Identity Verification

Marketing communications that frame CC as enabling one to enjoy a minimalistic lifestyle may attract minimalists to verify their identity through CC adoption. Indeed, practitioners have leveraged the synergy between CC and minimalism to make profits. For instance, an Airbnb house listing titled "Admire the Minimalist Style of This Excellent Penthouse" earned an average score of 4.86 stars in 251 reviews (Lima, n.d.).

Since minimalists verify their identity by buying minimalism-style products (Wilson & Bellezza, 2022), the demand for minimalistic offerings or the lifestyle is likely to increase. As upward trendiness is an effective way to nudge people to adopt recommended behaviors through greater inferred normality (Costello et al., 2023), those who have not adopted a minimalistic lifestyle (while others in the same social groups have) may feel themselves falling behind. Therefore, we argue that marketers should first communicate the uptrend of minimalist lifestyles in target consumers' identity-relevant social groups and then frame CC as a choice for minimalists to attract consumers through an identity-verification mechanism. Hence, we propose:

P5: Marketing communications that increase the inferred normality of minimalism achieved by CC may attract consumers to adopt CC.

Status Signaling

CC offers multiple ways to enable minimalists to be distinct from others. We first discuss an intangible status symbol innate in minimalism and CC: non-conformity (Eckhardt & Bardhi, 2020a; Warren & Campbell, 2014). Scholars argue that the success of CC is evidence of the death of "ownership" as the normative means of consumption (Lamberton & Goldsmith, 2020). Since acquiring ownership of possessions is the conventional consumption mode, being a minimalist with fewer possessions displays nonconformity (Makri et al., 2020; Ubbenga, 2021). Prior research shows that individuals judge others as having to have higher competence and social status when they don't follow the conventional norm in a social group (Bellezza et al., 2014). Similarly, individuals may judge minimalists as having higher social status due to them not conforming to the mainstream. Therefore, CC might be more attractive for minimalists as a means to stand out as non-conformists with higher perceived social status relative to conformists.

Since nonconformity is an intangible status symbol, it facilitates inconspicuous consumption, which is preferred by those who have reached a higher level in their social networks (Berger & Ward, 2010; Eckhardt et al., 2015). Coincidentally, many existing minimalists are better educated and higher on the social hierarchy (Pangarkar et al., 2021), as are those who prefer CC (Aspara & Wittkowski, 2019). So, we observe a three-way synergy (i.e., symbol, CC, and minimalism). Due to this synergy, those having higher social status may be especially interested in adopting CC to become a minimalist if doing so is framed as a non-conforming consumption style. Further, we argue that the high-status image of earlier adopters may naturally form an upward comparison trend, boosting one's desire to climb the social ladder by becoming a minimalist through CC. Thus, we propose:

P6: Framing CC as elites' non-conforming choices to become minimalists may increase consumers' interest in CC.

DIGITALIZATION

Digitalization is the third social trend that may facilitate the adoption of CC (Morewedge et al., 2020). This trend not only facilitates the development of CC but also generates new digital products that are not available offline. For instance, some consumers value the co-creation opportunities among group members (Nohutlu et al., 2022), such as music streaming provided by YouTubers (Zimmermann et al., 2022), digital music albums created by Spotify users (Hagen, 2015), and consumers' product reviews on Yelp (Luo et al., 2012). Others share their digital assets to enable fellow members to temporarily access digital goods, such as the rental services in the Metaverse and NFT rentals through reNFT – Rental Infrastructure for the Metaverse. Individuals can also lend money to strangers through CC platforms such as Kiva.org to support other people's dreams.

Identity Verification

Online CC platforms give their users many opportunities to express themselves. The most appealing is to express one's ideal self as on social media platforms (Seidman, 2013). With digitalization intertwined with almost all aspects of our lives, an individual's digital self becomes more important and central to their self-concept (Morewedge et al., 2020). This allows one to achieve their pursued identity by simply engaging in a digital version of goods. For instance, researchers find that liking a brand's Pinterest content reduces consumers' likelihood of buying that brand because their brand-related identity has been satisfied by that simple gesture online (Grewal et al., 2019). Like one's social media engagement, practicing CC through online communities (e.g., crowdsourcing platforms, unique digital marketplaces) offers individuals a way to construct their digital selves (Venkatesh, 2016). However, differing from the mere engagement in social media platforms, we argue that the beauty of online CC platforms is the ability for users to achieve multiple roles that they may not be able to realize in the real world. Considering the following scenarios, a music lover who does not have the resources to become a musician may curate their music playlists and share them publicly on Spotify to attract followers and even fans who admire their musical taste (Malik, 2022). Loyal music listeners on Spotify will also be able to identify with famous playlist curators when talking to friends to verify their music-lover identity. So, the collaboration among different parties via CC platforms helps one realize their musical dream.

Engaging in digital CC becomes a substitute for individuals to realize certain identities in other cases also. For instance, an environmentalist or minimalist who chooses not to purchase or consume any excessive material goods but is interested in a specific area, such as fashion, can participate in a blockchain-enabled circular fashion platform to rent digital clothing and build their digital persona to display their fashion-lover identity. SPIN, a rental company led by H&M Mitte Garten and Lablaco, allows users to buy or rent digital fashion items to curate their digital images in the Metaverse (Magunje, 2021). Therefore, given that online CC platforms allow individuals to realize their ideal identities in a digitalized style, we propose:

P7: Framing CC as a unique opportunity for one to verify their ideal identities in a digital world may increase consumers' interest in an online CC platform in general.

Status Signaling

Other than the materialized display of one's status, digital collaborative platforms bring consumers alternative ways to signal status to a large audience through expertise, which is an inconspicuous status symbol (Eckhardt & Bardhi, 2020a). Sharing one's knowledge, resources, and tastes is a display of cosmopolitan competence (Figueiredo et al., 2021). On digital CC platforms, one's competence in a small area is more likely to be recognized and appreciated by a much larger audience. For instance, Yelp bestows reviewers who provide a large number of high-quality reviews with the "elite" status, thus enabling them to receive social respect on the platform (Luca, 2012). But, beyond such a badge system, how could online CC platforms offer status-signaling values to users?

We posit that online CC platforms may benefit from offline engagement. There are situations when users share content on digital platforms, with the platform audience including their colleagues and friends in real life. For instance, programmers and scholars on GitHub (the largest code-sharing online platform) spend numerous hours offering free solutions to challenging projects, constantly updating codes or programming packages, and providing high-quality reusable codes for others to learn and download freely (Badashian & Stroulia, 2016). Research finds that such behaviors help these individuals gain social influence, thereby elevating their status in their online and offline communities (Badashian & Stroulia, 2016). Therefore, online CC platforms may motivate more individuals to engage in sharing by offering various ways for other users to express gratitude toward those sharing their unique expertise both online and offline (e.g., award recognitions at high-end professional conferences). Hence, we propose:

P8: Consumers may raise their interest in an online CC platform that offers offline meeting opportunities to recognize users' high-quality online sharing.

In other cases, marketers may boost CC adoption by highlighting how much a user's sharing has helped others. For instance, Yelp reviewers disclose positive or negative restaurant dining experiences, and users on Sephora beauty forums share make-up tips and product-related information (Cheung & Lee, 2012). Some people join microfinancing companies to lend money with a very low or free interest rate, such as Kiva ($25 or more), to provide collective financial help to students and entrepreneurs worldwide that enables them to achieve big dreams (Schwittay, 2014). Therefore, if a CC platform can highlight how users' generous behaviors may help others, more people may choose to join CC as a virtue signal. Hence, we propose:

P9: Promoting online CC platforms by highlighting how much a user's sharing has helped others may increase users' interest in continuously sharing on that platform.

CONCLUSION

As the CC business model is thriving, a more nuanced understanding is needed for marketing purposes. This chapter draws on the theories and findings related to social influence as a means of shaping consumer behaviors. In doing so, it offers a theoretical framework for studying different communication mechanisms that could promote the adoption of CC. Specifically, we derive nine propositions based on the interaction between three social trends (sustainability, minimalism, and digitalization) and two social motives (identity verification and status signaling) for future empirical studies. We discuss how CC synergizes with each of the three social trends, and then consider how CC may be marketed as a way to either verify identity or signal status. Across these social trends, we propose that communications need to include content that can first make consumer identity salient (e.g., environmentalist) and then market the associated benefits of CC. Additionally, we propose that marketers highlight intangible status symbols that consumers may use to distinguish themselves from others by engaging in CC under each social trend.

Although our proposed framework has a few limitations, these challenges can spur future research opportunities. First, we primarily focus on the environmental aspect of sustainability. However, sustainability also involves people and profits that are not discussed in the current chapter. Though some of our positions involve the environment aspect, future work may examine how the remaining two (i.e., people and profit) may relate to CC. Second, while we do not specify the type of resources being rotated in CC, we recognize that they are substantially different (Wirtz et al., 2019; i.e., capacity-unconstrained assets, such as music and documents, under digitalization, and capacity-constrained assets, such as cars and clothing). Given different types of resources, further work may explore if CC communications should follow divergent promotional strategies.

REFERENCES

Anderson, C., Hildreth, J. A. D., & Howland, L. (2015). Is the desire for status a fundamental human motive? A review of the empirical literature. *Psychological Bulletin, 141*(3), 574–601. https://doi.org/10.1037/a0038781

Aspara, J., & Wittkowski, K. (2019). Sharing-dominant logic? Quantifying the association between consumer intelligence and choice of social access modes. *Journal of Consumer Research, 46*(2), 201–222. https://doi.org/10.1093/jcr/ucy074

Badashian, A. S., & Stroulia, E. (2016). Measuring user influence in GitHub: The million follower fallacy. In *Proceedings of the 3rd International Workshop on CrowdSourcing in Software Engineering, CSI-SE 2016* (pp. 15–21). Association for Computing Machinery. https://doi.org/10.1145/2897659.2897663

Bagwell, L. S., & Bernheim, B. D. (1996). Veblen effects in a theory of conspicuous consumption. *American Economic Review, 86*(3), 349–373. https://doi.org/10.2307/2118201

Bai, F., Ho, G. C. C., & Yan, J. (2019). Does virtue lead to status? Testing the moral virtue theory of status attainment. *Journal of Personality and Social Psychology, 118*(3), 501–531. https://doi.org/10.1037/pspi0000192

Ballard, J. (2019, August 28). *What do Americans think of minimalism?* YouGov. https://today.yougov.com/topics/society/articles-reports/2019/08/28/simplify-life-stress-marie-kondo-poll

Bardhi, F., & Eckhardt, G. M. (2012). Access-based consumption: The case of car sharing. *Journal of Consumer Research, 39*(4), 881–898. https://doi.org/10.1086/666376

Bardhi, F., & Eckhardt, G. M. (2017). Liquid consumption. *Journal of Consumer Research, 44*(3), 582–597. https://doi.org/10.1093/jcr/ucx050

Belk, R. (1988). Possessions and the extended self. *Journal of Consumer Research, 15*(2), 139–168. https://doi.org/10.1086/209154

Belk, R. (2014). You are what you can access: Sharing and collaborative consumption online. *Journal of Business Research, 67*(8), 1595–1600. https://doi.org/10.1016/j.jbusres.2013.10.001

Bellezza, S. (2022). Distance and alternative signals of status: A unifying framework. *Journal of Consumer Research, 50*(2), 322–342. https://doi.org/10.1093/jcr/ucac049

Bellezza, S., Gino, F., & Keinan, A. (2014). The red sneakers effect: Inferring status and competence from signals of nonconformity. *Journal of Consumer Research, 41*(1), 35–54. https://doi.org/10.1086/674870

Berger, J. (2019). Signaling can increase consumers' willingness to pay for green products. Theoretical model and experimental evidence. *Journal of Consumer Behaviour, 18*(3), 233–246. https://doi.org/10.1002/cb.1760

Berger, J., & Heath, C. (2007). Where consumers diverge from others: Identity signaling and product domains. *Journal of Consumer Research, 34*(2), 121–134. https://doi.org/10.1086/519142

Berger, J., & Ward, M. (2010). Subtle signals of inconspicuous consumption. *Journal of Consumer Research, 37*(4), 555–569. https://doi.org/10.1086/655445

Boniface, E. A. (2019, September 10). *The changing consumer behind Rent the Runway's success.* Commerce Next. https://commercenext.com/the-changing-consumer-behind-rent-the-runways-success/

Brewer, M. B. (1991). The social self: On being the same and different at the same time. *Personality and Social Psychology Bulletin, 17*(5), 475–482.

Brough, A. R., Wilkie, J. E. B., Ma, J., Isaac, M. S., & Gal, D. (2016). Is eco-friendly unmanly? The green-feminine stereotype and its effect on sustainable consumption. *Journal of Consumer Research, 43*(4), 567–582. https://doi.org/10.1093/jcr/ucw044

Cakanlar, A., Nikolova, H., & Nenkov, G. Y. (2023). I will be green for us: When consumers compensate for their partners' unsustainable behavior. *Journal of Marketing Research, 60*(1), 110–129. https://doi.org/10.1177/00222437221108891

Cakanlar, A., & Ordabayeva, N. (2023). How economic system justification shapes demand for peer-to-peer providers. *Journal of Consumer Psychology, 33*(3), 602–612. https://doi.org/10.1002/jcpy.1344

Cheung, C. M. K., & Lee, M. K. O. (2012). What drives consumers to spread electronic word of mouth in online consumer-opinion platforms. *Decision Support Systems, 53*(1), 218–225. https://doi.org/10.1016/j.dss.2012.01.015

Costello, J. P., Garvey, A. M., Germann, F., & Wilkie, J. E. B. (2023). The uptrend effect: Encouraging healthy behaviors through greater inferred normativity. *Journal of Marketing Research, 61*(1), 110–127. https://doi.org/10.1177/00222437231167832

Davidson, A., Habibi, M. R., & Laroche, M. (2018). Materialism and the sharing economy: A cross-cultural study of American and Indian consumers. *Journal of Business Research, 82*, 364–372. https://doi.org/10.1016/j.jbusres.2015.07.045

Davies, I., Oates, C. J., Tynan, C., Carrigan, M., Casey, K., Heath, T., Henninger, C. E., Lichrou, M., McDonagh, P., McDonald, S., McKechnie, S., McLeay, F., O'Malley, L., & Wells, V. (2020). Seeking sustainable futures in marketing and consumer research. *European Journal of Marketing, 54*(11), 2911–2939. https://doi.org/10.1108/EJM-02-2019-0144

Dolly. (2018, January 15). *Minimalist living: How to live a minimalist lifestyle with less stuff.* https://dolly.com/blog/minimalist-living/

Eastman, J. K., Goldsmith, R. E., & Flynn, L. R. (1999). Status consumption in consumer behavior: Scale development and validation. *Journal of Marketing Theory and Practice, 7*(3), 41–52. https://doi.org/10.1080/10696679.1999.11501839

Eckhardt, G. M., & Bardhi, F. (2020a). New dynamics of social status and distinction. *Marketing Theory, 20*(1), 85–102. https://doi.org/10.1177/1470593119856650

Eckhardt, G. M., & Bardhi, F. (2020b). The value in de-emphasizing structure in liquidity. *Marketing Theory, 20*(4), 573–580. https://doi.org/10.1177/1470593120941038

Eckhardt, G. M., Belk, R. W., & Wilson, J. A. J. (2015). The rise of inconspicuous consumption. *Journal of Marketing Management, 317*(8), 807–826. https://doi.org/10.1080/0267257X.2014.989890

Eckhardt, G. M., Houston, M. B., Jiang, B., Lamberton, C., Rindfleisch, A., & Zervas, G. (2019). Marketing in the sharing economy. *Journal of Marketing, 83*(5), 5–27. https://doi.org/0022242919861929

Feather. (n.d.). *Feather.* https://www.livefeather.com/

Figueiredo, B., Larsen, H. P., & Bean, J. (2021). The cosmopolitan servicescape. *Journal of Retailing, 97*(2), 267–287. https://doi.org/10.1016/j.jretai.2020.09.001

Frey, S., Am, J. B., Doshi, V., Malik, A., & Noble, S. (2023). *Consumers care about sustainability – and back it up with their wallets.* McKinsey. https://www.mckinsey.com/

industries/consumer-packaged-goods/our-insights/consumers-care-about-sustainability -and-back-it-up-with-their-wallets#/

Fritze, M. P., Benkenstein, M., Belk, R., Peck, J., Wirtz, J., & Claus, B. (2021). Commentaries on the sharing economy: Advancing new perspectives. *Journal of Service Management Research*, 5(1), 3–19. https://doi.org/10.15358/2511-8676-2021 -1-3

Gao, H., Winterich, K. P., & Zhang, Y. (2016). All that glitters is not gold: How others' status influences the effect of power distance belief on status consumption. *Journal of Consumer Research*, 43(2), 265–281. https://doi.org/10.1093/jcr/ucw015

Gibbs, E., Patel, M., & Siccardo, G. (2023, January 9). *Solving the other half of the climate equation: Removing carbon*. Utility Dive. https://www.utilitydive.com/news/ carbon-dioxide-removal-Mckinsey-greenhouse-gas-reduction/639429/

Grewal, L., Stephen, A. T., & Coleman, N. V. (2019). When posting about products on social media backfires: The negative effects of consumer identity signaling on product interest. *Journal of Marketing Research*, 56(2), 197–210. https://doi.org/10 .1177/0022243718821960

Griffiths, M. A., Perera, B. Y., & Albinsson, P. A. (2022). Lives of the lonely: How collaborative consumption services can alleviate social isolation. *Frontiers in Psychology*, 13, 826533. https://doi.org/10.3389/fpsyg.2022.826533

Griskevicius, V., Tybur, J. M., & Van den Bergh, B. (2010). Going green to be seen: Status, reputation, and conspicuous conservation. *Journal of Personality and Social Psychology*, 98(3), 392–404. https://doi.org/10.1037/a0017346

Guo, Y. J., & Lamberton, C. (2021). When does sharing stigmatize? Saving money (vs. seeking variety) through access-based consumption. *Frontiers in Psychology*, 12, 778290. https://doi.org/10.3389/fpsyg.2021.778290

Guo, Y., Lamberton, C., & Goldsmith, K. (2023). The role of product acquisition mode in self- and social-signals of status. *Marketing Letters*. https://doi.org/10.1007/ s11002-023-09688-1

Hagen, A. N. (2015). The playlist experience: Personal playlists in music streaming services. *Popular Music and Society*, 38(5), 625–645. https:// doi .org/ 10 .1080/ 03007766.2015.1021174

Han, Y. J., Nunes, J. C., & Drèze, X. (2010). Signaling status with luxury goods: The role of brand prominence. *Journal of Marketing*, 74(4), 15–30. https:// doi .org/ 10 .1509/jmkg.74.4.015

Hartl, B., Kamleitner, B., & Holub, S. (2020). Take me on a ride: The role of environmentalist identity for carpooling. *Psychology and Marketing*, 37(5), 663–676. https://doi.org/10.1002/mar.21340

Haws, K. L., & Reczek, R. W. (2022). Optimizing the possession portfolio. *Current Opinion in Psychology*, 46, 101325. https://doi.org/10.1016/j.copsyc.2022.101325

Lamberton, C., & Goldsmith, K. (2020). Ownership: A perennial prize or a fading goal? A curation, framework, and agenda for future research. *Journal of Consumer Research*, 47(2), 301–309. https://doi.org/10.1093/jcr/ucaa027

Lamberton, C. P., & Rose, R. L. (2012). When is ours better than mine? A framework for understanding and altering participation in commercial sharing systems. *Journal of Marketing*, 76(4), 109–125. https://doi.org/10.1509/jm.10.0368

Lawson, S. J., Gleim, M. R., Perren, R., & Hwang, J. (2016). Freedom from ownership: An exploration of access-based consumption. *Journal of Business Research*, 69(8), 2615–2623. https://doi.org/10.1016/j.jbusres.2016.04.021

Lee, M. S. W., & Ahn, C. S. Y. (2016). Anti-consumption, materialism, and consumer well-being. *Journal of Consumer Affairs, 50*(1), 18–47. https://doi.org/10.1111/joca .12089

Lima, P. (n.d.). Admire the minimalist style of this excellent penthouse. https:// www.airbnb.com/rooms/plus/8078557?source_impression_id=p3_1672946420 _V93TQHiX3o1q7Q4e

Liu, S. Q., & Mattila, A. S. (2017). Airbnb: Online targeted advertising, sense of power, and consumer decisions. *International Journal of Hospitality Management, 60*, 33–41. https://doi.org/10.1016/j.ijhm.2016.09.012

Luca, M. (2012). Reviews, reputation, and revenue: The case of Yelp.com. *Harvard Business School*, Working Paper 12-016. https://doi.org/10.2139/ssrn.1928601

Luo, Y., Hawkley, L. C., Waite, L. J., & Cacioppo, J. T. (2012). Loneliness, health, and mortality in old age: A national longitudinal study. *Social Science and Medicine, 74*(6), 907–914. https://doi.org/10.1016/j.socscimed.2011.11.028

Magunje, D. (2021, October 19). *H&M and lablaco launch the first blockchain-based iot rental service powered by SPIN*. Business Wire. https://www.businesswire.com/ news/ home/ 20211019005528/ en/ HM -and -lablaco -Launch -the -First -Blockchain -Based-IoT-Rental-Service-Powered-by-SPIN

Makri, K., Schlegelmilch, B. B., Mai, R., & Dinhof, K. (2020). What we know about anticonsumption: An attempt to nail jelly to the wall. *Psychology and Marketing, 37*(2), 177–215. https://doi.org/10.1002/mar.21319

Malik, A. (2022, April 4). *Spotify is testing a way to promote popular user-created playlists*. TechCrunch. https://techcrunch.com/2022/04/04/spotify-testing-promote -popular-user-created-playlists/

Mick, D. G. (1996). Are studies of dark side variables confounded by socially desirable responding? The case of materialism. *Journal of Consumer Research, 23*(2), 106–119. https://doi.org/10.1086/209470

Moeller, S., & Wittkowski, K. (2010). The burdens of ownership: Reasons for preferring renting. *Managing Service Quality, 20*(2), 176–191. https://doi.org/10.1108/ 09604521011027598

Morewedge, C. K., Monga, A., Palmatier, R. W., Shu, S. B., & Small, D. A. (2020). Evolution of consumption: A psychological ownership framework. *Journal of Marketing, 85*(1), 196–218. https://doi.org/10.1177/0022242920957007

Morhart, F., Wilcox, K., Czellar, S., Bardhi, F., Eckhardt, G. M., & Samsioe, E. (2020). Liquid luxury. In F. Morhart, K. Wilcox, & S. Czellar (Eds.), *Research handbook on luxury branding* (pp. 22–43). Edward Elgar Publishing https://doi.org/10.4337/ 9781786436351.00011

Nault, K., & Yap, A. J. (2022). The social perception of virtue signaling. *Academy of Management Proceedings, 2022*(1). https:// doi .org/ 10 .5465/ ambpp .2022 .13613abstract

Nelissen, R. M. A., & Meijers, M. H. C. (2011). Social benefits of luxury brands as costly signals of wealth and status. *Evolution and Human Behavior, 32*(5), 343–355. https://doi.org/10.1016/j.evolhumbehav.2010.12.002

Nie, X., Yang, Z., Zhang, Y., & Janakiraman, N. (2022). How does global–local identity affect consumer preference for access-based consumption? Investigating the mediating role of consumption openness. *Journal of Marketing Research, 59*(3), 555–577. https://doi.org/10.1177/00222437211055130

Nohutlu, Z. D., Englis, B. G., Groen, A. J., & Constantinides, E. (2022). Customer cocreation experience in online communities: Antecedents and outcomes. *European*

Journal of Innovation Management, 25(2), 630–659. https://doi.org/10.1108/EJIM-08-2020-0313

Ozanne, L. K., & Ballantine, P. W. (2010). Sharing as a form of anti-consumption? An examination of toy library users. *Journal of Consumer Behaviour, 9*(6), 485–498. https://doi.org/10.1002/cb.334

Pangarkar, A., Shukla, P., & Taylor, C. R. (2021). Minimalism in consumption: A typology and brand engagement strategies. *Journal of Business Research, 127*, 167–178. https://doi.org/10.1016/j.jbusres.2021.01.033

Puska, P., Kurki, S., Lähdesmäki, M., Siltaoja, M., & Luomala, H. (2018). Sweet taste of prosocial status signaling: When eating organic foods makes you happy and hopeful. *Appetite, 121*, 348–359. https://doi.org/10.1016/j.appet.2017.11.102

Reed, A., Forehand, M. R., Puntoni, S., & Warlop, L. (2012). Identity-based consumer behavior. *International Journal of Research in Marketing, 29*(4), 310–321. https://doi.org/10.1016/j.ijresmar.2012.08.002

Schaefers, T., Lawson, S. J., & Kukar-Kinney, M. (2016). How the burdens of ownership promote consumer usage of access-based services. *Marketing Letters, 27*, 569–577. https://doi.org/10.1007/s11002-015-9366-x

Schwittay, A. F. (2014). Making poverty into a financial problem: From global poverty lines to kiva.org. *Journal of International Development, 26*(4), 508–519. https://doi.org/10.1002/jid.2966

Seidman, G. (2013). Self-presentation and belonging on Facebook: How personality influences social media use and motivations. *Personality and Individual Differences, 54*(3), 402–407. https://doi.org/10.1016/j.paid.2012.10.009

Shrivastava, A., Jain, G., Kamble, S. S., & Belhadi, A. (2021). Sustainability through online renting clothing: Circular fashion fueled by Instagram micro-celebrities. *Journal of Cleaner Production, 278*, 123772. https://doi.org/10.1016/j.jclepro.2020.123772

Stough, R. A., & Carter, E. P. (2023). What was yours is (for now) mine: Prior user knowledge reduces product satisfaction but can improve experiential satisfaction in access-based consumption. *Journal of Consumer Behaviour, 22*(4), 833–847. https://doi.org/10.1002/cb.2164

Ubbenga, J. (2021, October 16). Minimalism is countercultural. Here are 7 reasons to do it anyway. https://richinwhatmatters.com/2021/10/16/minimalism-is-countercultural-here-are-7-reasons-to-do-it-anyway/

Venkatesh, A. (2016). Social media, digital self, and privacy: a socio-analytical perspective of the consumer as the digital avatar. *Journal of the Association for Consumer Research, 1*, 378–391. DOI: 10.1086/686914

Warren, C., & Campbell, M. C. (2014). What makes things cool? How autonomy influences perceived coolness. *Journal of Consumer Research, 41*(2), 543–563. https://doi.org/10.1086/676680

White, K., Habib, R., & Hardisty, D. J. (2019). How to SHIFT consumer behaviors to be more sustainable: A literature review and guiding framework. *Journal of Marketing, 83*(3), 22–49. https://doi.org/10.1177/0022242919825649

Wilson, A. V., & Bellezza, S. (2022). Consumer minimalism. *Journal of Consumer Research, 48*(5), 796–816. https://doi.org/10.1093/jcr/ucab038

Wirtz, J., So, K. K. F., Mody, M. A., Liu, S. Q., & Chun, H. H. (2019). Platforms in the peer-to-peer sharing economy. *Journal of Service Management, 30*(4), 452–483. https://doi.org/10.1108/JOSM-11-2018-0369

Woods, M. (2021, March 12). *More, or less? Minimalism an avenue to bliss for many amid pandemic.* Spectrum News. https://spectrumnews1.com/wi/green-bay/news/2021/03/12/minimalism-gaining-traction

Zimmermann, D., Noll, C., Gräßer, L., Hugger, K. U., Braun, L. M., Nowak, T., & Kaspar, K. (2022). Influencers on YouTube: A quantitative study on young people's use and perception of videos about political and societal topics. *Current Psychology, 41*(10), 6808–6824. https://doi.org/10.1007/s12144-020-01164-7

Index